Business B

Essential Excel Skills to Streamline Your Business

SHELLEY FISHEL

MOLTEN PUBLISHING

Business Barista
Essential Excel Skills to Streamline Your Business

First published in 2017 in Great Britain by Molten Publishing Ltd
Molten Publishing Ltd, 14 Clachar Close, Chelmsford, Essex, CM2 6RX

ISBN 978 0 9935929 4 2 (Paperback)
ISBN 978 0 9935929 5 9 (E-book)

www.moltenpublishing.co.uk
www.businessbaristabook.com

Business Barista

This, my first book in print, is dedicated to my husband, David.
My rock and best friend. For all your support – Always!

Contents

Acknowledgements

I would like to thank all the brilliant trainers who have helped me to learn along with the students who helped me find new ways of explaining things.

Thank you to Henry Stewart of Happy Computers who took a chance and gave me my first training job.

I would also like to thank Molly of Molten Publishing, who has been a great support throughout this project and has eagle eyes!

About the Author

Shelley Fishel is a Microsoft Certified Trainer and owner of The IT Training Surgery.

She has worked as an IT Trainer since 1998 and loves nothing more than simplifying a process. She has worked internationally both in person and remotely. Shelley has published several e-books around Microsoft Office, and this is her first printed book, which she is very excited about!

Shelley is married to David, a Chartered Accountant, and lives in London. They have three grown-up children and five grandchildren.

When Shelley is not tinkering with new versions of software, she can be found reading detective stories or in her kitchen as she and David love entertaining their friends and family.

Introduction

Microsoft Excel is a wonderful business tool that many small businesses overlook. The information you can glean from Excel can be a game-changer, as Matt, our dedicated entrepreneur, is about to find out.

We'll be following Matt's progress as he identifies his business needs and the best and most efficient ways of meeting them. As you track Matt's journey, you'll find a wealth of practical advice and examples that can be directly related back to your own business.

This book is also a distillation of everything I've taught in the classroom over my nineteen years of delivering IT training on Excel. This is the information I impart over and over, simply because it's the tried, tested, and solid foundation on which successful businesses are built.

This is not an Excel Bible, it doesn't contain every formula or function, but I hope it will be a rich source of information you can use to take your own business wherever you want it to go.

I have added lots of screenshots to help explain and show you what I mean. Some of them have been turned around so we can show them full size – otherwise you would need a magnifying glass to read them!

Man on a Mission

Matt is a man with a dream. He wants to create the perfect coffee shop. He loves his coffee, relishes the whole coffee shop experience, and has spent time in lots of different coffee outlets. But whilst they all have great points, not one of them seems to have everything.

Apart from the money to launch such a venture, he also needs systems in place so the running of the business will be as smooth as the coffee they plan to serve. He opts for Office 365. It has all the programs he needs: Word, Excel, PowerPoint, and Outlook. It can be used on a computer, laptop, smartphone, or tablet – in fact, on any device and operating system. This is a huge plus factor as his staff can work on the device they are most used to using.

Because Office 365 can be used both locally and online, it's the perfect package for working away from the office. Plus, it has in-built collaboration features. Matt and his team will be able to work on a shared document together or at different times.

What's in a Name?

Having decided what's needed for the back end of the business, Matt now needs a name for the front end! It needs to be both memorable and to the point. He wants customers to feel as though they've been transported to an island, an oasis in the midst of city hustle and bustle. So he opts for Koffee Island, the K making the name quirky and different, exactly what Matt intends the Koffee Island experience to be.

One Step at a Time

Rome wasn't built in a day, and Matt knows his business needs all sorts of things in place before the hard work really begins. He needs to get hold of Office 365 for himself first, and then get licences for each of his staff. Microsoft are continually updating the range of offerings, so we won't go into them here.

Matt opts for the E3 plan, which allows him to use Office 365 online and install it on up to five devices for each person who has a licence. So Matt now has Office on his desktop in the office at Koffee Island as well as on his laptop for home use. He also has a tablet and a smartphone which he uses when out and about, so he installs it on those too.

Scenarios – What We Will Learn

Matt has put a lot of thought into what he needs to know to run his business. He lists a series of scenarios or challenges that need to be resolved. We'll discover how he overcomes these challenges with the help of Koffee the chimp from the Koffee Island logo. Look out for Koffee as you continue onwards. He'll be a great source of helpful suggestions and tips.

To be done:

- Set up the menu and price list
- Work out item costs
- Work out the profit margin
- Create a list of staff with all contact details
- Work out staff payment
- Gain confidence with calculations
- Understand formulas
- Work out daily sales totals
- Work out weekly and quarterly sales figures
- Set up reordering system
- Create an order form for meeting room bookings

Now Matt knows what he wants to achieve, it's time to open Excel.

Formatting and Printing – Setting Up the Menu and Price List

Day one, and Matt needs to list everything that's on sale at Koffee Island along with their prices. He's going to list the items in Excel and organise them into drink types. The list needs to be accurate and clear as well as appealing to customers.

Start Excel 2016

You'll see this book is about Excel 2016, and Matt's using Windows 10. You may be using a different version of Windows or Excel, but don't panic. Most of what you will learn is the same for all versions.

Click or tap the Excel icon on the Start menu (1), or the shortcut on the desktop (2), or the shortcut on the task bar (3), and Excel will open.

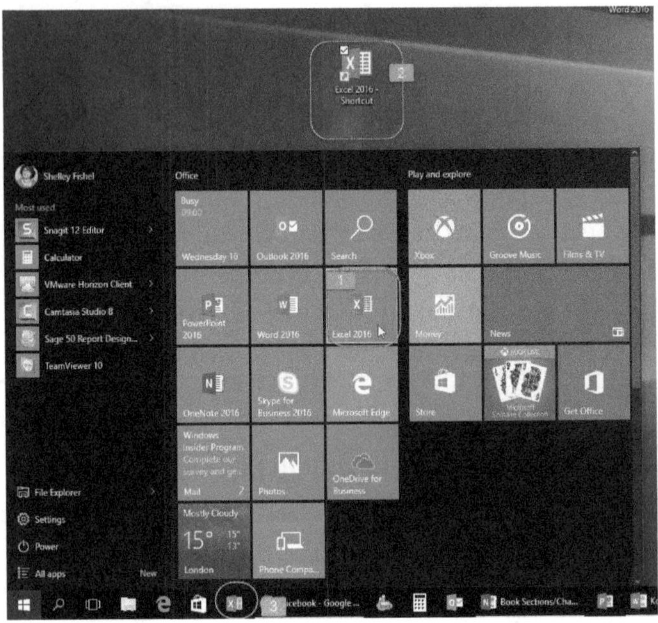

Figure 1

When Excel is first installed, you will only have a shortcut tile on the Start menu. To place a shortcut on your desktop, simply drag the tile to the desktop.

To place a shortcut on the task bar, right-click on the Excel tile on the Start menu and select *More*, then choose *Pin to taskbar*.

The Excel 2016 Screen

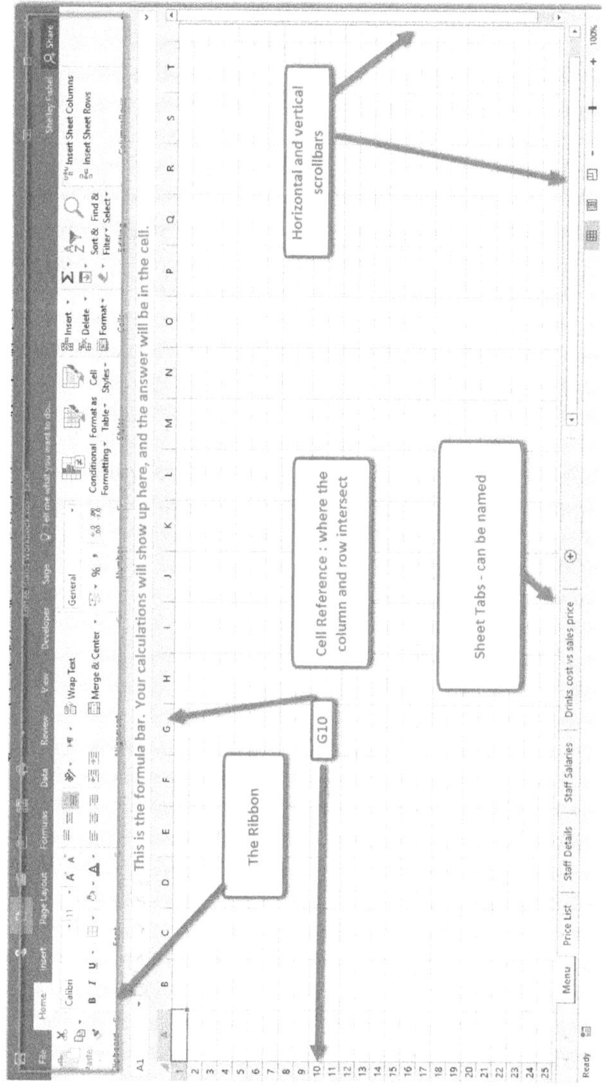

Figure 2

Excel 2016 continues with the familiar ribbon interface. Each ribbon tab has a different functionality, and some pop up only when you need them. These are called contextual ribbons. For example, if you insert a chart, the *Chart Format* and *Design* ribbons will appear.

Excel opens a workbook made up of a series of worksheets. You can have as many worksheets as your computer memory can handle. However, it's never a great idea to have just one workbook with all your worksheets in it. It's far better to create different workbooks for different topics. That will make things much easier to find and manage.

When you start, you will have just the one worksheet. You can add more by clicking on the + sign at the right of the sheet tabs.

Koffee Says:

If you always need four worksheets when you start a workbook, you can set Excel to do this. Click ***File >>Options>>General*** and change the number in *Include this many sheets* to the number you want.

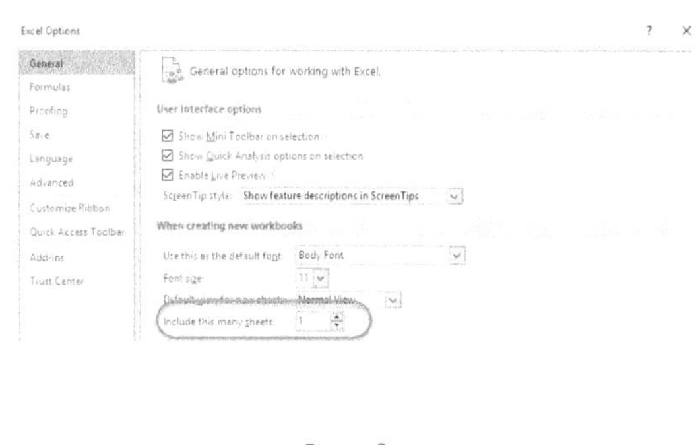

Figure 3

You'll see the working area of Excel is a grid, and like a map, it will have vertical and horizontal references. Vertical are columns with letters. Horizontal are rows referenced by numbers.

Click on a cell in column B and row 4, and your reference will be B4. References are always written with the column first and row second. You can see where your cursor is by looking at the Name Box, which is to the left of the Formula Bar.

Here you can see the number 27 in the cell called B4. In the Formula Bar, you can see the calculation – more on that later – and in the Name Box it says B4 because that's the cell you've clicked on.

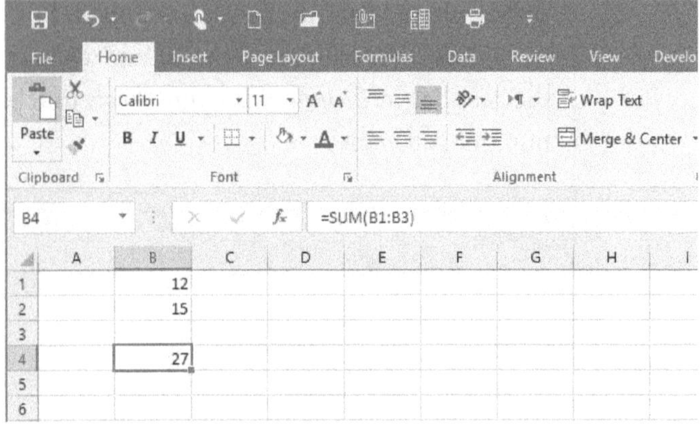

Figure 4

Different Devices

Matt and his team can use Excel 2016 on a variety of devices. Matt uses a tablet because it's portable. Lisa, as office manager, uses a desktop with the luxury of a 23-inch monitor, and the baristas will use Office on their phones or tablets. The joy of Office 365 is that it works across different devices.

If the text and numbers appear small on the screen you're using, you need to know how to magnify. When the magnification is changed, only the on-screen display is affected.

Zoom in to What's on Screen

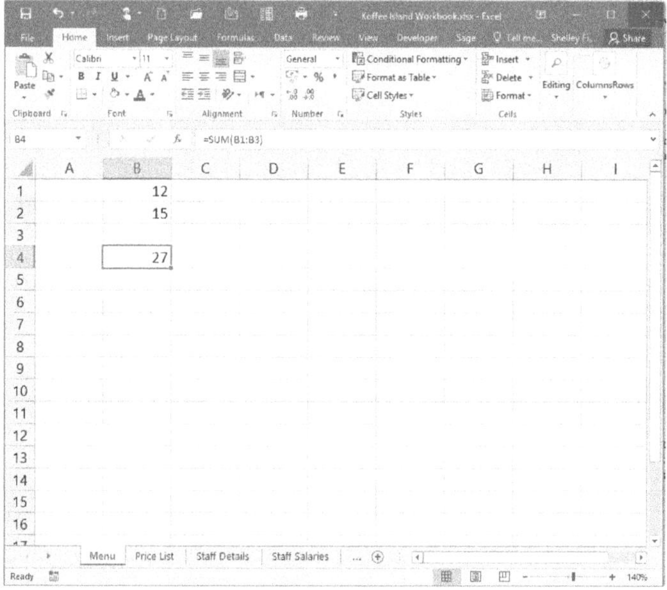

Figure 5

To zoom in, click on the percentage – where it says *100%* – and you will be offered a dialogue box with some pre-set percentages or the option to type in your own.

An easier option is to drag the slider or press the + or – signs. This is known as the Zoom Slider because that's what it does!

Start Adding Text and Numbers

Now that Matt's starting to find his way around and is comfortable with how the grid references work, he can start building his all-important menu and price list.

Add Text

All Matt needs to do is start typing where he wants the text to appear. Cell A1 is a good place to begin. Here he will have the name of the coffee shop, and underneath he will start to fill in the items on sale along with their individual prices.

Items for sale are in column A as you can see in Figure 6.

I11

	A	B	C	D	E
1	Koffee Island				
2					
3	Coffee				
4	Americano				
5	Cappuccino				
6	Koffee Island Special				
7	Macchiato				
8	Hot Chocolate				
9	Latte				
10					
11	Tea				
12	Breakfast				
13	Camomile				
14	Earl Grey				
15	Mint				
16	Very Berry				
17					
18	Cold Drinks				
19	Apple Juice				
20	Orange Juice				
21	Cola				
22					
23	Milkshakes				
24	Chocolate				
25	Vanilla				
26	Strawberry				
27					

Figure 6

However, Matt's concerned it's not looking right. The items look as if they're spilling over to the second column, which is where he wants to put the prices. It's essential the whole thing is presented as professionally as possible. Matt wants to:

- Centre the heading across the data

- Resize the first column so the text fits exactly
- Make the drink groups bold and coloured
- Sort the items alphabetically in each group of drinks
- Add borders to enhance the appearance of the spreadsheet
- Print the menu and price list

Centre the Heading Across the Data

If you want to centre a heading across multiple cells, you can use *Merge & Centre.* It's on the *Home* ribbon in the *Alignment* group of icons.

To make it work, you need to specify which cells you want to merge so the text can be centred. If there is already text in the cell, as Matt has here, it will immediately merge the cells he picks and move the text to the centre of the highlighted cells.

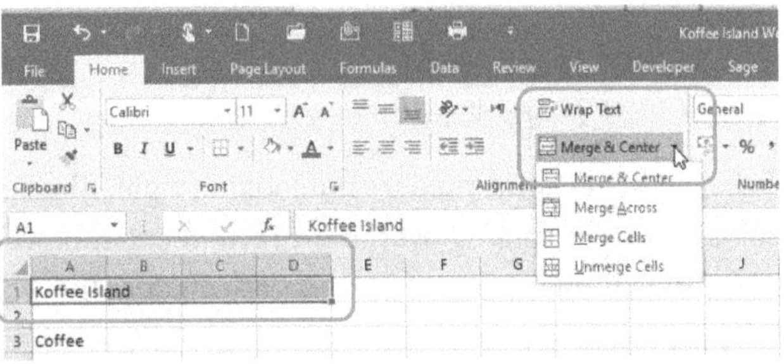

Figure 7

You'll see Matt has selected cells A1 through to D1. This is where he wants the heading to be. Next, he will select *Merge & Centre.* Note the button has a drop-down with various options. If you want to merge and centre, you simply click on the icon. However, if you want to use one of the other options, click the drop-down and choose the one you want.

Merge & Centre	Merges the selected cells together and centres any text across them.
Merge Across	Merges each row of selected cells separately without centring the text.
Merge Cells	Merges the cells without centring the text.
Unmerge Cells	Removes the merging, splitting the cell into multiple cells and returning them to their original size.

Resize the First Column to Fit the Data

It may be that when you add text or numbers to a cell, the cell is not wide enough to display what you've entered, so it may appear to flow into the cell or cells to the right. If there are too many numbers to fit in the cell, you may see ##### in the cell. This is a kind of code that simply means *please make the column wider.*

So how is this done?

Double Click to Resize

With the double click method, Excel will resize the column to fit the widest text. It will look down the column and find the text with the most characters and fit to that.

This is why we needed to merge and centre first. We want to resize column A to fit the widest item in the list, but we don't want it to resize the heading!

Before

	A	B	C	D	E	F
1	Koffee Island					
2						
3	Coffee					
4	Americano					
5	Cappuccino					
6	Koffee Island Special					
7	Macchiato					
8	Hot Chocolate					
9	Latte					

Figure 8

After

	A	B	C	D
1	Koffee Island			
2				
3	Coffee			
4	Americano			
5	Cappuccino			
6	Koffee Island Special			
7	Macchiato			
8	Hot Chocolate			
9	Latte			

Figure 9

Change the Formatting

The next task is to change the formatting of the group headings. This can be done heading by heading or all at once.

Heading by Heading

- Select the heading you want to apply the format to
- Choose the format

All at Once

- Select all the headings at the same time
- Choose the format

Selecting Cells in Excel

Cells That Are Next to Each Other

Click on a single cell. Now whatever you do format-wise will apply to that cell. To select a range of cells, click and drag. As you drag, they turn dark grey. The mouse will look like a white plus sign as you drag.

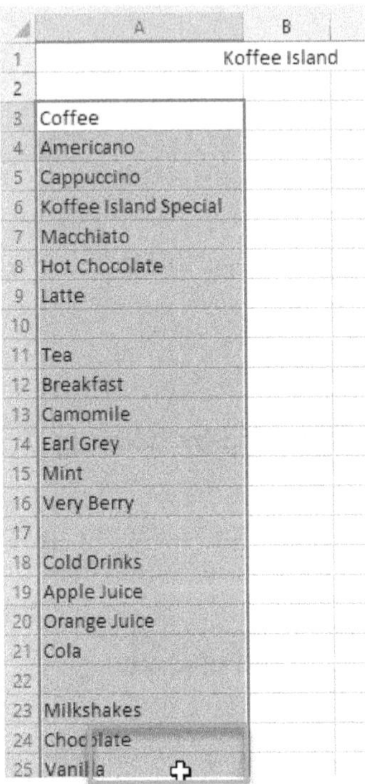

Figure 10

Cells Not Next to Each Other

Use the *Control* key on your keyboard to select cells that are not next to each other.

Click on the first cell, hold the *Control* key, and click on the next cell you want.

Figure 11

Now Apply Formatting

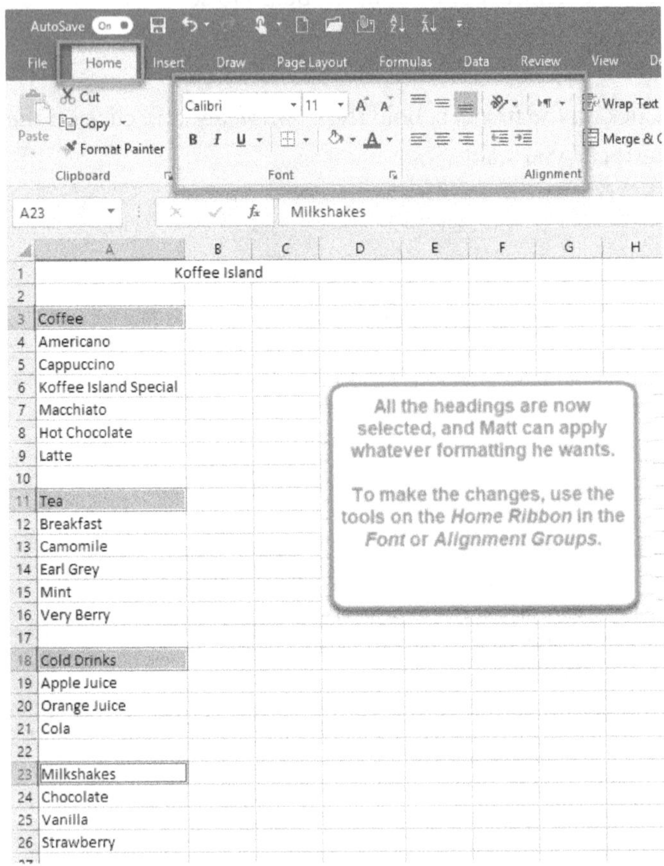

Figure 12

Text Formatting Options

Formatting text in Excel is more or less the same as any other package. There are options to change the font, the font size, increase the size by two points automatically (the larger A), decrease the size by two points automatically (the smaller A), and apply bold, italic, and underline.

Adding borders and shading and changing the colour of the font is all possible. Then there's alignment: *Top*, *Middle,* and *Bottom*, and *Left*, *Centre,* and *Right*. What Matt doesn't initially realise is he can also indent text inside a cell. We can see this in action in the next section.

Text can also be angled using the slanting tab, and we have already visited *Merge & Centre*. The remaining option here is *Wrap Text.* Matt can use this when the text is too wide for the column, but he doesn't want to resize that column.

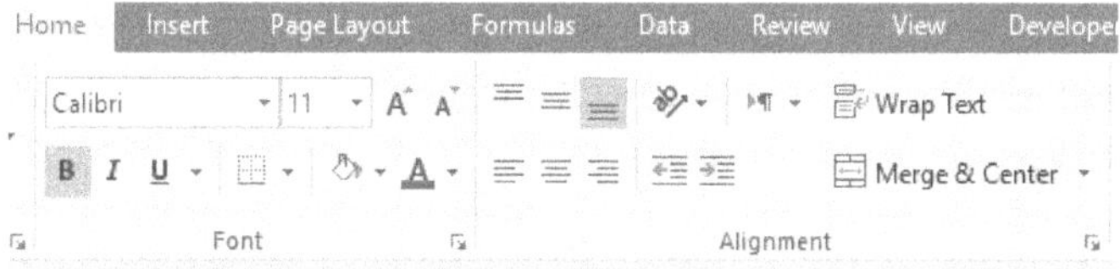

Figure 13

Angled Text

To change text from horizontal to something else, Matt can select one of the options from the *Orientation* icon.

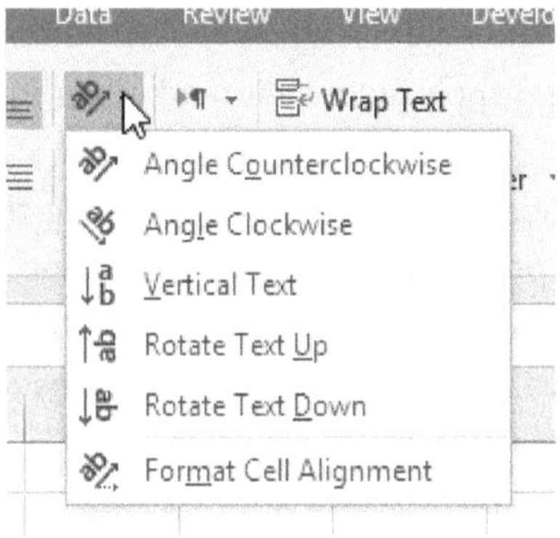

Figure 14

Add Shading to Cells

To add shading to the headings, Matt can select the headings and apply a colour from the list to match his Koffee Island branding.

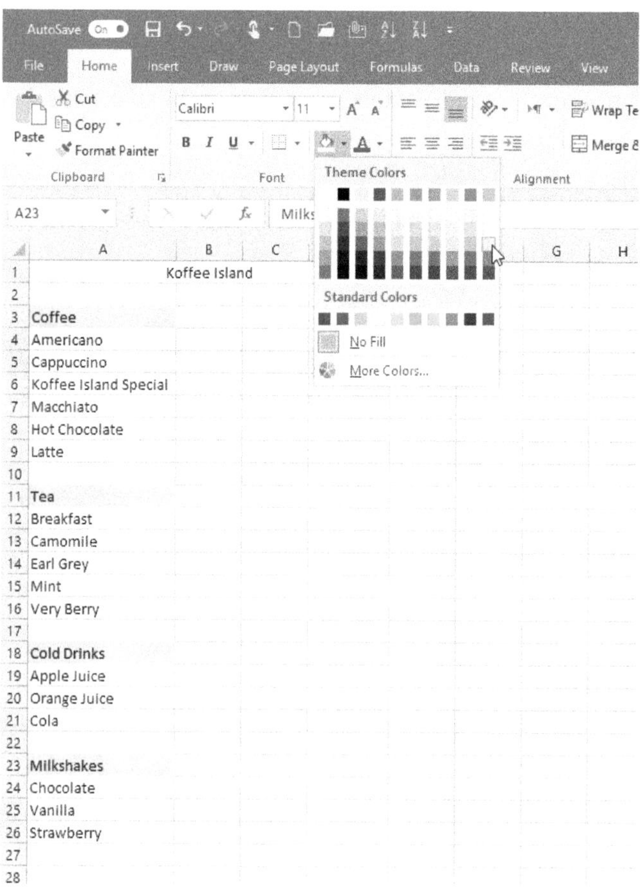
AutoSave
On
File
Home
Insert
Draw
Page Layout
Formulas
Data
Review
View
Cut
Copy
Format Painter
Paste
Clipboard
Calibri
11
Font
Wrap Te
Merge &
Alignment
Theme Colors
Standard Colors
No Fill
More Colors...
A23
Milks
A
B
C
G
H
1 Koffee Island
2
3 Coffee
4 Americano
5 Cappuccino
6 Koffee Island Special
7 Macchiato
8 Hot Chocolate
9 Latte
10
11 Tea
12 Breakfast
13 Camomile
14 Earl Grey
15 Mint
16 Very Berry
17
18 Cold Drinks
19 Apple Juice
20 Orange Juice
21 Cola
22
23 Milkshakes
24 Chocolate
25 Vanilla
26 Strawberry
27
28

Figure 15

Indent Text

Matt wants to indent the listed drinks to make his list interesting and easier to read.

To do this, he will select the cells he wants to indent and use the *Indent* icon.

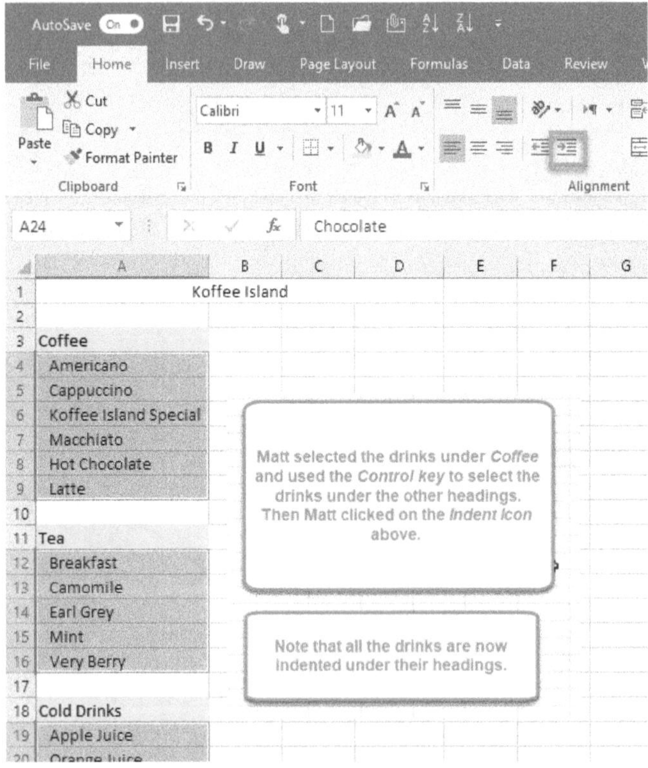

Figure 16

Next, Matt needs to add and format the prices.

Adding Numbers

As with text, simply click and type. However, it's important to consider what the numbers represent. Excel is built to calculate using numbers and mathematical symbols along with a whole host of built-in functions which we'll see later in the book.

When typing numbers in Excel, there's no need to type notation. For example, if Matt wants to charge £2.20 for a cappuccino, he only needs to type *2.2*. Excel will take care of the rest with the formatting applied.

Number formats can be applied to a single cell, a range of cells, a whole row or column, or even the whole spreadsheet. However, it's unlikely the whole spreadsheet will have the same format.

Number Formats

As stated, just type in the numbers, and then format them using the drop-down. Here's a picture of what each format looks like.

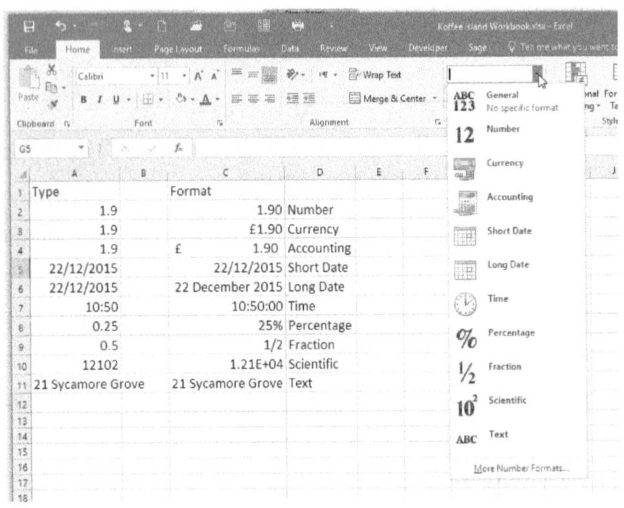

	A	B	C	D
1	Type		Format	
2	1.9		1.90	Number
3	1.9		£1.90	Currency
4	1.9		£ 1.90	Accounting
5	22/12/2015		22/12/2015	Short Date
6	22/12/2015		22 December 2015	Long Date
7	10:50		10:50:00	Time
8	0.25		25%	Percentage
9	0.5		1/2	Fraction
10	12102		1.21E+04	Scientific
11	21 Sycamore Grove		21 Sycamore Grove	Text

Figure 17

Dates are particularly important. When performing a calculation using a date, Excel needs to know it's a date. For example, Matt needs to work out when Bob's trial employment period will end. As Bob's on a one-month trial, Matt can simply add thirty days on to Bob's start date, and Excel will work it out. More on that one later.

Here is Matt's price list with three different formats to choose from. The first is the plain number simply typed into the cell. Matt then copies the numbers to the other columns and applies each of the formats so he can see them all side by side and decide which to use.

	A	B	C	D	E	F	G
1		Koffee Island					
2							
3	**Coffee**	**No Notation**	**Number**	**Currency**	**Accounting**		
4	Americano	1.9	1.90	£1.90	£ 1.90		
5	Cappuccino	1.95	1.95	£1.95	£ 1.95		
6	Hot Chocolate	2.1	2.10	£2.10	£ 2.10		
7	Koffee Island Special	2.5	2.50	£2.50	£ 2.50		
8	Latte	1.9	1.90	£1.90	£ 1.90		
9	Macchiato	2	2.00	£2.00	£ 2.00		
10							
11	**Tea**						
12	Breakfast	1.5	1.50	£1.50	£ 1.50		
13	Camomile	1	1.00	£1.00	£ 1.00		
14	Earl Grey	1.5	1.50	£1.50	£ 1.50		
15	Mint	1	1.00	£1.00	£ 1.00		
16	Very Berry	1	1.00	£1.00	£ 1.00		
17							
18	**Cold Drinks**						
19	Apple Juice	0.8	0.80	£0.80	£ 0.80		
20	Cola	0.6	0.60	£0.60	£ 0.60		
21	Orange Juice	0.8	0.80	£0.80	£ 0.80		
22							
23	**Milkshakes**						
24	Chocolate	2.5	2.50	£2.50	£ 2.50		
25	Strawberry	2.5	2.50	£2.50	£ 2.50		
26	Vanilla	2.5	2.50	£2.50	£ 2.50		
27							
28							

Figure 18

Matt decides to use the *Accounting* format, so he needs to remove the other three columns.

Delete Content

To delete content, simply select it and either use the *Delete* key or the *Clear* icon.

Koffee Island
No Notation
Number
Currency
Accounting
Coffee
Americano
Cappuccino
Hot Chocolate
Koffee Island Special
Latte
Macchiato
Tea
Breakfast
Camomile
Earl Grey
Mint
Very Berry
Cold Drinks
Apple Juice
Cola
Orange Juice
Milkshakes
Chocolate
Strawberry
Vanilla

Figure 19

Clear All – clears everything, including text, numbers, formatting, comments, and hyperlinks.

Clear Formats – clears all formatting and leaves the text or numbers in the cell.

Clear Contents – clears the contents and leaves the formatting in the cell.

Clear Comments – clears only the comments from selected cells.

Clear Hyperlinks – clears only hyperlinks from the selected cells.

Deleting Columns and Rows

Now Matt has removed the content, he has three blank columns. He wants to remove two of them so he only has one blank column between the name of the drink and its price.

Deleting Columns Within the Data

First, Matt will select the cells to delete, then right-click where the *Delete* option will be found. Clicking that will bring up this dialogue box. Matt will choose *Shift cells left*, and the whole lot will move left.

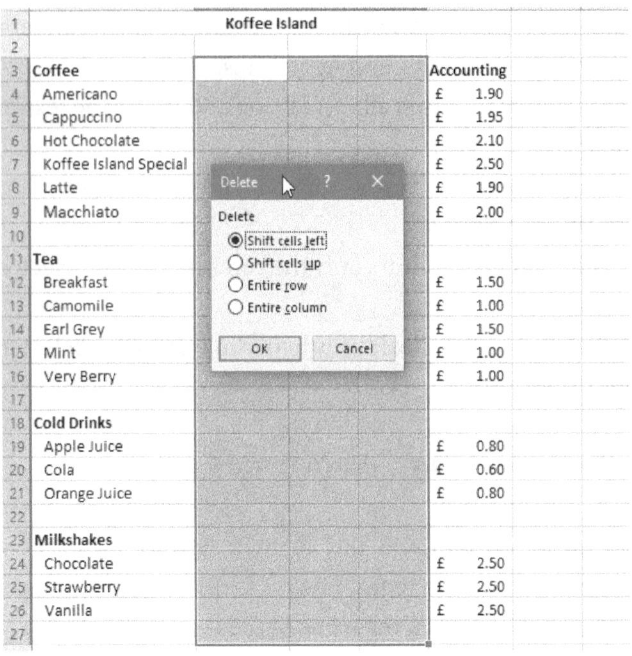

Figure 20

Deleting Columns from the Top

Simply click on the column letter, and the whole column is selected. Then right-click and choose *Delete*. The column will disappear.

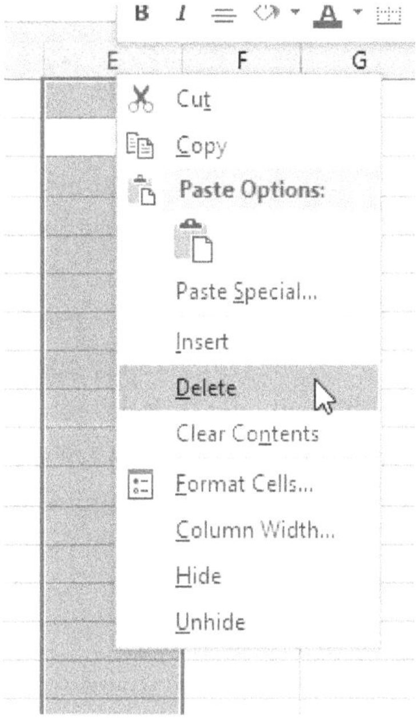

Figure 21

Deleting Rows

Click on the row number to select the row, then right-click and choose *Delete*. That's it, the row is removed.

Inserting Columns or Rows

Matt realises he needs to add another type of coffee. He wants to add *Flat White* above the *Latte* entry. To do this, he needs to right-click on the row number that has *Latte* and select *Insert*. A new row will appear above *Latte*.

If Matt simply places his cursor on the *Latte* entry and right-clicks, choosing *Insert*, he will have the option to shift cells down. However, this will only shift the current cell, not any that are adjacent. So, if Matt wants to keep the price column lined up, he would be better off inserting a whole row.

Koffee Says:

Remember that new rows always appear above the row you are in, and columns are always inserted to the left of the current column.

Remember to place your cursor correctly first!

Right-click on a cell

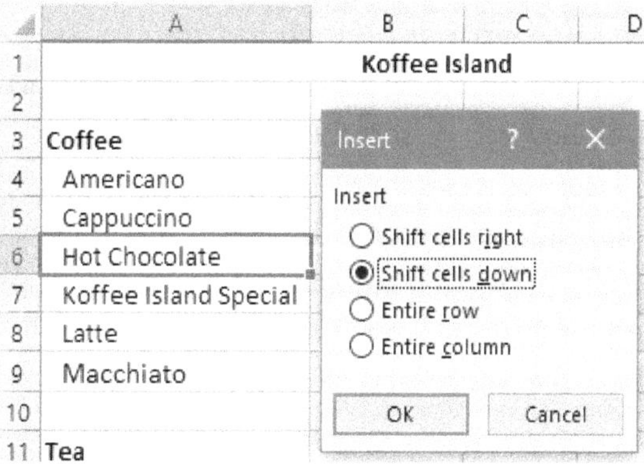

Figure 22

Right-click on the row number

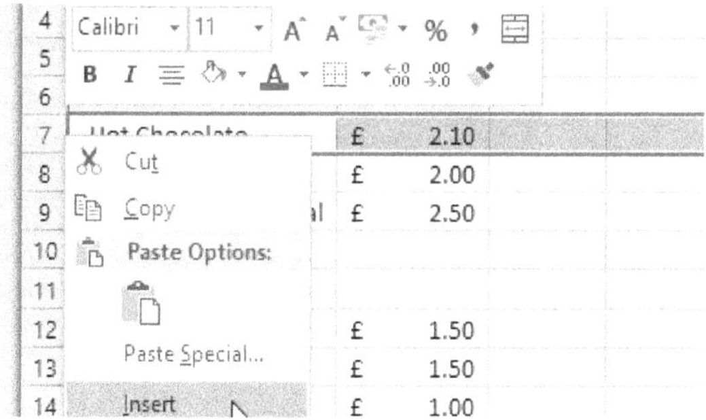

Figure 23

Sorting

Before Matt goes on to add borders and finish formatting the menu and price list, he notices the drinks aren't in alphabetical order. Being a methodical chap, this irks him no end. So how can he sort the groups of drinks?

When sorting a spreadsheet, Excel will sort alphabetically, numerically, or by date. You can sort A-Z, which is smallest to largest, or Z-A, in reverse order, largest to smallest. For dates, it's earliest to latest date or latest to earliest.

In this scenario, we are going to select the small groups of drinks along with their prices. Selecting the prices ensures each price stays with the corresponding drink.

Before Sorting

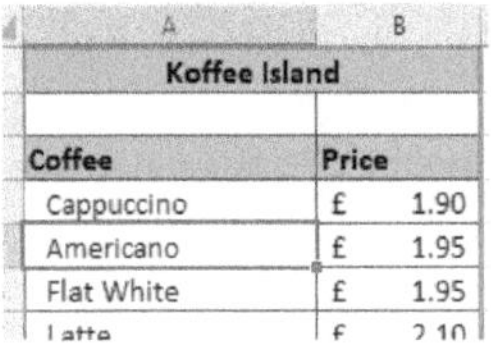

A	B	
Koffee Island		
Coffee	Price	
Cappuccino	£	1.90
Americano	£	1.95
Flat White	£	1.95
Latte	£	2.10

Figure 24

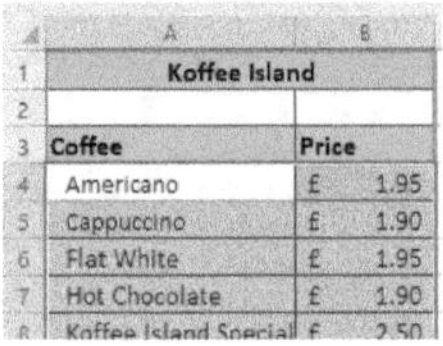

After Sorting

	A	B	
1	Koffee Island		
2			
3	Coffee	Price	
4	Americano	£	1.95
5	Cappuccino	£	1.90
6	Flat White	£	1.95
7	Hot Chocolate	£	1.90
8	Koffee Island Special	£	2.50

Figure 25

Perform the Sort

Matt is discovering there are often several ways of doing any one thing in Excel, and sorting is no different. We can sort via:

- Right-click
- Option on a drop-down on the *Home* ribbon
- *Icon* on the *Data* ribbon

Here they are, one by one.

Right-Click to Sort

1. Select the data to sort – in our case the drinks and their prices.
2. Right-click on the selection.
3. Select *Sort*.
4. Choose how the data should be sorted.

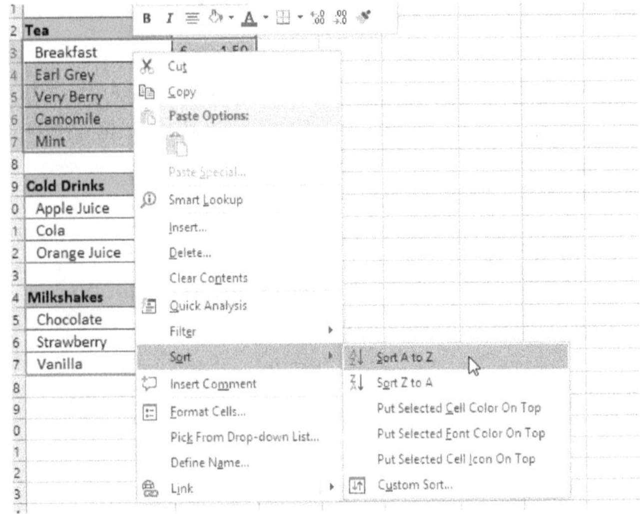

Figure 26

Drop-Down on the Home Ribbon

1. Select the data to sort.
2. Click on the drop-down under *Sort & Filter*, which is in the *Editing* group.
3. Pick *Sort A to Z, Sort Z to A,* or *Custom Sort.*

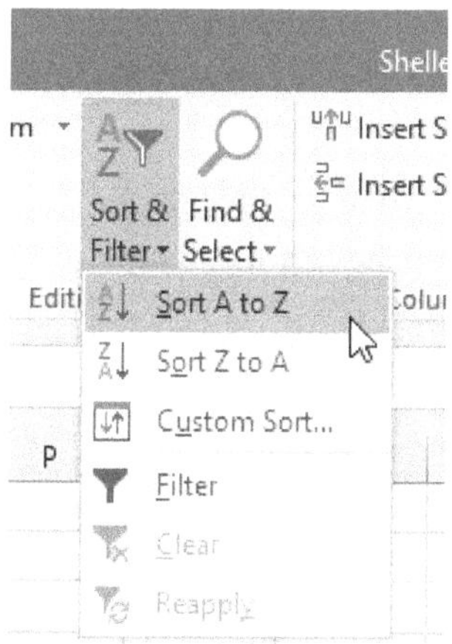

Figure 27

Custom Sort

When Matt chooses *Custom Sort* from the drop-down, he is offered an option to expand the selection. This has happened because, as you can see in the screenshot, Matt only selected the names of the drinks to sort. Excel has detected there is adjacent data and wants to make sure Matt wants to sort only the list of drinks.

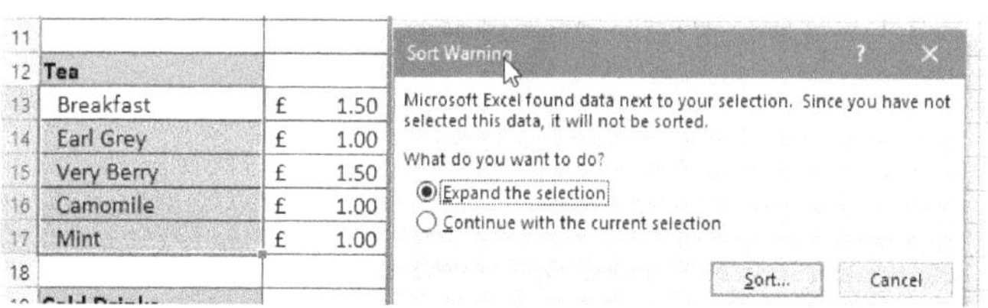

Figure 28

By selecting to *Expand the selection*, Excel will also include the numbers in the sort, so Matt will get an accurate result.

By clicking *Sort*, Matt is then taken to the custom sort dialogue box where he can specify the sort order and which columns to sort by.

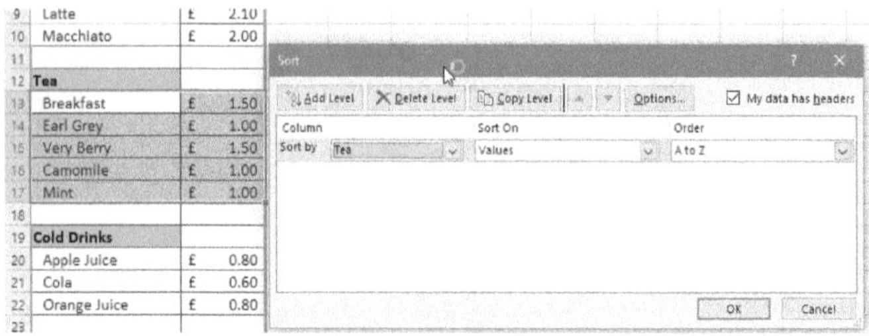

Figure 29

We'll look at sorting in more detail later in the book.

Adding Borders

Now the price list for the drinks at Koffee Island is ready. Well, almost. Before printing, Matt wants to add borders. Again, there are several ways of doing this.

The Icon

There's an icon with a drop-down menu. From here, you can choose which borders to apply, whether you want just the right or left border, or all borders.

Note: it is possible to draw a border and change the line colour and style too.

Let's say Matt decides to add a border all around and wants inside borders as well. That choice is not available from here. To apply more than one option, Matt will need to pick from the drop-down each time.

To apply a border:

- Select the cells to apply it to
- Choose the type of border to apply

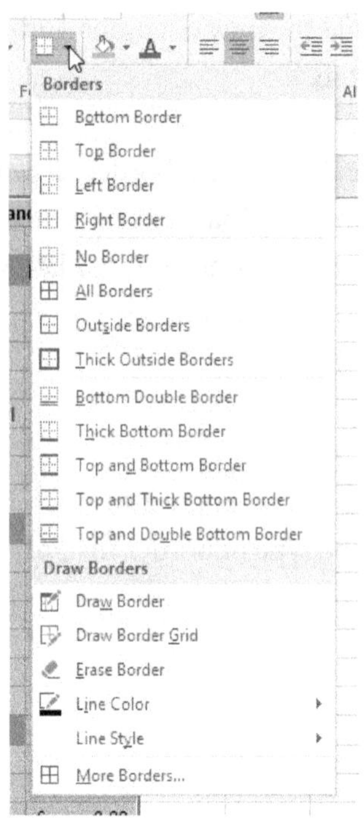

Figure 30

To change the options for borders, Matt needs to go into the borders dialogue box. This is accessed via *Format Cells* and the *Border* tab.

To get there, click *More Borders* at the bottom of the list.

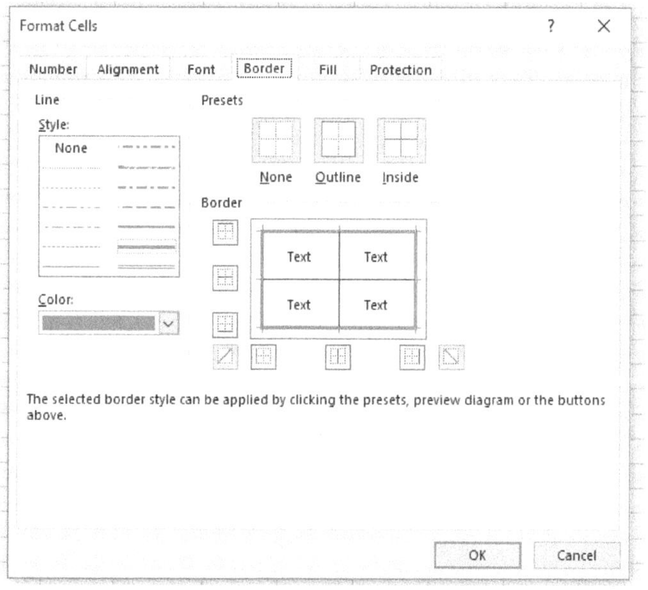

Figure 31

Firstly, Matt needs to decide which line style and colour he wants.

He can click on the three icons at the top: *None*, *Outline*, *Inside*. This will apply borders to those areas. Matt's going to go for a heavy orange line and apply this to the outside by clicking on the *Outline* icon.

Next, he opts for a thin line style and a green colour. He clicks on the *Inside* icon this time. Now the outer border will be heavy orange and the inner border green. Clicking *OK* will apply his selections to the cells he highlighted.

The advantage of using *More Borders* is that all the border styles can be applied at the same time. For it to work, first select the line style and colour, and then click on the icons to apply the style to the relevant borders.

Once Matt clicks *OK*, the border styles will be applied to whatever area he has highlighted.

	A	B	
1	**Koffee Island**		
2			
3	**Coffee**	**Price**	
4	Americano	£	1.95
5	Cappuccino	£	1.90
6	Flat White	£	1.95
7	Hot Chocolate	£	1.90
8	Koffee Island Special	£	2.50
9	Latte	£	2.10
10	Macchiato	£	2.00
11			
12	**Tea**		
13	Breakfast	£	1.50
14	Camomile	£	1.00
15	Earl Grey	£	1.00
16	Mint	£	1.00
17	Very Berry	£	1.50
18			
19	**Cold Drinks**		
20	Apple Juice	£	0.80
21	Cola	£	0.60
22	Orange Juice	£	0.80
23			
24	**Milkshakes**		
25	Chocolate	£	2.50
26	Strawberry	£	2.50
27	Vanilla	£	2.50
28			

Figure 32

Now Matt has applied a heavy orange border around the outside and lighter weight green borders inside.

These borders were selected and applied together.

Now that Matt has the price list formatted exactly as he wants it, it's time to think about printing.

Printing

Printing on a simple level is easy. However, there are options to consider. Matt wants to see how it will look first. To do this, he can click *File* and then *Print*. The spreadsheet will be displayed on the right of the screen.

- The *Print* option is on the left when you click *File*
- In the middle panel are all the print options
- On the right is the preview of how it will look with the number of pages at the bottom so you can move between them

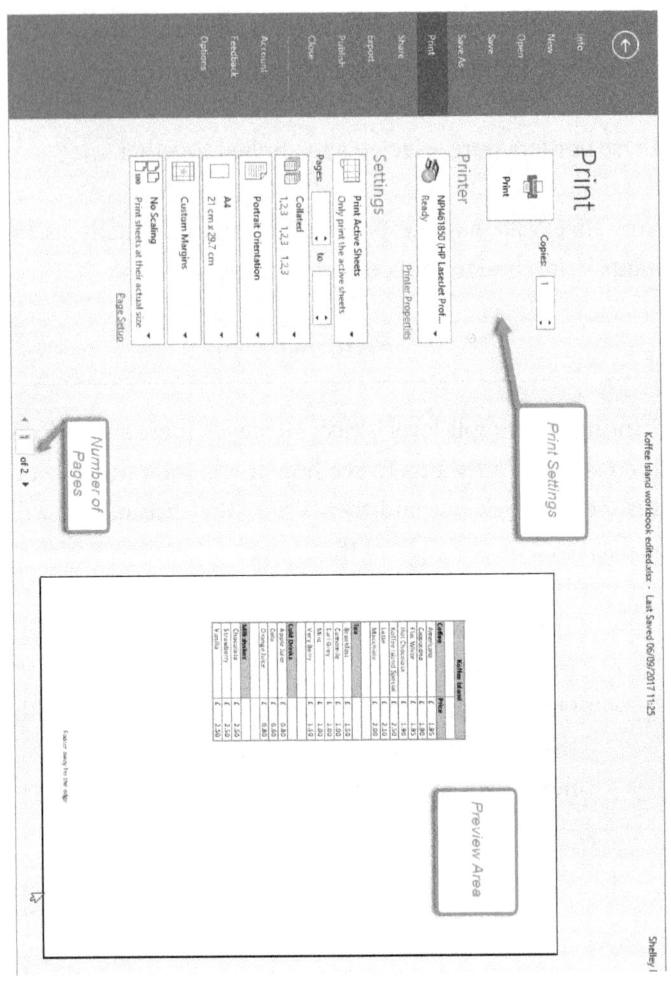
Print Settings
Number of Pages
Preview Area
Print
Copies:
Printer
Printer Properties
Settings
Print Active Sheets
Only print the active sheets
Pages:
to
Collated
1,2,3 1,2,3 1,2,3
Portrait Orientation
A4
21 cm x 29.7 cm
Custom Margins
No Scaling
Print sheets at their actual size
Page Setup
Koffee Island workbook edited.xlsx - Last Saved 06/09/2017 11:25
Info
New
Open
Save
Save As
Share
Export
Publish
Close
Account
Feedback
Options
of 2

Figure 33

Print Options

Print Icon – the big print button will go ahead and print to the selected printer.
Copies – if you want more than one copy, you change the number here.
Printer – under *Printer*, you can choose the correct printer. The printer here is showing a LaserJet printer and should be changed to a colour printer.

Settings

Under *Settings*, there are a variety of other options.

Print Active Sheets – this is the default setting on this button and will print whichever sheets you have selected.
Print Entire Workbook – this prints all worksheets in the workbook whether they are selected or not.
Print Selection – this prints only the items you have selected on the worksheet.
Ignore Print Area – if you have set a print area, this will ignore it. This selection will remain in place until you deselect it.

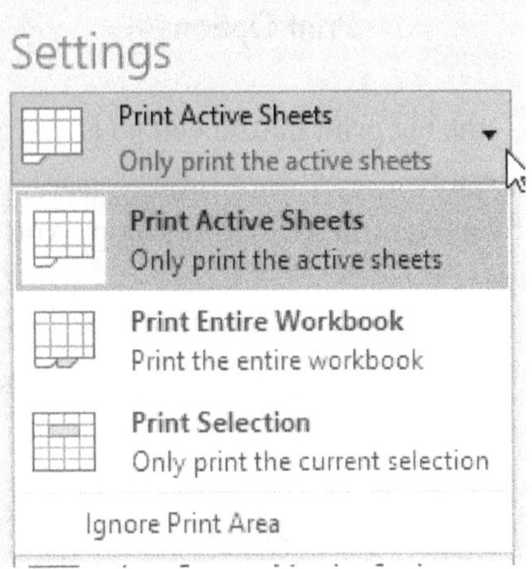

Figure 34

What is a Print Area?

This is the area you set to print automatically when you click *Print*. Say you always need to print the same area of a spreadsheet. You don't want to have to select it each time; you want to hit *Print* and get exactly what you want. Once you've set a print area, that's what will happen.

Once you've set this up, whenever you print, only the print area will be printed. Should you need to print other things, you will need to *Ignore Print Area*. Clicking on this ticks the option and leaves it selected until you deselect it.

Pages

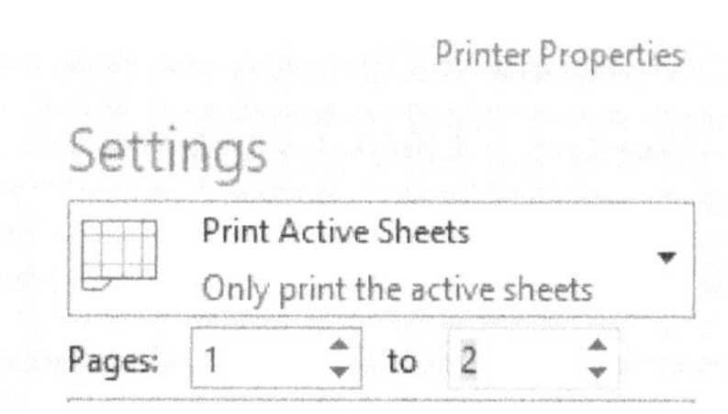

Figure 35

If your data is going to print on lots of pages, it is possible to tell Excel exactly which pages you want. For example, if you had printed six pages and then found an error on page 4, you could correct the error and then re-print only page 4.

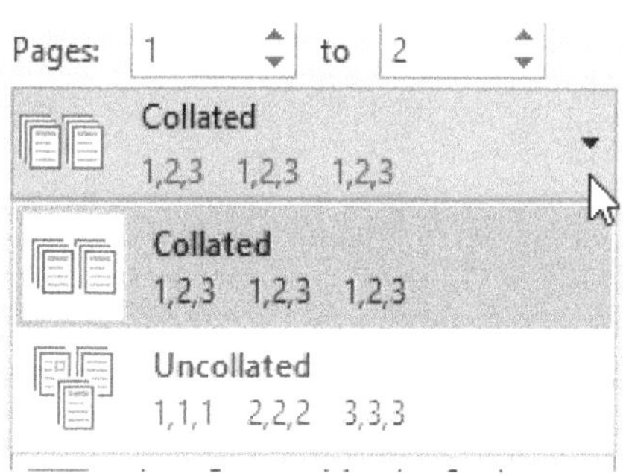

Figure 36

Let's say Matt has a report with six pages, and he needs six copies. He hits *Print* and chooses *Collated*, which is the default setting. This will print pages 1-6. It will then start at page 1 again.

If the setting is *Uncollated*, all six copies of page 1 will print, followed by all six copies of page 2 and so on.

As a rule, Matt will want things collated unless the pages are going to be put into different packs for a promotion or report and are not consecutive.

Orientation

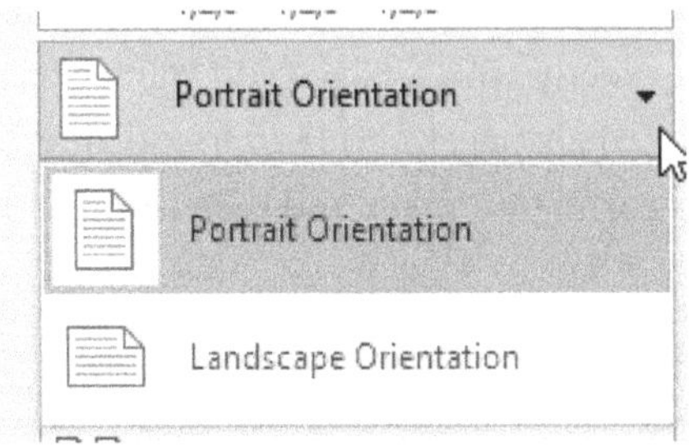

Figure 37

Often when printing, it is only when the preview is on screen that you realise the orientation is wrong. It should be landscape instead of portrait. Instead of going back into the *Layout* ribbon to change this, Matt can change it here.

Paper Size

This is very important. In Europe, we use A4 sized paper; in the USA, Letter is the default size.

Why Does It Matter?

The actual size of the paper is different, which means the margins will come out differently when you print. If you set a one-inch margin from the edge of the page, and the page width is different for different paper sizes, the margins will be placed differently. This can be very frustrating when you print and the sheets don't come out as you wish.

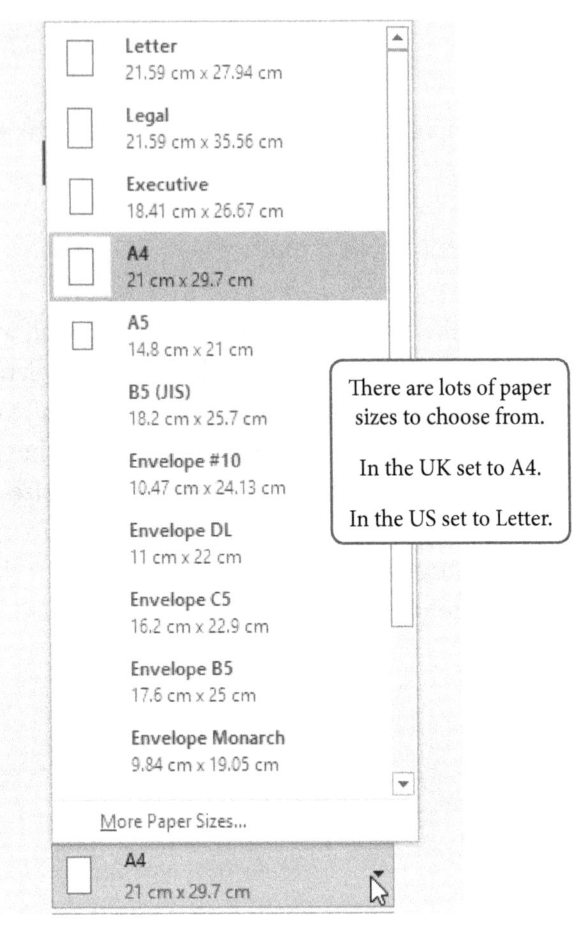

Figure 38

Margins

You may only realise the margins are not right when you see the preview. You can select from three settings plus the last custom setting, or you can go into *Custom Margins* and change them to whatever you want.

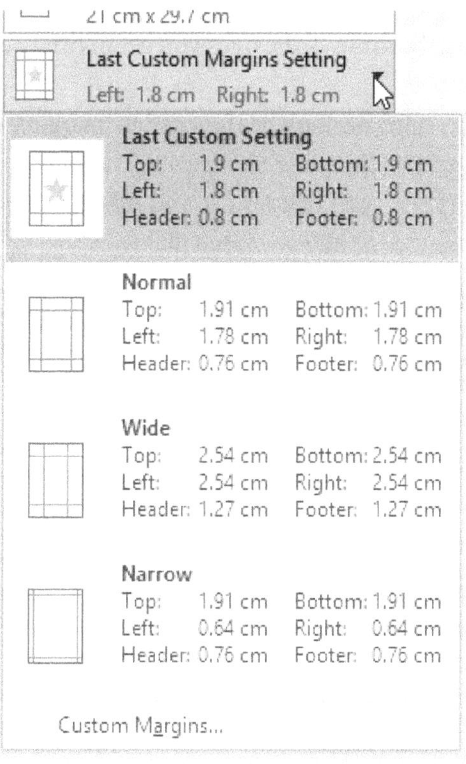

Figure 39

Custom Margins

Margins can be set from the *Custom Margins* option shown here.

Change Margins in the Worksheet

Because margins are to do with the layout of the worksheet, you will find them on the *Layout* ribbon. Note, the first options are the same as the ones you get in print settings.

Now we're going to look at the custom margins dialogue box. This will be the same dialogue box no matter how you access it. When you click on *Custom Margins*, it brings up the *Margins* tab in the *Page Setup* dialogue box.

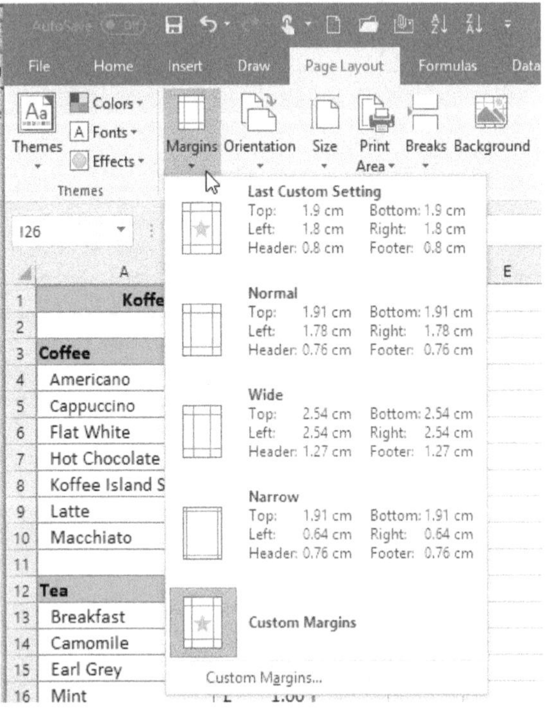

Figure 40

The Page Setup Dialogue Box

Margins have their own tab in the *Page Setup* dialogue box. Here you can set the top, left, right, and bottom margins.

You can also set the header and footer distance from the top or the bottom edge. Keep these within the margins.

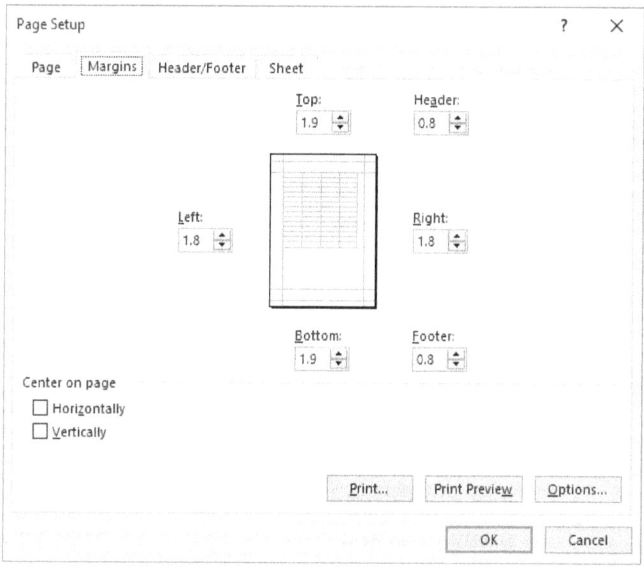

Figure 41

Often when previewing a spreadsheet, we realise it doesn't all fit on the page. We don't want to delete anything, but we do want it to fit on the page. Scaling can help here.

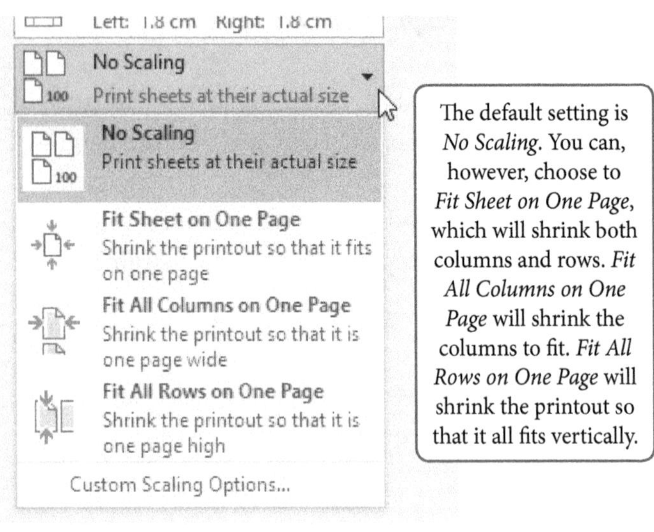
Left: 1.8 cm Right: 1.8 cm
No Scaling
Print sheets at their actual size
No Scaling
Print sheets at their actual size
Fit Sheet on One Page
Shrink the printout so that it fits on one page
Fit All Columns on One Page
Shrink the printout so that it is one page wide
Fit All Rows on One Page
Shrink the printout so that it is one page high
Custom Scaling Options...
The default setting is *No Scaling*. You can, however, choose to *Fit Sheet on One Page*, which will shrink both columns and rows. *Fit All Columns on One Page* will shrink the columns to fit. *Fit All Rows on One Page* will shrink the printout so that it all fits vertically.

Figure 42

Koffee Says:

Remember, when you choose scaling, the text will shrink to fit the page. If you have too many rows and columns to fit on a page, you may need a magnifying glass to read it – this is not good!

Matt's Printout

Here, we have a preview of Matt's price list.

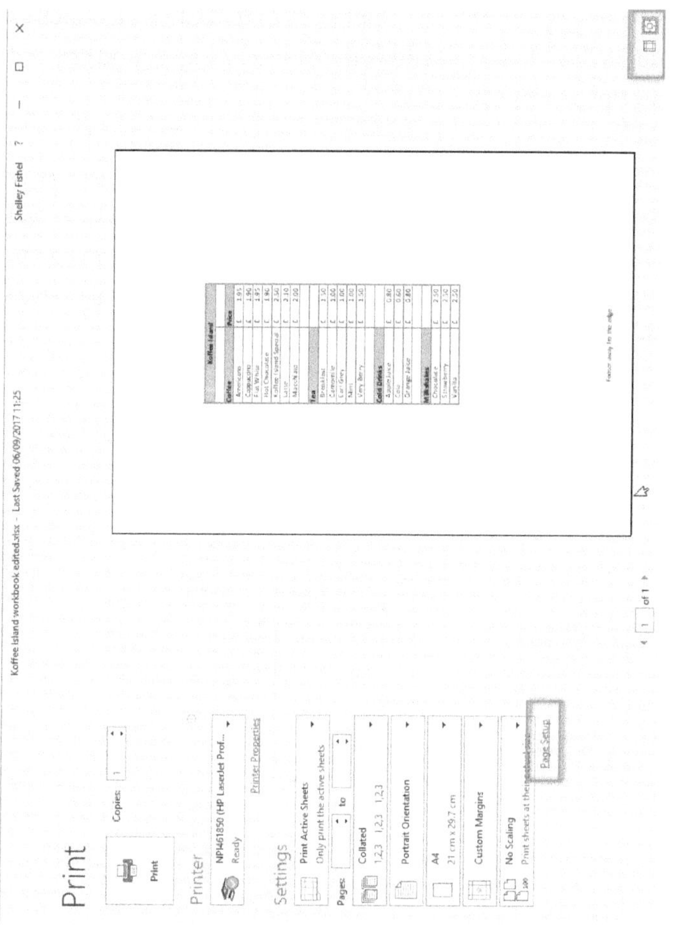

Figure 43

To see the margins on the preview, click on the icon in the bottom right corner. This will put lines on the preview which you can drag around to move the margins.

Looking at this preview, Matt realises the data is all bunched up on the left. It could do with being a bit bigger and centred on the page.

He clicks the blue *Page Setup* link. This opens the *Page Setup* dialogue box. It opens on the *Page* tab where you can change paper size and scale the worksheet. Matt needs to centre the text, so he goes over to the *Margins* tab. Here there are two checkboxes at the bottom.

Centre on the page horizontally, vertically, or both.

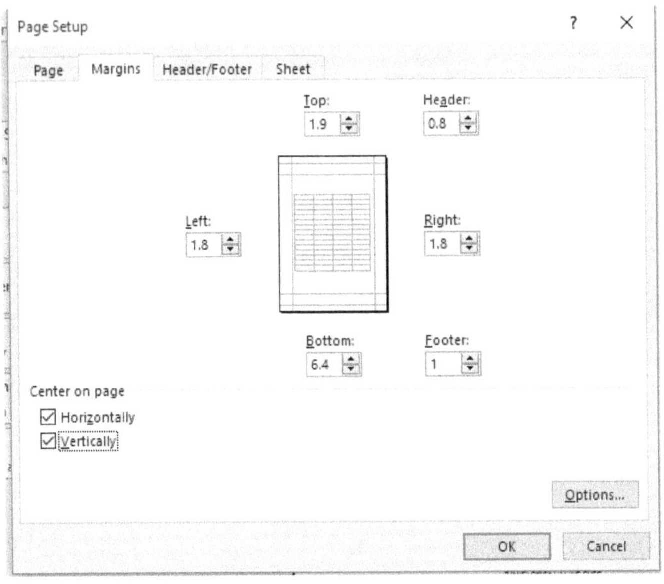

Figure 44

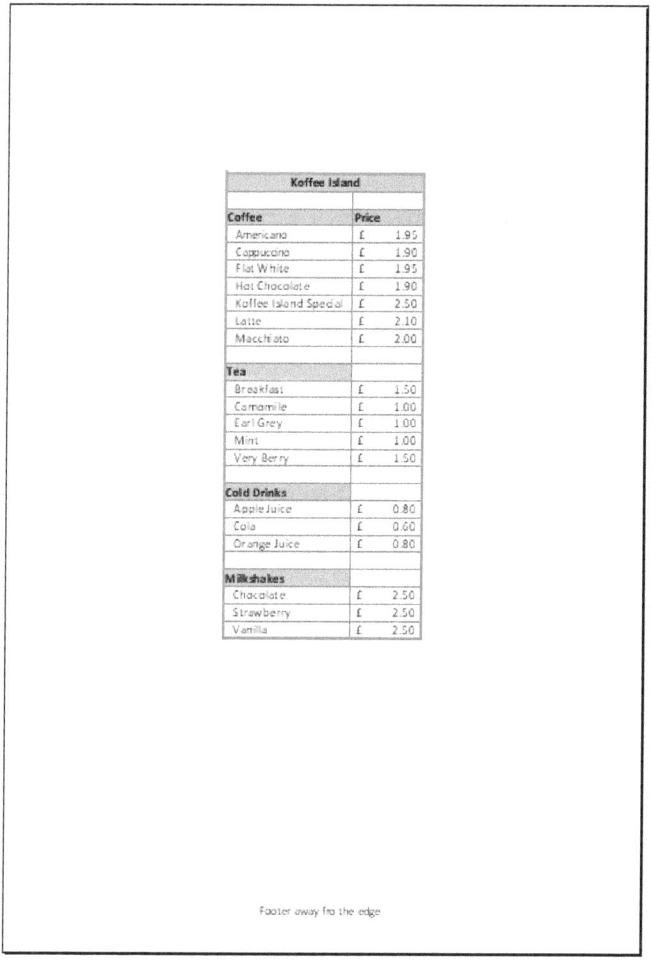

Koffee Island		
Coffee	**Price**	
Americano	£	1.95
Cappuccino	£	1.90
Flat White	£	1.95
Hot Chocolate	£	1.90
Koffee Island Special	£	2.50
Latte	£	2.10
Macchiato	£	2.00
Tea		
Breakfast	£	1.50
Camomile	£	1.00
Earl Grey	£	1.00
Mint	£	1.00
Very Berry	£	1.50
Cold Drinks		
Apple Juice	£	0.80
Cola	£	0.60
Orange Juice	£	0.80
Milkshakes		
Chocolate	£	2.50
Strawberry	£	2.50
Vanilla	£	2.50

Footer away fro the edge

Figure 45

That's better. He can now go ahead and print, ready for Koffee Island's wall.

More About Printing

There are a few other things to consider when thinking about printing.

- Headers and footers
- Reorganising the spreadsheet so it fits on a page
- Printing lists and making the header row print on every page

Add a Header or Footer

Adding fixed text to the header is simple, just type where you want it to appear.

To add other elements, click into the header area, and the *Header & Footer Tools* ribbon will appear.

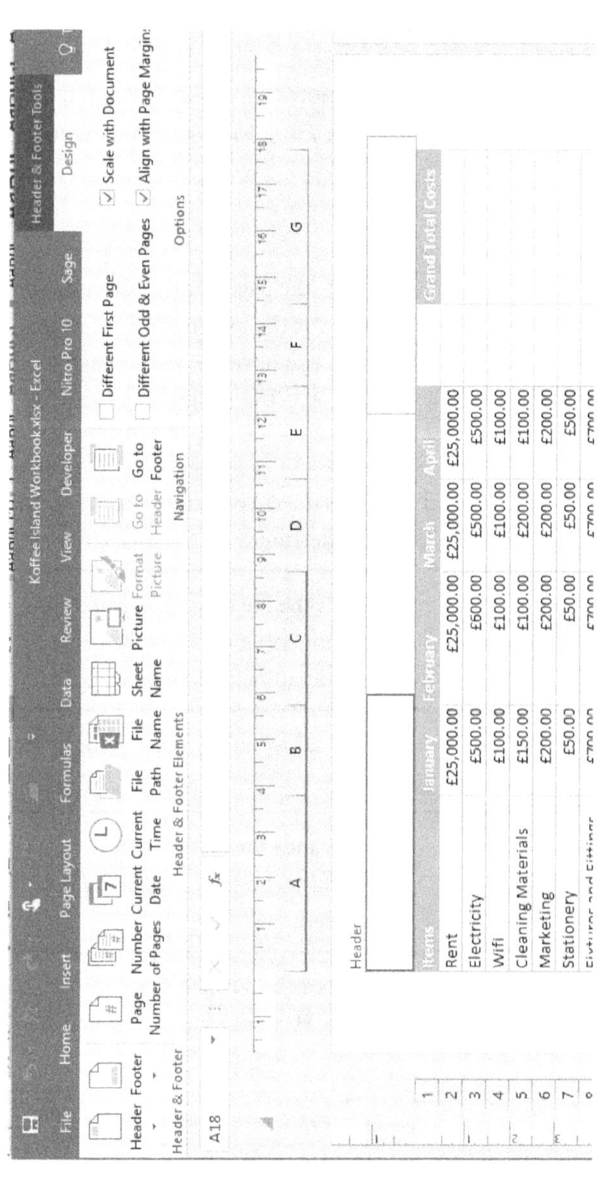
Koffee Island Workbook.xlsx - Excel
Header & Footer Tools
File
Home
Insert
Page Layout
Formulas
Data
Review
View
Developer
Nitro Pro 10
Sage
Design
Header
Footer
Page Number
Number of Pages
Current Date
Current Time
File Path
File Name
Sheet Name
Picture
Format Picture
Go to Header
Go to Footer
Different First Page
Different Odd & Even Pages
Scale with Document
Align with Page Margins
Header & Footer
Header & Footer Elements
Navigation
Options
A18
Header
Items
January
February
March
April
Grand Total Costs
Rent
£25,000.00
£25,000.00
£25,000.00
£25,000.00
Electricity
£500.00
£600.00
£500.00
£500.00
Wifi
£100.00
£100.00
£100.00
£100.00
Cleaning Materials
£150.00
£100.00
£200.00
£100.00
Marketing
£200.00
£200.00
£200.00
£200.00
Stationery
£50.00
£50.00
£50.00
£50.00

Figure 46

The first two icons, *Header* and *Footer*, will show you some ready-made headers and footers to pick from. There are also other elements such as *Page Numbers* and *Number of Pages*.

Page Numbers and Number of Pages	Adds the page number. *Number of Pages* is the total number of pages, so if you have 2/3, that is page 2 out of 3. The 3 is the number of pages.
Current Time and Current Date	Puts the current time or date in the header/footer.
File Path	Adds the file name and path to the document. It tells you the name of the document and where it is filed.
File Name	This adds the file name without the path.
Sheet Name	This adds the name of the worksheet or will say *Sheet 1* if not named.
Picture	You can add a picture such as a logo. However, it is best to resize it before adding.

Format Picture	When a picture is added, this becomes live. A picture can be resized and cropped. If you do resize or crop a picture in the header or footer, you will not see what it looks like until you go back to *Page Layout* view.
Go to Footer	This button switches between the header and footer.
Different First Page	When creating a report with several pages, set the first page to be different to the rest.
Different Odd and Even Pages	Have different headers and footers on odd or even pages.
Scale with Document	Makes sure everything is proportional. If you scale content, this scales headers and footers too.
Align with Page Margins	Makes sure that the header and footer align with the page margins.

Page Layout View

This is a view that shows how the pages will print, and it is here that headers and footers are added.

To get to *Page Layout View,* you will need to click on the icon at the bottom of the Excel window or access it via the *View* menu.

Page Layout View icon at the bottom of the window

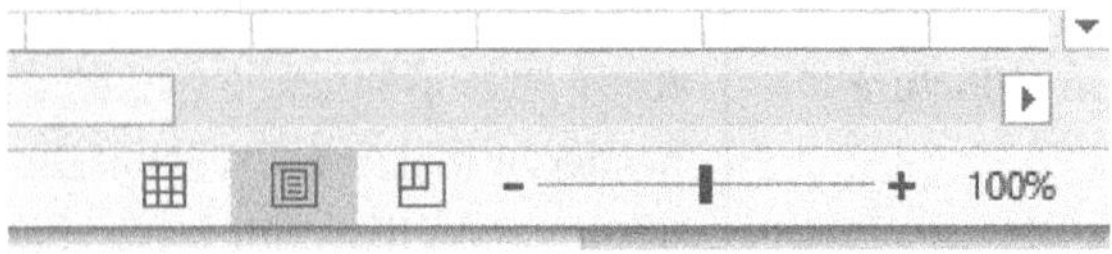

Figure 47

Page Layout icon on the *View* ribbon

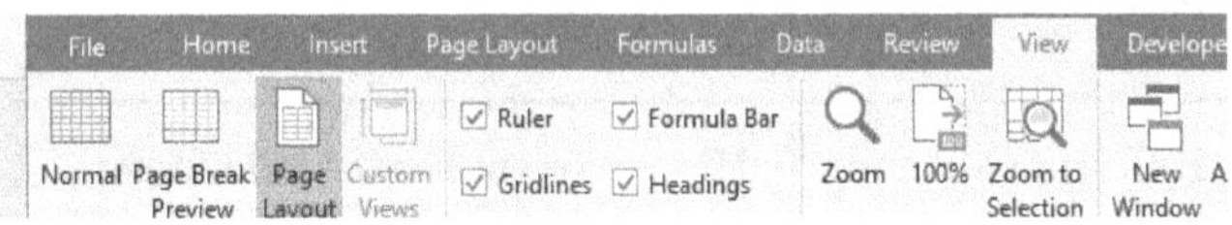

Figure 48

There is an area to add a header, and there is a corresponding one at the bottom of the page to add a footer. Margins are clearly visible, so it's easy to see how it will look when printed.

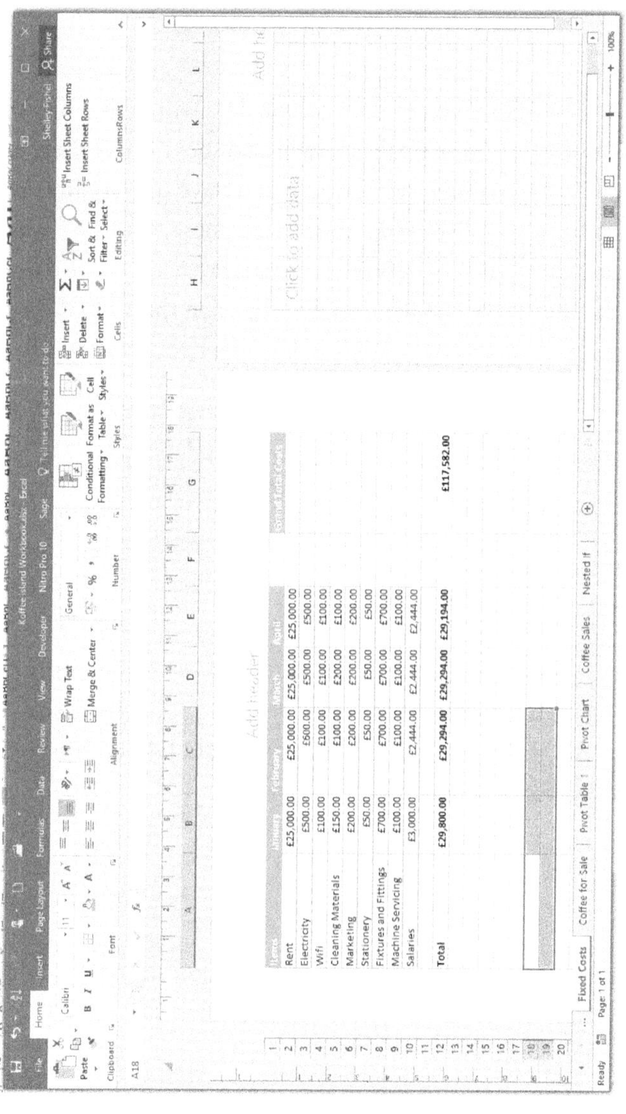
Koffee Island Workbook.xlsx - Excel
Rent £25,000.00 £25,000.00 £25,000.00 £25,000.00
Electricity £500.00 £600.00 £500.00 £500.00
Wifi £100.00 £100.00 £100.00 £100.00
Cleaning Materials £150.00 £100.00 £200.00 £100.00
Marketing £200.00 £200.00 £200.00 £200.00
Stationery £50.00 £50.00 £50.00 £50.00
Fixtures and Fittings £700.00 £700.00 £700.00 £700.00
Machine Servicing £100.00 £100.00 £100.00 £100.00
Salaries £3,000.00 £2,444.00 £2,444.00 £2,444.00
Total £29,800.00 £29,294.00 £29,294.00 £29,194.00 £117,582.00
Fixed Costs
Coffee for Sale
Pivot Table
Pivot Chart
Coffee Sales
Nested If

Figure 49

Page Break Preview

This view allows you to see how the data will sit and if it will print on one or more pages. It will also show where there are rogue columns or rows – where you have one column too many or a couple of rows too many. These can be adjusted by dragging the borders. *Page Break Preview* can be found at the bottom of the window as well as on the *View* ribbon.

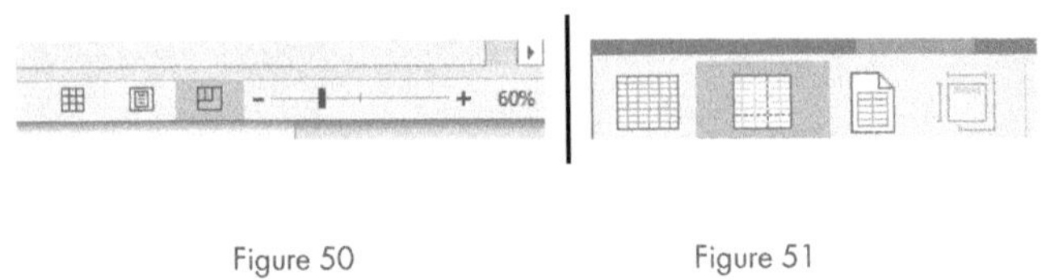

Figure 50

Figure 51

Here you can see dashed blue lines. These can be dragged to resize the content. However, be aware you will be scaling the text and numbers, and the text could end up too small for comfortable reading.

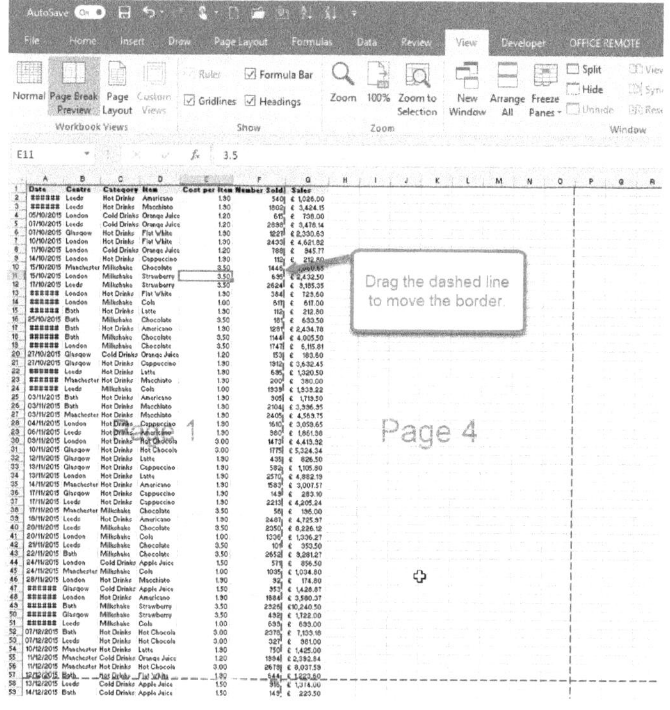

Figure 52

Print Titles on Every Page

When a spreadsheet contains a large amount of data and is printed, the headings are normally only printed on the first piece of paper, so if it runs onto several sheets, reading the columns can be tricky.

Tell Excel which rows or columns to repeat, and they will be printed on every page.

Click *Print Titles* on the *Page Layout* ribbon.

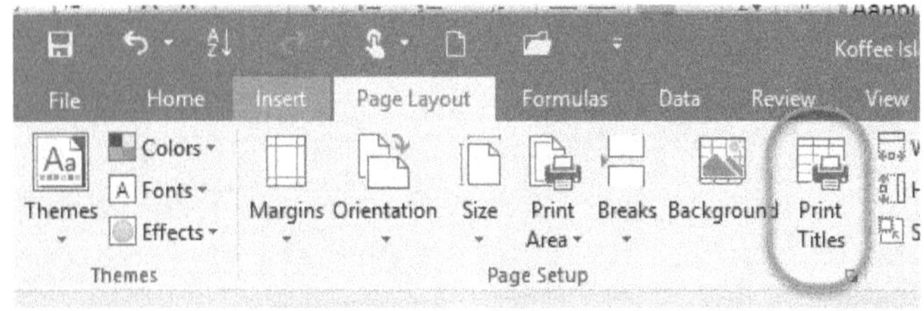

Figure 53

Tell Excel exactly what to repeat. You can click with the mouse on the row number of the row to repeat, and Excel will automatically add $row number (row number being the row you wish to fix).

Now when you print, no matter how long the document is, that row will print on every page. Columns can be repeated too.

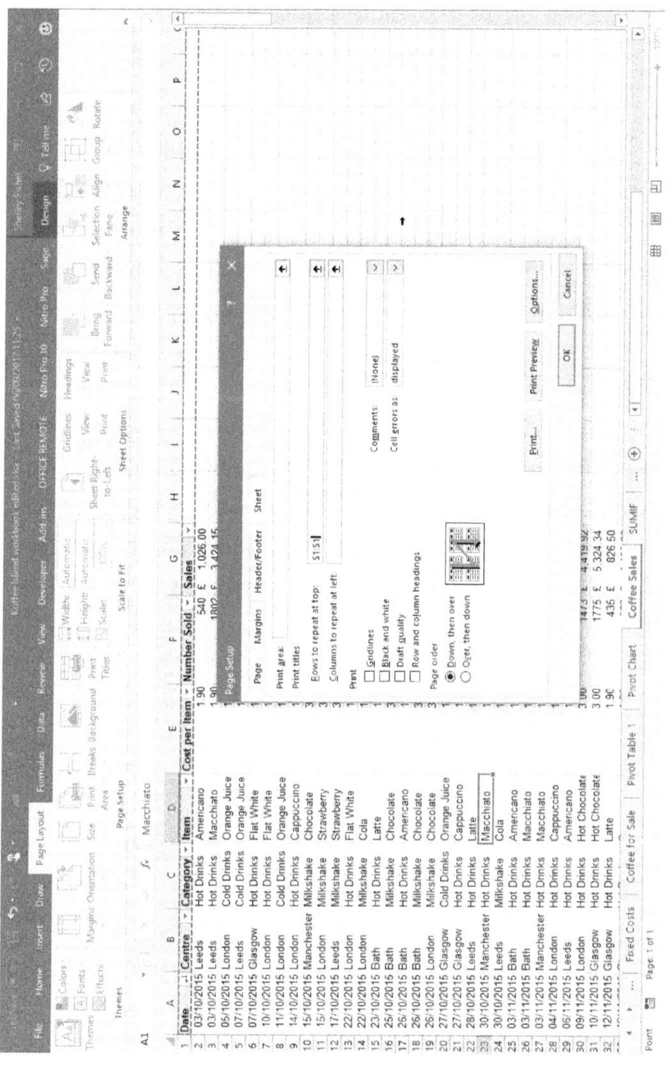
Page Setup
Page
Margins
Header/Footer
Sheet
Print area:
Print titles
Rows to repeat at top:
$1:$1
Columns to repeat at left:
Print
Gridlines
Black and white
Draft quality
Row and column headings
Comments:
(None)
Cell errors as:
displayed
Page order
Down, then over
Over, then down
Print...
Print Preview
Options...
OK
Cancel

Figure 54

Lists in Excel

A list in Excel consists of a grid comprising columns and rows. Koffee Island will have various lists, and one of these will be for staff details. Matt needs a couple of different columns: one for names and contact details, and one so he can calculate weekly pay, tax, and PAYE.

Matt plunges in with his staff details list. In the top row are the headings for each type of data. Before he does anything else, Matt needs to format the header row in bold. It's always good to make the headings different to the rest of the list so Excel will recognise that this row is the heading row. Then the data can be entered in the rows below. There are no blank columns or rows in a good list.

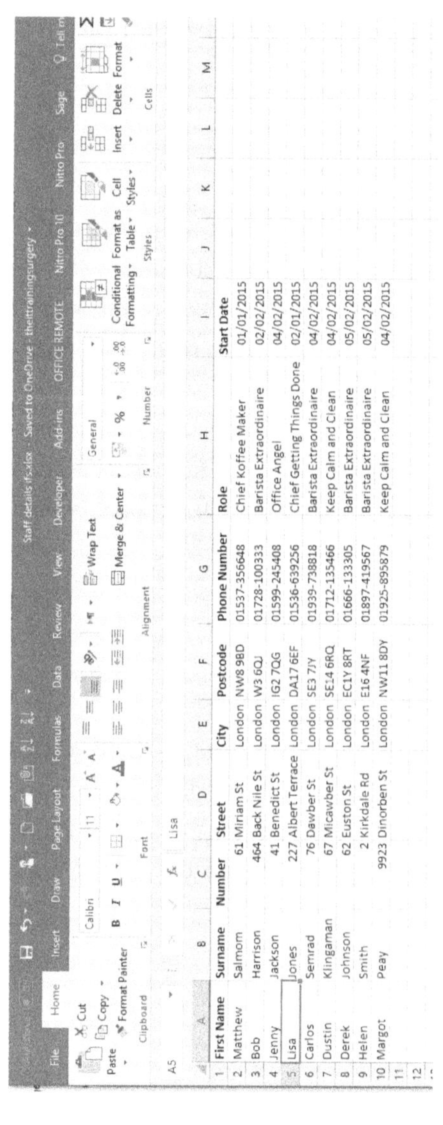

First Name	Surname	Number	Street	City	Postcode	Phone Number	Role	Start Date
Matthew	Salmom	61	Miriam St	London	NW8 9BD	01537-356648	Chief Koffee Maker	01/01/2015
Bob	Harrison	464	Back Nile St	London	W3 6QJ	01728-100333	Barista Extraordinaire	02/02/2015
Jenny	Jackson	41	Benedict St	London	IG2 7QG	01599-245408	Office Angel	04/02/2015
Lisa	Jones	227	Albert Terrace	London	DA17 6EF	01536-639256	Chief Getting Things Done	02/01/2015
Carlos	Semrad	76	Dawber St	London	SE3 7JY	01939-738818	Barista Extraordinaire	04/02/2015
Dustin	Klingaman	67	Micawber St	London	SE14 6RQ	01712-135466	Keep Calm and Clean	04/02/2015
Derek	Johnson	62	Euston St	London	EC1Y 8RT	01666-133305	Barista Extraordinaire	05/02/2015
Helen	Smith	2	Kirkdale Rd	London	E16 4NF	01897-419567	Barista Extraordinaire	05/02/2015
Margot	Peay	9923	Dinorben St	London	NW11 8DY	01925-895879	Keep Calm and Clean	04/02/2015

Figure 55

As it's looking a bit boring, Matt wants to jazz it up a bit and make it easier to read.

Koffee Suggests – *Format as a Table*

When you format a list as a table, automatic formatting is added. Shaded rows and columns make it easier to read. Additionally, if you add new columns or rows, the formatting will continue.

If working with numbers, automatic tables have even more functionality. We'll look at this later on.

To format the list as a table:

1. Click inside the list – so long as there are no blank columns or rows, it will work perfectly.
2. Click on *Format as Table* on the *Home* ribbon.
3. Select a style from the drop-down list offered.

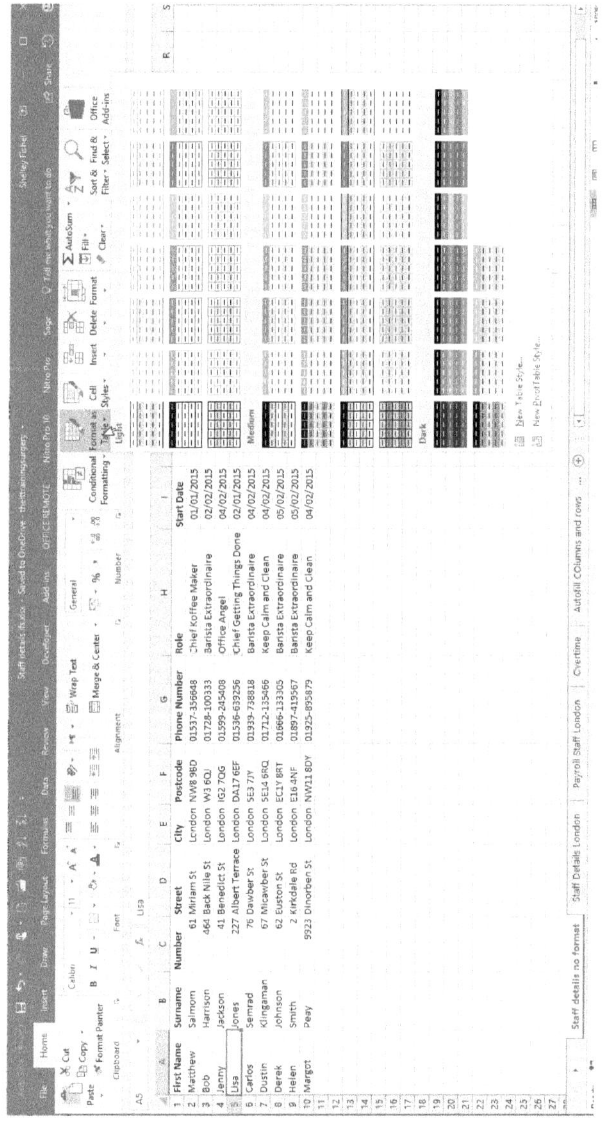

Figure 56

The formatting is applied, and the whole list looks a lot better.

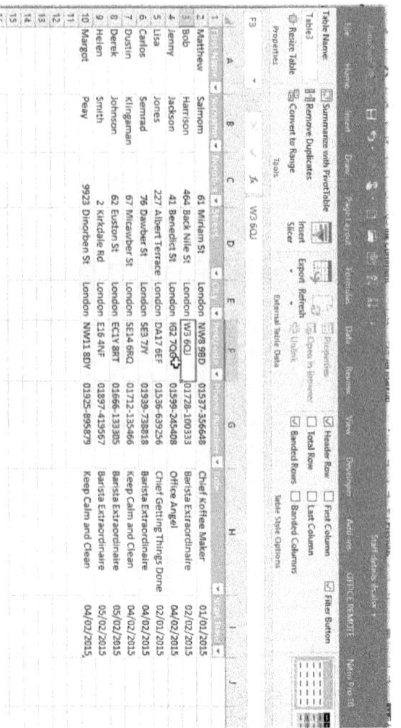

Figure 57

We will revisit *Format as Table* further on in the book.

Sums and Making Things Add Up

Matt is familiar with a normal handheld calculator and reasons that Excel can be thought of as a much larger and more advanced version. He needs to learn exactly how to make it do what he wants, so he asks Lisa, the Excel whizz, for help in setting up the spreadsheet he needs.

When we learn to do sums at school, we're told to write them like this:

3+2=5

The first number, then the mathematical symbol, then the second number, then an equals sign, then the answer. If you can do it in your head, great. If not, get your calculator out.

Excel works slightly differently.

In Excel, the numbers are written inside cells, and we already know the cells are referenced by grid numbers: A2, G4 etc.

Lisa also reminds Matt that he wants the spreadsheet to be automatic. He wants to plug in the hours each person works in a week, then let Excel do all the heavy-duty calculations.

To make this happen, calculations in Excel use cell references in the formula rather than the numbers themselves.

The sum above would look like this:

=A1+A2

Note that in each cell is a number. The answer is showing in the cell called A4, and the formula behind the answer is showing in the Formula Bar.

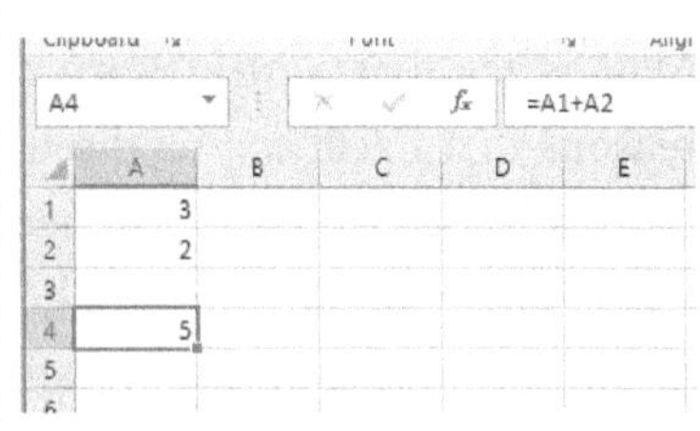

Figure 58

Koffee Says:

By using cell references in formulas, we can ensure that if the numbers change, so will the end calculation.

Add Up Two Numbers in Excel

1. Type an = (equals) sign.
2. Click on the first cell to add up.
3. Type a + (plus) sign.
4. Click on the second cell to add up.
5. Press *Enter* on your keyboard.

What Are the Mathematical Symbols?

=	Equals sign. All formulas start with this, no matter how simple or complex.
+	Addition to **add** up.
-	Minus to **subtract** one number away from another.
*	Asterisk, find this above the number 8 on the keyboard or on the top right corner of the numeric keypad. Use this to **multiply.**
/	Forward slash. Use this to **divide.**
( )	Brackets. Often a calculation will consist of several parts. Excel needs to know which parts to perform first. Anything in brackets will be done first.

Order of Precedence

Look at the following example. What would the answer be?

3+2*5=	It could be either: (3+2) *5 = 25 or 3+(2*5) = 13

Whatever is in the brackets gets calculated first. See Lisa's illustration for Matt.

(3+2)*5=25

5*5=25

3+(2*5)=13

3+10=13

Figure 59

BODMAS

The order of calculation is as follows:

Brackets – whatever is in brackets gets done first.
Order – work out anything to the power of next (a topic for a much more advanced book).
Divide – this is done first if there are no brackets or order.
Multiply – this is done next or first if there is no division, order, or brackets.
Add – this is done next or first if no multiplication, division, order, or brackets.
Subtract – this is done last.

If you need to make sure a calculation is done in a particular order, place whatever needs to be done first inside brackets. Excel will always perform that part first.

Now that Matt knows how to add up two single numbers by using the cell references, he wants to have a go at working out how much each member of staff has earned this week.

What Matt Needs to Know:

- The hourly rate for each member of staff
- The number of hours worked that week
- The bonus for each person
- The profit-related pay for each person (PRP)
- How much tax they need to pay
- Their net pay

The bonus, PRP rate, and tax rate are the same for each person. Matt needs to find a way of adding these figures to the spreadsheet so he can use them in each formula without having to key them into every cell. Lisa confirms he can put them down just once on the spreadsheet and reuse them.

But there are just a few things he needs to master first:

- Using AutoSum to add up a column or row
- Using Autofill
- Copying a formula to several columns or rows
- Creating an absolute cell reference

Once Matt has these under his belt, he'll be ready to complete this worksheet every week, doing each calculation just once.

Here is the spreadsheet Lisa and Matt created:

	A	B	C	D	E	F	G	H	I
1	Bonus on Gross	5%							
2	PRP Rate	2%							
3	Tax Rate	20%							
4									
5									
6	Name	Hours	Rate	Basic Gr	Bonus	PRP	Taxable Incom	Tax	Net
7	Matthew	15	£10.00	£150.00	£7.50	£3.00	£160.50	£32.10	£128.40
8	Bob	20	£15.00	£300.00	£15.00	£6.00	£321.00	£64.20	£256.80
9	Jenny	26	£20.00	£520.00	£26.00	£10.40	£556.40	£111.28	£445.12
10	Lisa	35	£7.00	£245.00	£12.25	£4.90	£262.15	£52.43	£209.72
11	Carlos	14	£9.00	£126.00	£6.30	£2.52	£134.82	£26.96	£107.86
12	Dustin	30	£10.00	£300.00	£15.00	£6.00	£321.00	£64.20	£256.80
13	Derek	26	£11.00	£286.00	£14.30	£5.72	£306.02	£61.20	£244.82
14	Helen	25	£13.00	£325.00	£16.25	£6.50	£347.75	£69.55	£278.20
15		12	£16.00	£192.00	£9.60	£3.84	£205.44	£41.09	£164.35
16	Total			**£2,444.00**	**£122.20**	**£48.88**	**£2,615.08**	**£523.02**	**£2,092.06**
17									
18									
19	**Summary**								
20	Average								
21	Highest								
22	Lowest								
23	Number of Staff								
24	Count Number of Staff								
25									

Figure 60

All the variables are in one location at the top of the worksheet, ready to be used once in each calculation.

Each person has a row with the number of hours worked and their hourly rate.

Matt will also want to see the largest, smallest, and average salary paid, and he will also want to count how many people are included.

Matt spots some tiny red triangles in the top right-hand corners of some of the heading cells. Lisa tells him these are comments. They're useful for adding information that is needed at some point. In this case, the comments tell Matt how to calculate each column.

To see the comment, hover the mouse over the cell with the comment.

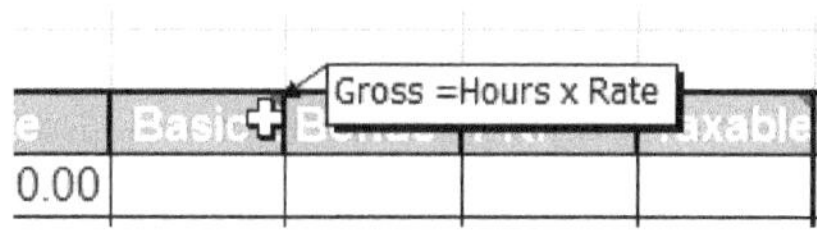

Figure 61

To Add Comments

Right-click or use the *Review* ribbon.

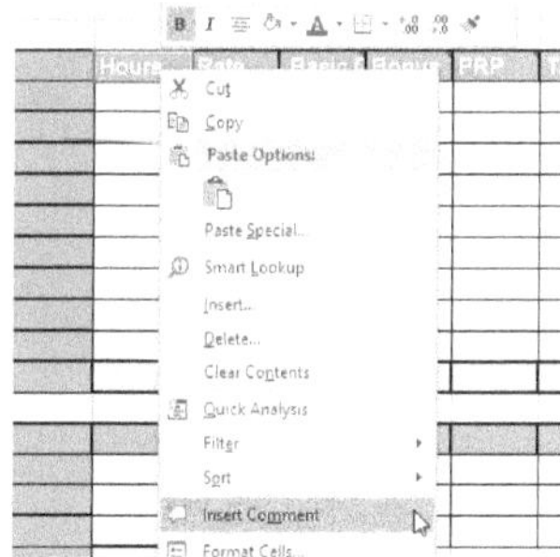

Figure 62

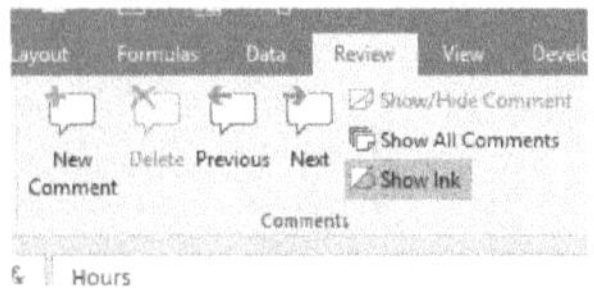

Figure 63

Click *Insert Comment* or *New Comment*, and add your text to the yellow box that appears. When you click away, you will be left with a red triangle.

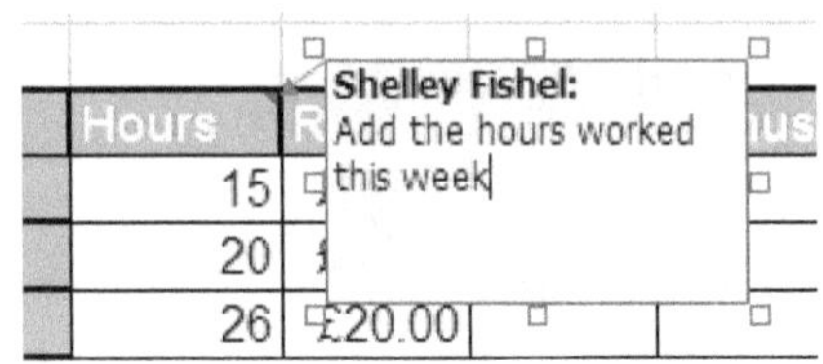

Figure 64

AutoSum

AutoSum adds up a whole range of cells automatically.

Here is a monthly sales list with figures for January through April. To add up the total sales for each month, use AutoSum.

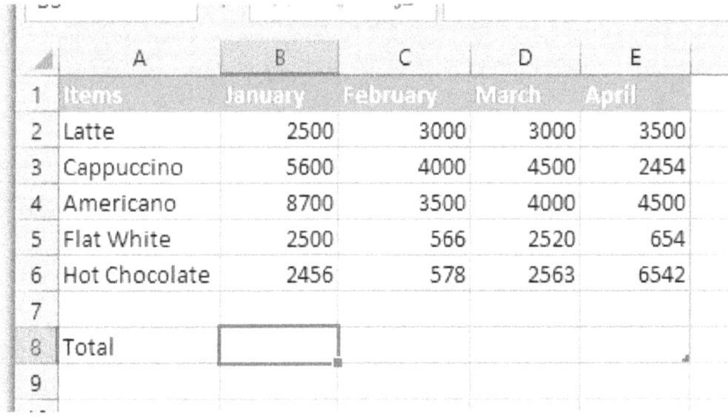

	A	B	C	D	E
1	Items	January	February	March	April
2	Latte	2500	3000	3000	3500
3	Cappuccino	5600	4000	4500	2454
4	Americano	8700	3500	4000	4500
5	Flat White	2500	566	2520	654
6	Hot Chocolate	2456	578	2563	6542
7					
8	Total				
9					

Figure 65

Lisa shows Matt two ways to find the *AutoSum* icon and how to write the formula from scratch.

The *Home* ribbon – here the *AutoSum* icon can be found at the far right-hand side in the *Editing* group of icons.

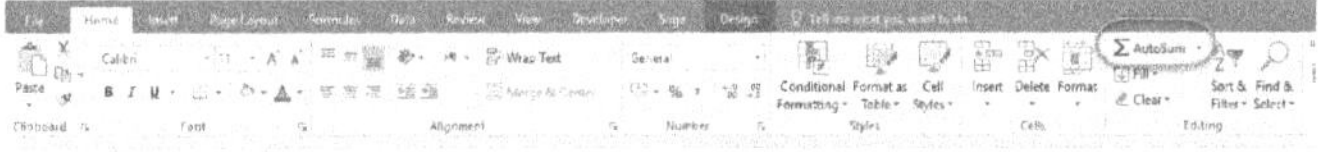

Figure 66

The *Formula* ribbon – there is a whole ribbon devoted to functions and formula, plus some other functionality. Here the *AutoSum* icon is on the left.

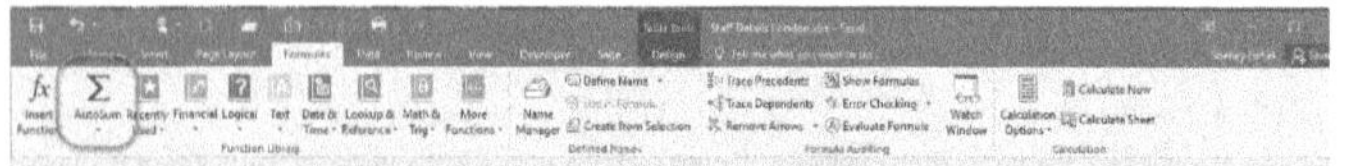

Figure 67

To use the AutoSum feature:

1. Click into the cell you want the answer to appear in.
2. Click the *AutoSum* icon – note the formula that appears in the cell.
3. If the cells the AutoSum identified are not quite right, drag over the ones that are.
4. Press *Enter* on your keyboard.

	A	B	C	D	E
1	Items	January	February	March	April
2	Latte	2500	3000	3000	3500
3	Cappuccino	5600	4000	4500	2454
4	Americano	8700	3500	4000	4500
5	Flat White	2500	566	2520	654
6	Hot Chocolate	2456	578	2563	6542
7					
8	Total	=SUM(B2:B7)			
9		SUM(**number1**, [number2], ...)			

Figure 68

In this case, Excel has picked up all the cells in the January list, and when Matt presses the *Enter* key, it will add them up. Notice the function in Cell B8.

=SUM(B2:B7)

Lisa unpicks this for Matt.

=	The = sign tells Excel a calculation is coming.
SUM	SUM tells Excel they are going to add up. It could be any formula here: average, minimum, maximum.
(B2:B7)	This is the range of cells that Excel will use in the formula. The colon means from cell to cell. In this case, from cell B2 to B7.

Koffee Says:

Remember there are no spaces when writing a formula. You can write the formula in the cell instead of using the *AutoSum* icon, and it will work. As you become an Excel expert, you may find you write the formula in the cell instead of using the icon!

Now Matt knows how to use AutoSum, he can use it on every column in this list until he has filled them all in.

Or can he?

	A	B	C	D	E	F
1	Items	January	February	March	April	
2	Latte	2500	3000	3000	3500	
3	Cappuccino	5600	4000	4500	2454	
4	Americano	8700	3500	4000	4500	
5	Flat White	2500	566	2520	654	
6	Hot Chocolate	2456	578	2563	6542	
7						
8	Total	21756	11644	=SUM(B8:C8)		
9				SUM(number1, [number2], ...)		
10						

Figure 69

Look what happens when Matt gets to the third column. Excel seems to have decided not to look above for the cells. It is going from left to right. This is *not* what Matt wants.

Matt is ready to panic, but Lisa explains. Excel is programmed to work with numbers. This means it looks left first – imagine a number line. It goes from left to right. Excel will look to its left first, and if there are two cells with numbers in, it will add them up. If Excel finds only one number, it will then look up and down.

When Excel does this, it's easy to override it. Simply drag over the cells you do want to add up, and Excel will behave itself.

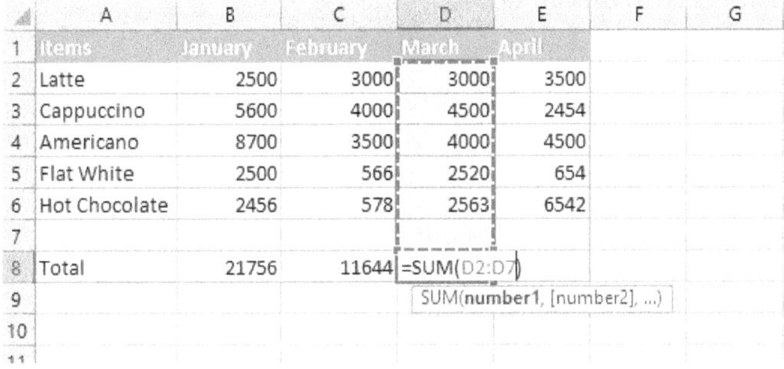

	A	B	C	D	E	F	G
1	Items	January	February	March	April		
2	Latte	2500	3000	3000	3500		
3	Cappuccino	5600	4000	4500	2454		
4	Americano	8700	3500	4000	4500		
5	Flat White	2500	566	2520	654		
6	Hot Chocolate	2456	578	2563	6542		
7							
8	Total	21756	11644	=SUM(D2:D7)			
9				SUM(number1, [number2], ...)			
10							

Figure 70

Matt discovers that for just four columns it's easy to use AutoSum each time, but what if he had twenty columns or even more? That would be tedious.

That is where Autofill comes in. However, before using it to copy a formula from one column to another, see how it works and what else it can do.

Autofill

This is one of the most useful features of Excel. It can save so much time.

Things Autofill can do:

- Copy a value to many columns or rows
- Copy contents and formatting
- Create an automatic list – this can be a pre-built list or one you create yourself
- Copy formula across columns or down rows
- Create an incremented list of dates or numbers
- Create a list of days of the week with or without weekends
- Create a daily, monthly, or yearly incremented list of dates

Matt just needs Lisa to show him exactly how to do all that.

The first thing to do is identify the Autofill handle. It is a little black plus sign that appears when you hover over the bottom right-hand corner of a cell.

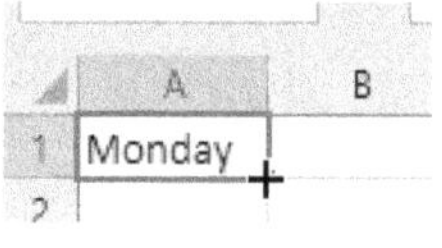

Figure 71

To see what it can do, Lisa suggests holding down the left mouse button when he sees the black plus sign and drag down the column. Then try dragging to the right.

Here is what Matt sees when he lets go.

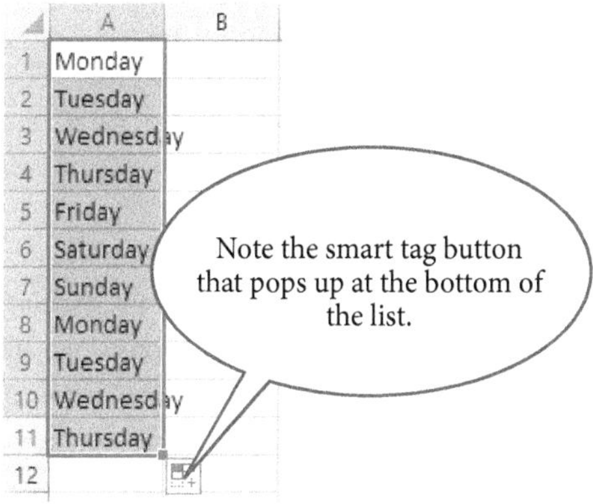

Figure 72

On the horizontal list, the smart tag pops up on the far right.

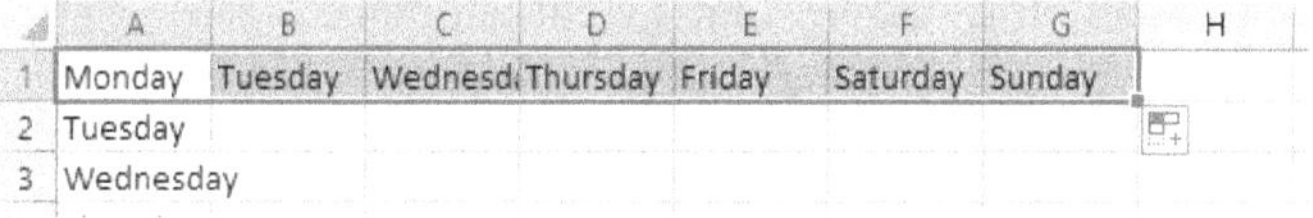

Figure 73

When clicking the smart tag, different options are offered. The options will change based on the type of data being filled.

Options for days of the week:

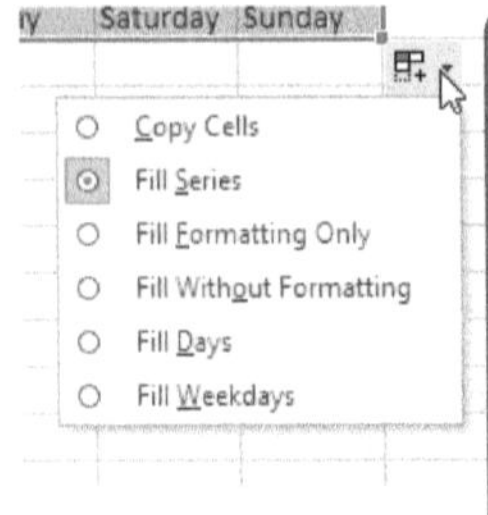

- Copy Cells – this will copy exactly what's in the first cell.
- Fill Series – this is the default, and wherever Excel recognises a series, it will complete it.
- Fill Formatting Only – copy only the formatting from the starting cell.
- Fill Without Formatting – fills only the content and not the formatting.
- Fill Days – fills days of the week including weekends.
- Fill Weekdays – removes Saturdays and Sundays from the list.

Figure 74

When you fill numbers, here's what happens:

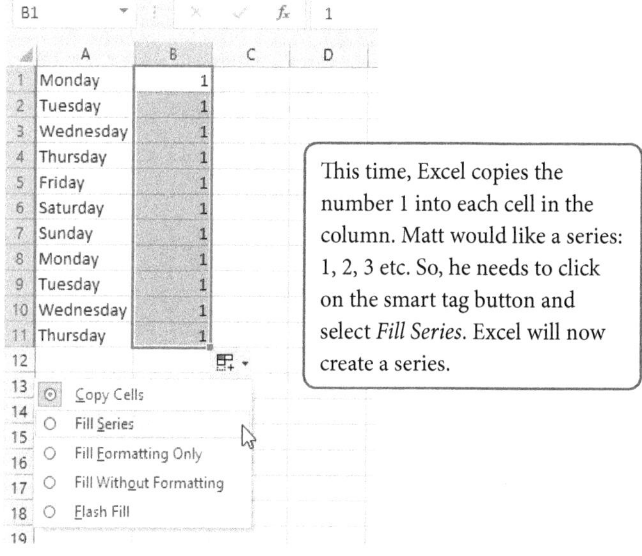

This time, Excel copies the number 1 into each cell in the column. Matt would like a series: 1, 2, 3 etc. So, he needs to click on the smart tag button and select *Fill Series*. Excel will now create a series.

Figure 75

To make Excel fill a series without having to click the smart tag button, Matt needs to give Excel the beginning of the series on the spreadsheet. Excel will then replicate what it sees.

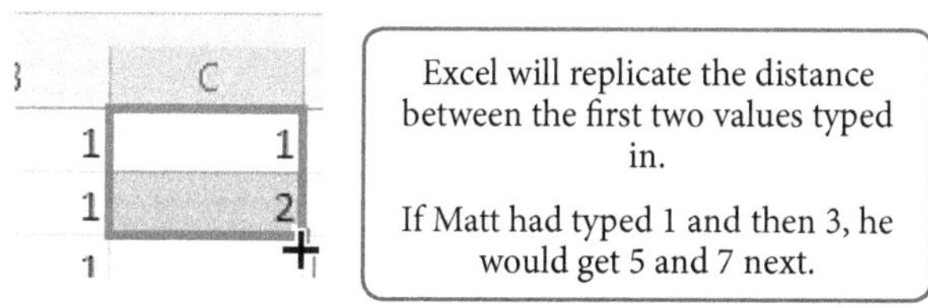

C
1
2
Excel will replicate the distance between the first two values typed in.
If Matt had typed 1 and then 3, he would get 5 and 7 next.

Figure 76

Filling Dates

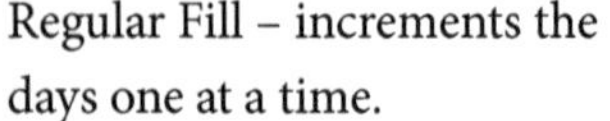 Regular Fill – increments the days one at a time. 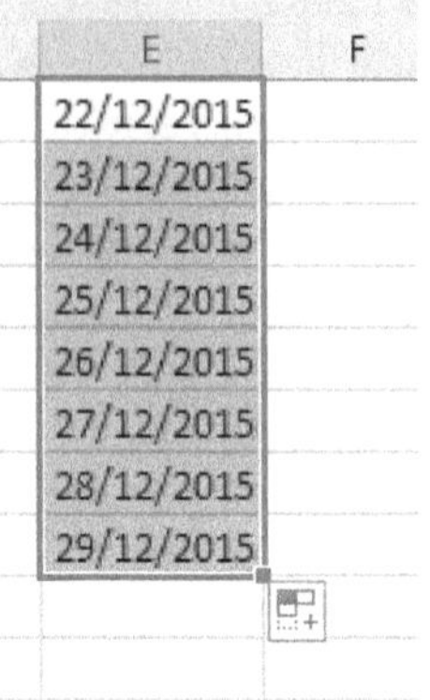 Figure 77	Fill Weekdays – removes Saturdays and Sundays from the list. 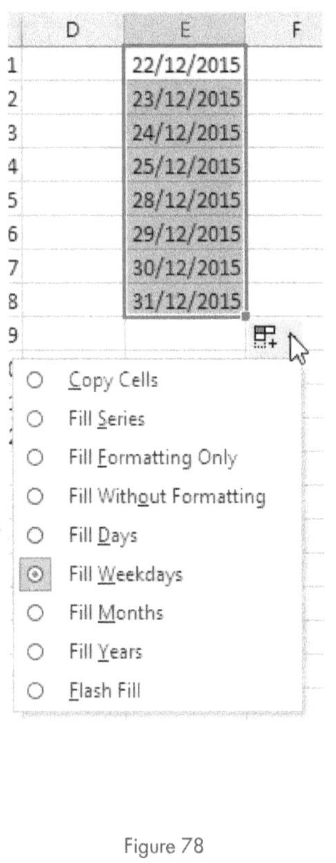 Figure 78

Fill Months – increments the months by one – 12, 01, 02 etc.	Fill Years – increments the year by one.

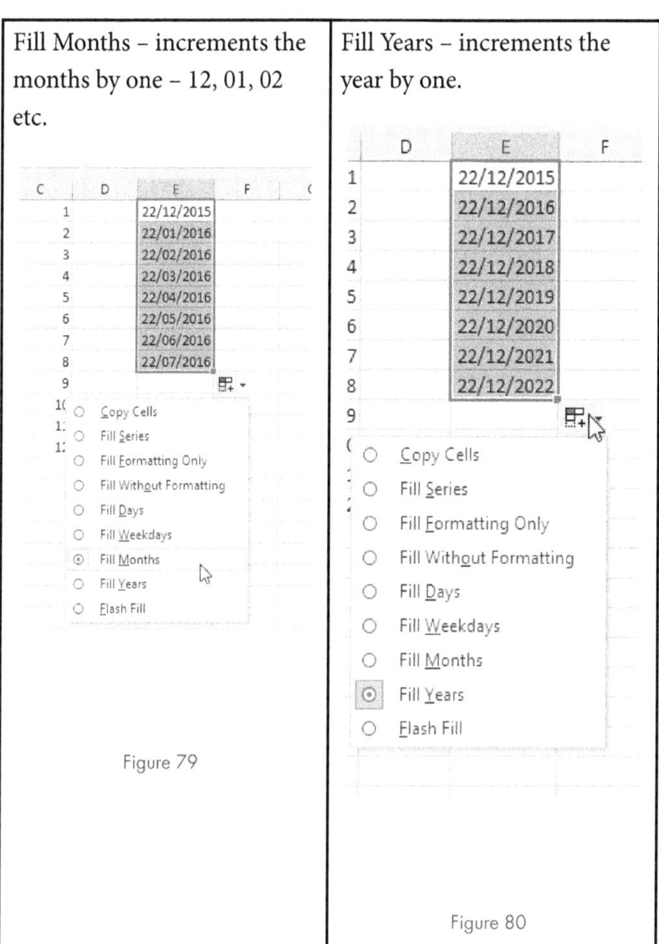

Figure 79

Figure 80

Here, Matt sets the first two times in an agenda, and Excel fills in the rest.

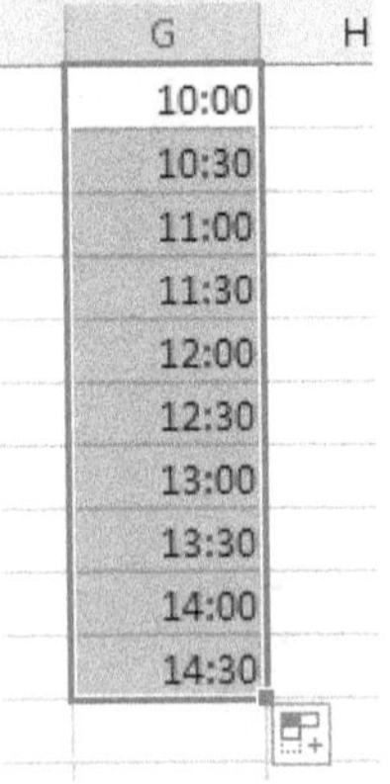

Figure 81

Here, Matt sets up the dates that correspond to Monday 28th December 2015 and Monday 4th January 2016. Excel fills in the list of dates of every Monday.

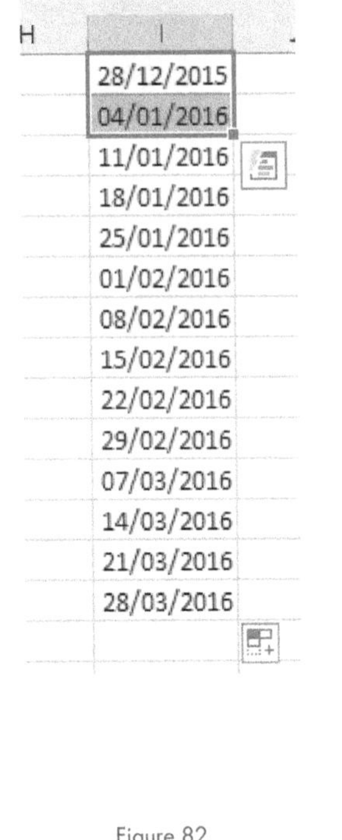

Figure 82

Matt now knows how to find Autofill and how to use it. Now he needs help with the calculations.

Here is where it gets magical, says Lisa. We can use Autofill to copy a formula across columns or down rows. Let me show you what I mean.

Autofill Formula

Going back to the example of the monthly sales numbers, Lisa shows Matt he can use Autofill to copy the formula from the January column across to the April column so he only needs to do that formula once.

	A	B	C	D	E	F
1	Items	January	February	March	April	
2	Latte	2500	3000	3000	3500	
3	Cappuccino	5600	4000	4500	2454	
4	Americano	8700	3500	4000	4500	
5	Flat White	2500	566	2520	654	
6	Hot Chocolate	2456	578	2563	6542	
7						
8	Total	21756	11644	16583	17650	
9						

Figure 83

As you'll remember, Matt wants to work out how much to pay each member of staff. Remember this spreadsheet? Here, Matt has started to work out the basic gross salary for himself by multiplying the hours worked by the rate.

	A	B	C	D	E
1	Bonus on Gross	5%			
2	PRP Rate	2%			
3	Tax Rate	20%			
4					
5					
6	Name	Hours	Rate	Basic Gr	Bonus
7	Matthew	15	£10.00	=B7*C7	
8	Bob	20	£15.00		
9	Jenny	26	£20.00		
10	Lisa	35	£7.00		
11	Carlos	14	£9.00		
12	Dustin	30	£10.00		
13	Derek	26	£11.00		
14	Helen	25	£13.00		
15		12	£16.00		
16	Total				
17					
18					
19	**Summary**				
20	Average				
21	Highest				
22	Lowest				
23	Number of Staff				
24	Count Number of Staff				
25					

Figure 84

He can now press *Enter* on the keyboard and use Autofill to copy the formula down the whole column.

5					
6	Name	Hours	Rate	Basic Gr	Bon
7	Matthew	15	£10.00	£150.00	
8	Bob	20	£15.00	£300.00	
9	Jenny	26	£20.00	£520.00	
10	Lisa	35	£7.00	£245.00	
11	Carlos	14	£9.00	£126.00	
12	Dustin	30	£10.00	£300.00	
13	Derek	26	£11.00	£286.00	
14	Helen	25	£13.00	£325.00	
15	Janice	12	£16.00	£192.00	
16	Total				

Figure 85

Matt is feeling pretty pleased with himself. Excel formulas aren't as scary as he thought. Now he just needs to complete the next few columns. Assuming it's all the same, he starts on the next column.

	A	B	C	D	E	F	G	H
1	Bonus on Gross	5%						
2	PRP Rate	2%						
3	Tax Rate	20%						
4								
5						Basic Gross x Bonus on Gross		
6	Name	Hours	Rate	Basic Gr	Bonu	PRP	Taxable Incom	Overtim
7	Matthew	15	£10.00	£150.00				
8	Bob	20	£15.00	£300.00				
9	Jenny	26	£20.00	£520.00				
10	Lisa	35	£7.00	£245.00				
11	Carlos	14	£9.00	£126.00				
12	Dustin	30	£10.00	£300.00				
13	Derek	26	£11.00	£286.00				
14	Helen	25	£13.00	£325.00				
15	Janice	12	£16.00	£192.00				
16	Total							
17								

Figure 86

The comment tells Matt to multiply the basic gross, which he just worked out, by the bonus on gross percentage. Easy peasy, says Matt. I type an = sign, then click on D7 (Matt's basic gross), type an *, then click on B1 (the bonus on gross rate). Then press *Enter* and use Autofill to copy to the whole column. No need to do it on every row.

	A	B	C	D	E	F	
1	Bonus on Gross	5%					
2	PRP Rate	2%					
3	Tax Rate	20%					
4							
5							
6	Name	Hours	Rate	Basic Gro	Bonus	PRP	Taxa
7	Matthew	15	£10.00	£150.00	=D7*B1		
8	Bob	20	£15.00	£300.00			

Figure 87

That is what Matt does, and this is what he sees as a result:

	A	B	C	D	E	F	
1	Bonus on Gross	5%					
2	PRP Rate	2%					
3	Tax Rate	20%					
4							
5							
6	Name	Hours	Rate	Basic Gr	Bonus	PRP	T
7	Matthew	15	£10.00	£150.00	£7.50		
8	Bob	20	£15.00	£300.00	£6.00		
9	Jenny	26	£20.00	£520.00	######		
10	Lisa	35	£7.00	£245.00	£0.00		
11	Carlos	14	£9.00	£126.00	£0.00		
12	Dustin	30	£10.00	£300.00	######		
13	Derek	26	£11.00	£286.00	######		
14	Helen	25	£13.00	£325.00	######		
15	Janice	12	£16.00	£192.00	######		
16	Total						

Figure 88

This is confusing. Matt knows Bob worked more hours at a higher rate. Why is his bonus shown as less? Then there are those funny ###### marks in some of the cells, and Lisa has a bonus of 0, which certainly isn't right.

Before Matt starts tearing his hair out, Lisa explains. The ###### signs mean the column is not wide enough. It needs resizing.

Now we can see what is going on. Lisa makes Matt click on the bonus for Jenny. Then looking in the Formula Bar, he can see where the result is coming from. Cell D9 is Jenny's basic gross salary, so that's OK. But the second part is not B1 any more. Now the second part is referencing B3, which has the tax rate in. No wonder Jenny has such a large bonus.

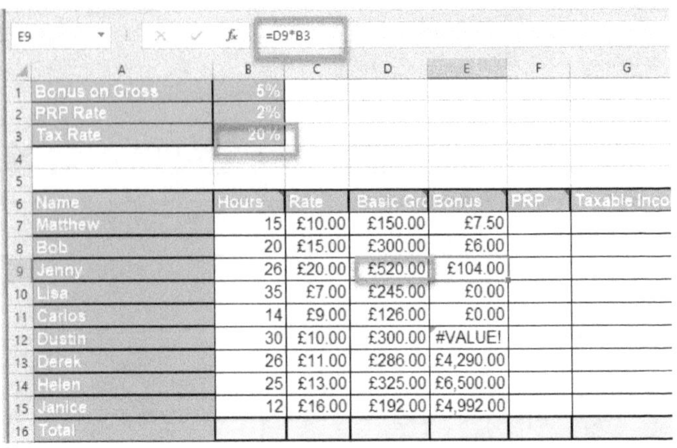

E9 =D9*B3

	A	B	C	D	E	F	G
1	Bonus on Gross	5%					
2	PRP Rate	2%					
3	Tax Rate	20%					
4							
5							
6	Name	Hours	Rate	Basic Gr	Bonus	PRP	Taxable Inco
7	Matthew	15	£10.00	£150.00	£7.50		
8	Bob	20	£15.00	£300.00	£6.00		
9	Jenny	26	£20.00	£520.00	£104.00		
10	Lisa	35	£7.00	£245.00	£0.00		
11	Carlos	14	£9.00	£126.00	£0.00		
12	Dustin	30	£10.00	£300.00	#VALUE!		
13	Derek	26	£11.00	£286.00	£4,290.00		
14	Helen	25	£13.00	£325.00	£6,500.00		
15	Janice	12	£16.00	£192.00	£4,992.00		
16	Total						

Figure 89

Absolute Cell References – Fixing the Reference

Matt realises he needs to fix the reference to B1 in every formula. Fixing the reference to B1 in each row will ensure that the correct figures are calculated. The basic gross salary is correct and needs to adjust down one row for each calculation.

Correct, says Lisa, that's exactly right. We make the reference to cell B1 absolute. It becomes an absolute cell reference and refers only to B1 and does not change in a formula using Autofill.

When a cell reference is absolute, it appears like this:

$B$1 – the dollar signs are code for Excel, telling it to refer to this cell and this cell only when using Autofill to copy a formula.

To make a cell absolute, we are going to use a keyboard shortcut. It's much faster than typing in the dollar signs, although you can do this if you wish.

The keyboard shortcut is **F4.**

Along the top of the keyboard is a range of what are known as function keys. They are labelled with *F* and a number. They often perform other functionality or enhance functionality as in this case.

Koffee Says:

On a laptop, the function keys may be used for different things. If you press the *F4* key and it doesn't work as you expect, you may need to press the *Function* key itself along with the *F4* key. You will find the *Function* key at the bottom of the keyboard next to the space bar. It may be on the left or the right; it depends on the laptop.

Now we can try this again.

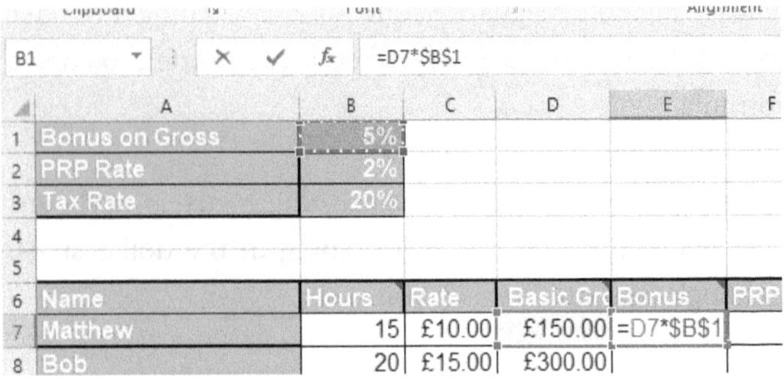

Figure 90

Once the F4 key is pressed, dollar signs appear in front of the B and the 1. Now Matt can use Autofill again and see a different result.

Matt places the cursor in cell E7 and types an = sign. Now to select the cells for the formula. He clicks on D7, then the asterisk to multiply, then once he clicks on B1, which is the cell to fix, he presses the F4 key. Once he sees $B$1 in the formula, he knows he can use the Autofill handle to copy it to the whole column.

E7 =D7*$B$1

	A	B	C	D	E	F	G
1	Bonus on Gross	5%					
2	PRP Rate	2%					
3	Tax Rate	20%					
4							
5							
6	Name	Hours	Rate	Basic Gr	Bonus	PRP	Taxable Incom
7	Matthew	15	£10.00	£150.00	£7.50		
8	Bob	20	£15.00	£300.00	£15.00		
9	Jenny	26	£20.00	£520.00	£26.00		
10	Lisa	35	£7.00	£245.00	£12.25		
11	Carlos	14	£9.00	£126.00	£6.30		
12	Dustin	30	£10.00	£300.00	£15.00		
13	Derek	26	£11.00	£286.00	£14.30		
14	Helen	25	£13.00	£325.00	£16.25		
15	Janice	12	£16.00	£192.00	£9.60		
16	Total						
17							
18							
19	Summary						
20	Average						
21	Highest						
22	Lowest						
23	Number of Staff						
24	Count Number of Staff						
25							

Figure 91

Each person now has the correct bonus rate.

Matt goes ahead and completes the next column for the PRP rate and uses the F4 key again to fix the reference to the PRP rate (B2). Before he does the calculation, he checks with the comment to make sure he's multiplying the correct cells together.

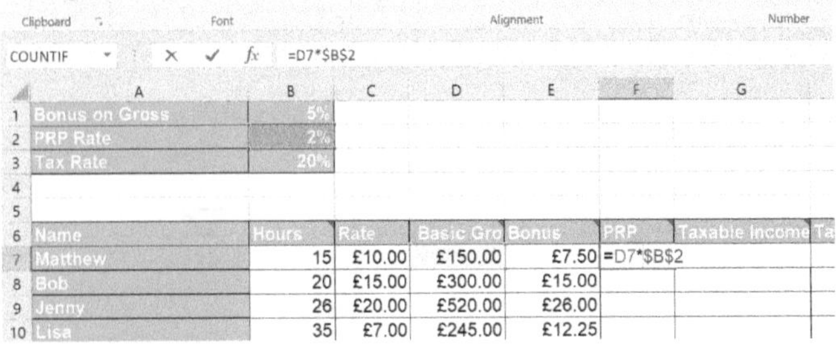

Figure 92

Using Autofill, he now completes the column.

Completing the Rest of This Spreadsheet

To complete the rest of this spreadsheet, Matt needs to work out the taxable salary, which is the basic gross + bonus + PRP. He uses AutoSum to add these up. As there are more than three columns to the left, Excel wants to add them all up. Matt only wants three. He uses the mouse to drag over the ones he wants to include.

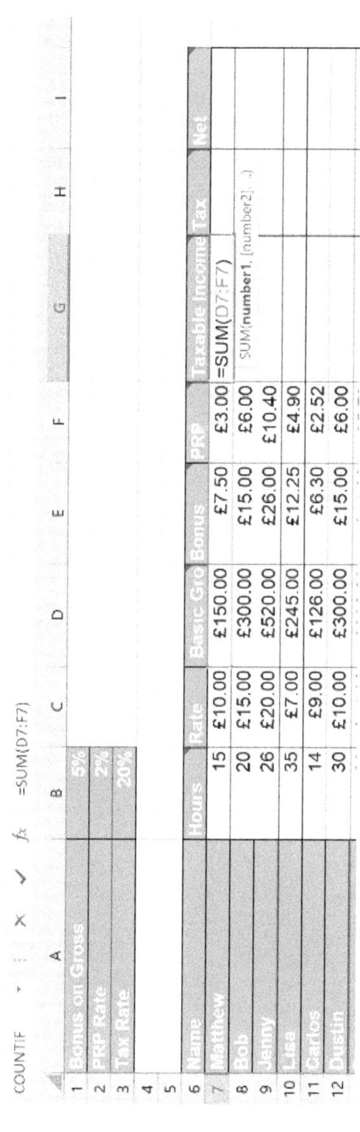

	A	B	C	D	E	F	G	H	I
1	Bonus on Gross	5%							
2	PRP Rate	2%							
3	Tax Rate	20%							
4									
5									
6	Name	Hours	Rate	Basic Gro	Bonus	PRP	Taxable Income	Tax	Net
7	Matthew	15	£10.00	£150.00	£7.50	£3.00	=SUM(D7:F7)		
8	Bob	20	£15.00	£300.00	£15.00	£6.00			
9	Jenny	26	£20.00	£520.00	£26.00	£10.40			
10	Lisa	35	£7.00	£245.00	£12.25	£4.90			
11	Carlos	14	£9.00	£126.00	£6.30	£2.52			
12	Dustin	30	£10.00	£300.00	£15.00	£6.00			

Figure 93

Then he can use Autofill to complete the column.

The tax column is calculated by multiplying the taxable income by the tax rate. Matt, being a fast learner, realises he needs to use his F4 key again to fix the reference to B3 so he can Autofill the column.

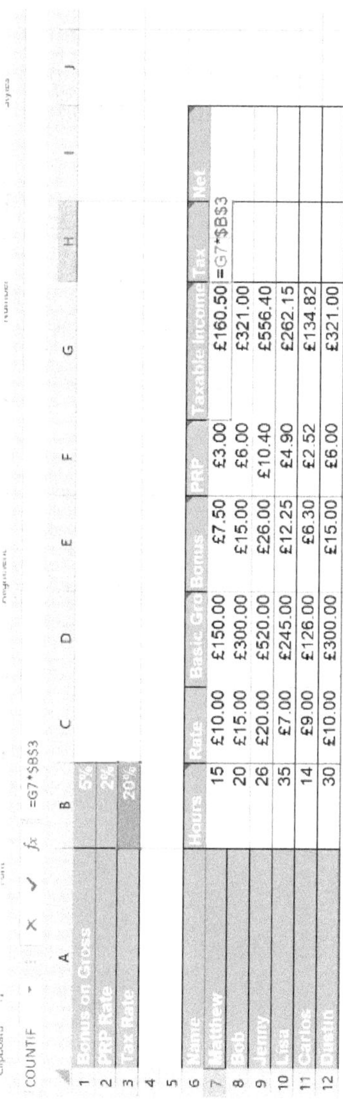

	A	B	C	D	E	F	G	H	I
1	Bonus on Gross	5%							
2	PRP Rate	2%							
3	Tax Rate	20%							
4									
5									
6	Name	Hours	Rate	Basic Gro	Bonus	PRP	Taxable Income	Tax	Net
7	Matthew	15	£10.00	£150.00	£7.50	£3.00	£160.50	=G7*$B$3	
8	Bob	20	£15.00	£300.00	£15.00	£6.00	£321.00		
9	Jenny	26	£20.00	£520.00	£26.00	£10.40	£556.40		
10	Lisa	35	£7.00	£245.00	£12.25	£4.90	£262.15		
11	Carlos	14	£9.00	£126.00	£6.30	£2.52	£134.82		
12	Dustin	30	£10.00	£300.00	£15.00	£6.00	£321.00		

Figure 94

The net is the total taxable amount minus the tax amount. This is a simple subtraction, so there's no need to fix any cells, and Matt can use Autofill as soon as he has worked out the first one.

	PRP	Taxable Income	Tax	Net
0	£3.00	£160.50	£32.10	=G7-H7
0	£6.00	£321.00	£64.20	
0	£10.40	£556.40	£111.28	

Figure 95

Now Matt has all the columns complete, he can start to see what the total salary bill and tax bill would be for everyone. To do this, he can use AutoSum to add up the basic gross salary, and then copy this across all the columns.

	A	B	C	D	E	F	G	H	I
1	Bonus on Gross	5%							
2	PRP Rate	2%							
3	Tax Rate	20%							
4									
5									
6	Name	Hours	Rate	Basic Gro	Bonus	PRP	Taxable Incom	Tax	Net
7	Matthew	15	£10.00	£150.00	£7.50	£3.00	£160.50	£32.10	£128.40
8	Bob	20	£15.00	£300.00	£15.00	£6.00	£321.00	£64.20	£256.80
9	Jenny	26	£20.00	£520.00	£26.00	£10.40	£556.40	£111.28	£445.12
10	Lisa	35	£7.00	£245.00	£12.25	£4.90	£262.15	£52.43	£209.72
11	Carlos	14	£9.00	£126.00	£6.30	£2.52	£134.82	£26.96	£107.86
12	Dustin	30	£10.00	£300.00	£15.00	£6.00	£321.00	£64.20	£256.80
13	Derek	26	£11.00	£286.00	£14.30	£5.72	£306.02	£61.20	£244.82
14	Helen	25	£13.00	£325.00	£16.25	£6.50	£347.75	£69.55	£278.20
15	Janice	12	£16.00	£192.00	£9.60	£3.84	£205.44	£41.09	£164.35
16	Total			**£2,444.00**	**£122.20**	**£48.88**	**£2,615.08**	**£523.02**	**£2,092.06**

Figure 96

Now Matt knows that he will need to have £2,615.08 available. There will be £523.02 to be set aside for tax and a total of £2,092.06 to be paid to the staff themselves.

At the bottom of the spreadsheet, Lisa has set up some other headings ready for information Matt might want to extrapolate from the data.

Average	To work out the average salary.
Highest	To see the highest number in the list – the maximum salary.
Lowest	To see the lowest number in the list – the minimum salary.
Number of Staff	How many staff are there in the list? This will enable Matt to check how many rows have numbers in them.
Count Number of Staff	Will count cells that have text in them.

Koffee Says:

When using a formula to count, you can count either numbers or text entries.
=Count( ) – this counts the number of cells that contain numeric values in the range of cells indicated.
=CountA( ) – this counts the number of cells that contain text.

Average

Lisa asks Matt how he would work out the average.

He thought he would:

- Count the entries in the list
- Add them up
- Divide the total by the number of entries

However, this is a several step operation that will take time. Plus, there's scope for error if Matt miscounts. Not to worry though, Excel has a function for this.

Lisa explains he could type the function in or use the drop-down on the AutoSum button.

Type the Formula

Matt starts to type the formula =*Ave.* At this point, a tool tip appears showing a list of formula that start with *AVE.* He uses the arrow key to move down the list, and the tab key to select *AVERAGE.* Then he drags over all the values in the column that he wants to include. Remember not to include the total!

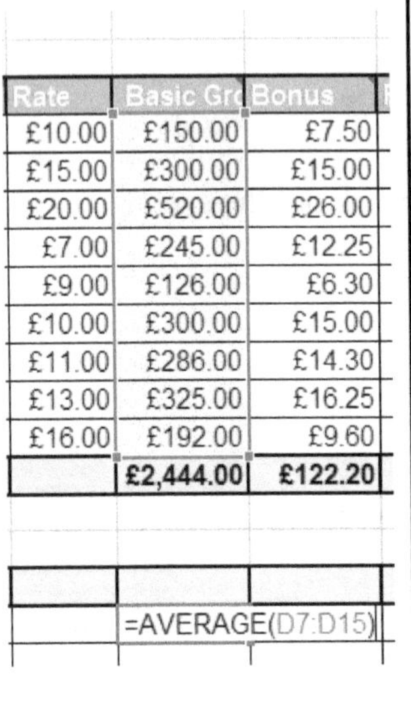

Rate	Basic Gro	Bonus
£10.00	£150.00	£7.50
£15.00	£300.00	£15.00
£20.00	£520.00	£26.00
£7.00	£245.00	£12.25
£9.00	£126.00	£6.30
£10.00	£300.00	£15.00
£11.00	£286.00	£14.30
£13.00	£325.00	£16.25
£16.00	£192.00	£9.60
	£2,444.00	**£122.20**
	=AVERAGE(D7:D15)	

Figure 97

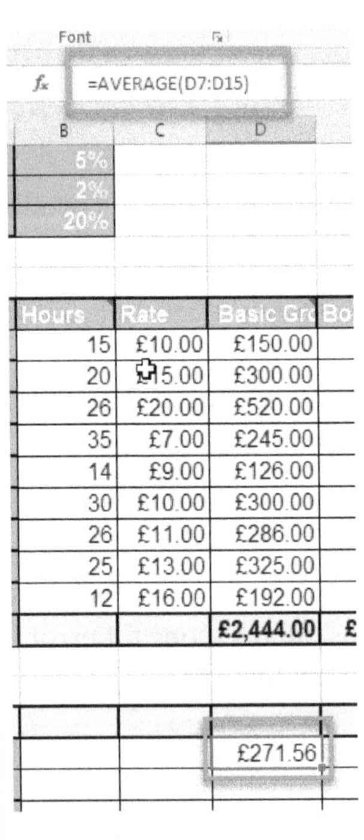

B	C	D
5%		
2%		
20%		

Hours	Rate	Basic Gro	Bo
15	£10.00	£150.00	
20	£15.00	£300.00	
26	£20.00	£520.00	
35	£7.00	£245.00	
14	£9.00	£126.00	
30	£10.00	£300.00	
26	£11.00	£286.00	
25	£13.00	£325.00	
12	£16.00	£192.00	
		£2,444.00	**£**
		£271.56	

Figure 98

When he presses *Enter*, Excel will work out the average. The formula can be seen in the Formula Bar and the result in the cell you performed the calculation in.

Minimum

Minimum is the function that picks up the smallest number in a list.

It follows the same process as average. This time, Matt uses the drop-down next to *AutoSum* so he can see the difference.

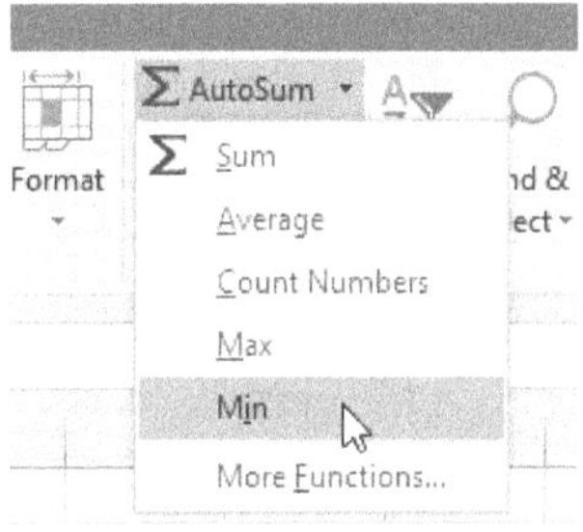

Figure 99

He clicks into the cell where the answer should be and clicks on the drop-down arrow next to the *AutoSum* icon. He chooses the *Min* function from the list, and Excel adds *=MIN(* to the cell. Now Matt just needs to drag over the cells he wants it to look in. He presses *Enter* and is left with the smallest number in the cell.

s	Rate	Basic Gr	Bonus	PRP
15	£10.00	£150.00	£7.50	£3.00
20	£15.00	£300.00	£15.00	£6.00
26	£20.00	£520.00	£26.00	£10.40
35	£7.00	£245.00	£12.25	£4.90
14	£9.00	£126.00	£6.30	£2.52
30	£10.00	£300.00	£15.00	£6.00
26	£11.00	£286.00	£14.30	£5.72
25	£13.00	£325.00	£16.25	£6.50
12	£16.00	£192.00	£9.60	£3.84
		£2,444.00	**£122.20**	**£48.88**
		£271.56		
		=MIN(D7:D15)		
		MIN(**number1**, [number2], ...)		

Figure 100

5%
2%
20%

Hours	Rate	Basic Gr	Bonu
15	£10.00	£150.00	£
20	£15.00	£300.00	£1
26	£20.00	£520.00	£2
35	£7.00	£245.00	£1
14	£9.00	£126.00	£
30	£10.00	£300.00	£1
26	£11.00	£286.00	£1
25	£13.00	£325.00	£1
12	£16.00	£192.00	£
		£2,444.00	**£12**
		£271.56	
		£126.00	

Figure 101

Maximum

Follow either process to work out the maximum. The formula will be: **=MAX(D7:D15)**

Count Numbers

To count how many number entries there are in a list, we will use a very similar process

AVERAGEIF =COUNT(B7:B15)

Bonus on Gross	5%
PRP Rate	2%
Tax Rate	20%

Name	Hours	Rate	Basic Gr	Bonus	PRP	Taxable Incom	Tax	Net
Matthew	15	£10.00	£150.00	£7.50	£3.00	£160.50	£32.10	£128.40
Bob	20	£15.00	£300.00	£15.00	£6.00	£321.00	£64.20	£256.80
Jenny	26	£20.00	£520.00	£26.00	£10.40	£556.40	£111.28	£445.12
Lisa	35	£7.00	£245.00	£12.25	£4.90	£262.15	£52.43	£209.72
Carlos	14	£9.00	£126.00	£6.30	£2.52	£134.82	£26.96	£107.86
Dustin	30	£10.00	£300.00	£15.00	£6.00	£321.00	£64.20	£256.80
Derek	26	£11.00	£286.00	£14.30	£5.72	£306.02	£61.20	£244.82
Helen	25	£13.00	£325.00	£16.25	£6.50	£347.75	£69.55	£278.20
Janice	12	£16.00	£192.00	£9.60	£3.84	£205.44	£41.09	£164.35
Total			**£2,444.00**	**£122.20**	**£48.88**	**£2,615.08**	**£523.02**	**£2,092.06**

Summary			
Average			£271.56
Highest			£520.00
Lowest			£126.00
Number of Staff			=COUNT(B7:B15)
Count Number of Staff			COUNT(value1, [value2], ...)

Figure 102

From the drop-down next to *AutoSum*, we pick *Count Numbers*. If typing this into the cell, note that the function is =**COUNT(**.

Matt wants to count how many people have worked this week, so he will count the cells that hold the hours. These values will change each week as he keeps track of how many hours each person has worked.

Count Text

Now Matt wants to count the number of staff in the list of names. He knows how many people worked this week, and now he wants to see if that is the total number of staff in the list.

As he is counting how many names are in the list, Matt will count the values in column A. The function is =**COUNTA(** – *CountA* tells Excel to count text values rather than numerical values.

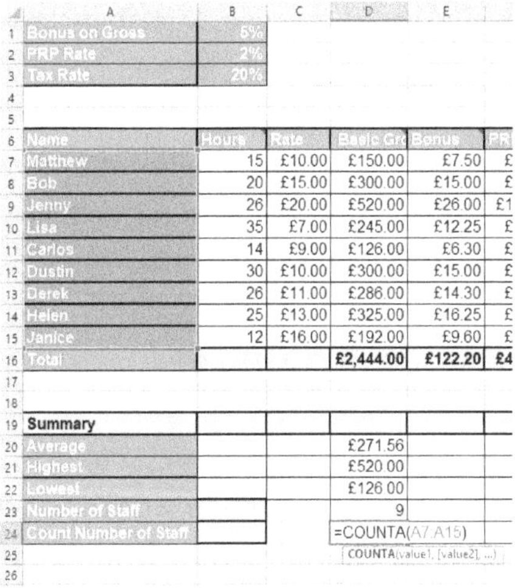

	A	B	C	D	E	
1	Bonus on Gross	5%				
2	PRP Rate	2%				
3	Tax Rate	20%				
4						
5						
6	Name	Hours	Rate	Basic Gr	Bonus	PR
7	Matthew	15	£10.00	£150.00	£7.50	£
8	Bob	20	£15.00	£300.00	£15.00	£
9	Jenny	26	£20.00	£520.00	£26.00	£1
10	Lisa	35	£7.00	£245.00	£12.25	£
11	Carlos	14	£9.00	£126.00	£6.30	£
12	Dustin	30	£10.00	£300.00	£15.00	£
13	Derek	26	£11.00	£286.00	£14.30	£
14	Helen	25	£13.00	£325.00	£16.25	£
15	Janice	12	£16.00	£192.00	£9.60	£
16	Total			**£2,444.00**	**£122.20**	**£4**
17						
18						
19	**Summary**					
20	Average			£271.56		
21	Highest			£520.00		
22	Lowest			£126.00		
23	Number of Staff			9		
24	Count Number of Staff			=COUNTA(A7:A15)		
25				COUNTA(value1, [value2], ...)		
26						

Figure 103

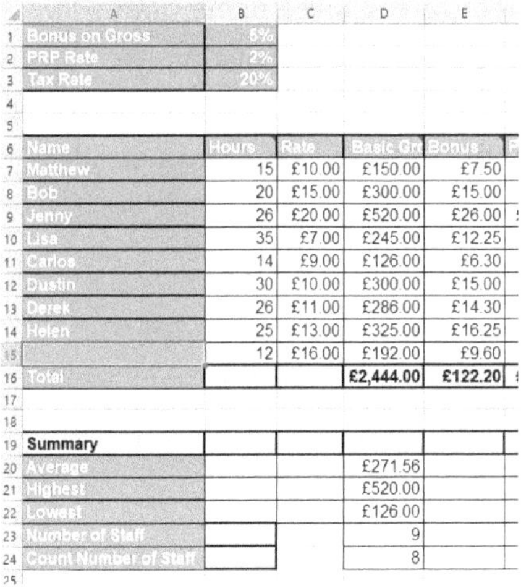

	A	B	C	D	E
1	Bonus on Gross	5%			
2	PRP Rate	2%			
3	Tax Rate	20%			
4					
5					
6	Name	Hours	Rate	Basic Gr	Bonus
7	Matthew	15	£10.00	£150.00	£7.50
8	Bob	20	£15.00	£300.00	£15.00
9	Jenny	26	£20.00	£520.00	£26.00
10	Lisa	35	£7.00	£245.00	£12.25
11	Carlos	14	£9.00	£126.00	£6.30
12	Dustin	30	£10.00	£300.00	£15.00
13	Derek	26	£11.00	£286.00	£14.30
14	Helen	25	£13.00	£325.00	£16.25
15		12	£16.00	£192.00	£9.60
16	Total			**£2,444.00**	**£122.20**
17					
18					
19	**Summary**				
20	Average			£271.56	
21	Highest			£520.00	
22	Lowest			£126.00	
23	Number of Staff			9	
24	Count Number of Staff			8	
25					

Figure 104

In the completed list on the right, Matt took the name *Janice* out of the list to see what would happen.

There are now 8 in the *Count Number of Staff* cell and 9 in the *Number of Staff* cell. This is because Matt did not remove the hours worked; he only removed her name.

Flash Fill

We covered copying a formula using Autofill to drag down a column. There is another option when you want to fill a data series. Excel is great at looking for patterns. Flash Fill is one of the tools that can help with finding and replicating a pattern.

Matt has a list of employee names and addresses, and he wants to extract certain information from the list. The first and last names are together, and Matt needs the first name in one column and the surname in another. He can use Flash Fill to help him.

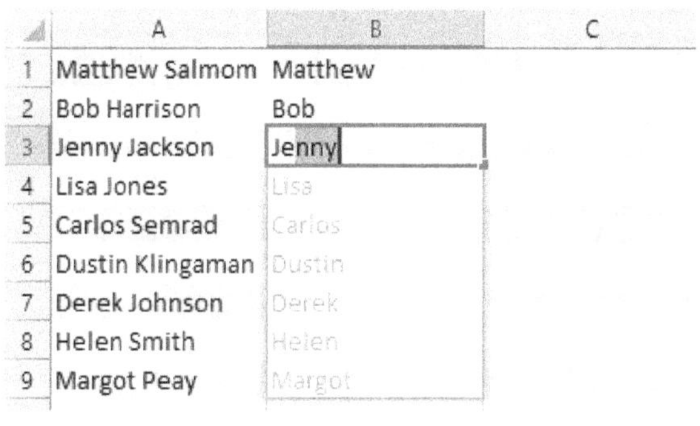

	A	B	C
1	Matthew Salmom	Matthew	
2	Bob Harrison	Bob	
3	Jenny Jackson	Jenny	
4	Lisa Jones	Lisa	
5	Carlos Semrad	Carlos	
6	Dustin Klingaman	Dustin	
7	Derek Johnson	Derek	
8	Helen Smith	Helen	
9	Margot Peay	Margot	

Figure 105

Note that in the column next to the one with the full names, Matt starts to type the first name only. He also did this in the second row of the column. By the time he gets to the third row, Excel realises there's a pattern being repeated and completes the rest of the column. The text shows up in grey and will be entered properly once Matt presses *Enter* to accept the suggestion.

He can then go on and do the same for the surname column.

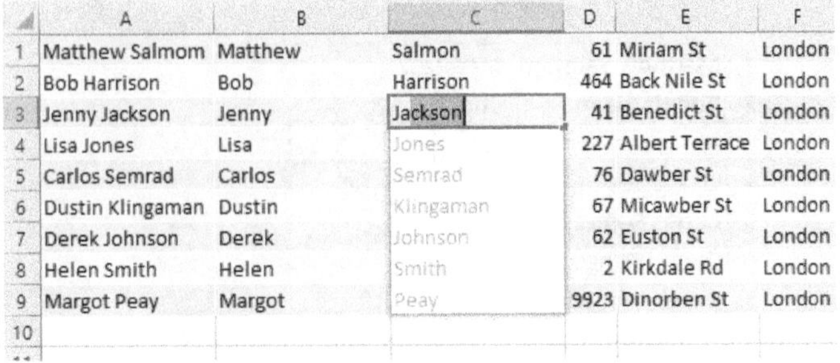

	A	B	C	D	E	F
1	Matthew Salmom	Matthew	Salmon	61	Miriam St	London
2	Bob Harrison	Bob	Harrison	464	Back Nile St	London
3	Jenny Jackson	Jenny	Jackson	41	Benedict St	London
4	Lisa Jones	Lisa	Jones	227	Albert Terrace	London
5	Carlos Semrad	Carlos	Semrad	76	Dawber St	London
6	Dustin Klingaman	Dustin	Klingaman	67	Micawber St	London
7	Derek Johnson	Derek	Johnson	62	Euston St	London
8	Helen Smith	Helen	Smith	2	Kirkdale Rd	London
9	Margot Peay	Margot	Peay	9923	Dinorben St	London
10						

Figure 106

Matt and Lisa now need to focus on what they are going to work out next. They need to figure out how much to charge for each beverage or food item and to do that they need some basic data.

They need to know:

- The cost of making a cup of coffee
- The different elements that make up the expenses of a coffee shop
- How to work it out on a spreadsheet
- What kind of mark-up there is
- How is profit calculated

Getting the Price Right

To get his pricing right (and he can't afford not to!), Matt needs to know the exact cost of every single cup of each type of drink. From this, he can calculate how many he needs to sell each day.

The first job is to find out the cost of the raw ingredients and work out how many cups of coffee can be made from each pack of coffee, milk, sugar etc.

Number of Cups per Kilo or Litre.

Coffee is sold in 1 kilogram bags, as is the chocolate for hot chocolate. Milk is priced per 4 litre bottle. To keep things simple, Matt's going to work out the cost based on 1L of milk and 1kg of each of the other ingredients.

Each cup of coffee is made with 7 grams of ground coffee beans and 150 millilitres of milk. If Matt divides the total weight of a bag of coffee beans by the weight per cup, he can work out how many cups of coffee he will be able to make per bag. The same applies to both milk and hot chocolate.

Here's the small spreadsheet Matt's created to work it out:

	A	B	C	D	E	F
1						
2		Per cup in grams or ml	Total Pack Size	Number of Cups	Rounded	
3	Coffee	7	1000			
4	Hot Chocolate	25	1000			
5	Milk	150	1000			
6						

Figure 107

To work out the number of cups, he needs to divide the pack size by the gram/ml per cup. Then as it is the same for each row, he can copy it down using Autofill.

	A	B	C	D	E	F
1						
2		Per cup in grams or ml	Total Pack Size	Number of Cups	Rounded	
3	Coffee	7	1000	=C3/B3		
4	Hot Chocolate	25	1000			
5	Milk	150	1000			
6						

Figure 108

Now Matt has the number of cups for each beverage in a list.

	A	B	C	D
1				
2		Per cup in grams or ml	Total Pack Size	Number of Cups
3	Coffee	7	1000	142.86
4	Hot Chocolate	25	1000	40.00
5	Milk	150	1000	6.67

Figure 109

As the totals for coffee and milk are not round numbers, he's decided to round them down and assume less per kg rather than more.

RoundDown

The *ROUNDDOWN* function takes a number with decimal points and rounds it down to the nearest whole number.

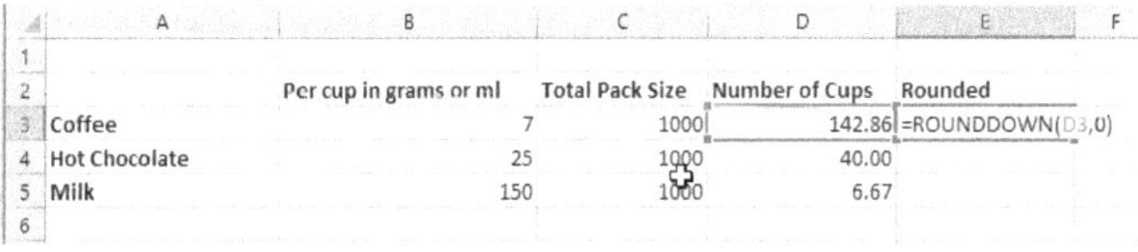

	A	B	C	D	E	F
1						
2		Per cup in grams or ml	Total Pack Size	Number of Cups	Rounded	
3	Coffee	7	1000	142.86	=ROUNDDOWN(D3,0)	
4	Hot Chocolate	25	1000	40.00		
5	Milk	150	1000	6.67		
6						

Figure 110

=ROUNDDOWN(D3,0)

In the example, Excel rounds the number down by 0 digits, which will round down to the nearest whole number. In our case, 142.00.

Now we have the numbers rounded down, it would be good to display them without the decimal places. Matt just wants to see the whole numbers. If you don't see the values following the decimal point, you won't need to decrease the decimals. However, in most cases, you will see the decimals even after rounding down.

Use the Increase or Decrease Decimal Icons

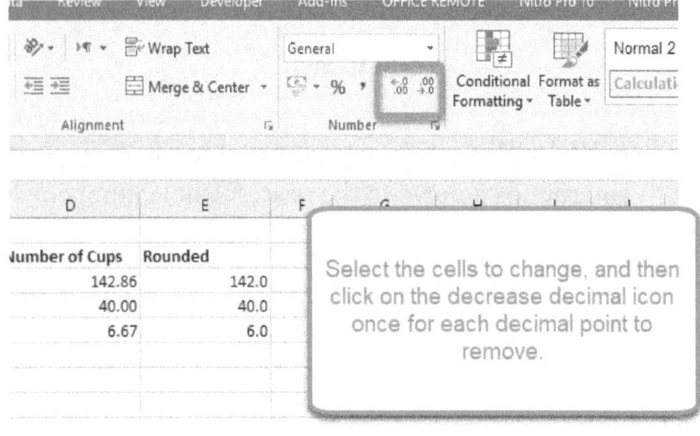

Figure 111

Now that the decimals have been hidden, Matt can continue with his calculations.

Cost Per Cup

Matt has the price per pack of coffee, milk, and hot chocolate and the number of cups each pack will make. He now needs to work out how much each individual cup will cost.

He knows this is a simple formula dividing the total cost of ingredients with the number of cups.

	Ingredients	Total cost per ingredient
11	Ingredients	Total cost per ingredient
12	Coffee Beans 1kg	26.00
13	Chocolate 1kg	30.00
14	Milk 1L	0.44

Figure 112

Display Formula

Matt wants to check what's going on in the cells without having to click into each one. Of course, there's a keyboard shortcut for this!

By pressing *Control* and *Pipe*, (the key on the keyboard in the top left, to the left of the number 1) the formula will be displayed in the cells instead of the results.

Figure 113

This can also be done by clicking on the *Show Formulas* icon on the *Formula* ribbon.

C	D	E
Total Pack Size	**Number of Cups**	**Rounded**
1000	=C3/B3	=ROUNDDOWN(D3,0)
1000	=C4/B4	=ROUNDDOWN(D4,0)
1000	=C5/B5	=ROUNDDOWN(D5,0)
Cost per cup		
=B12/$E3		
=B13/$E4		
=B14/$E5		

Figure 114

Matt can now see all the formulas in the cells themselves. This makes it easy for him to check for any problems.

Total Cost Per Cup

Now Mat has the cost per cup for each ingredient, he can add up the total cost per cup. It's a simple addition of coffee + milk or hot chocolate + milk. As we have used rounded numbers, the cost of coffee and milk with their original decimals comes to 0.2564 which is over 0.25, the cost we expected to see.

20		
21	**Coffee per cup**	
22	Coffee	0.18
23	Milk	0.07
24		
25		**0.25**
26		
27	**Hot Chocolate per cup**	
28	Hot Chocolate	0.75
29	Milk	0.07
30		
31		**0.82**

Figure 115

Partial Fixed Absolute Cell References

Matt couldn't stop his mind wandering. What if, he mused, he could open a branch of Koffee Island in another country? How about in the USA? Or France? He wondered if he could ever work out and show the costings in other currencies. He knew he was running before he could walk, but hey, it was dreaming big dreams that had got him where he was right now.

What Matt couldn't immediately fathom was how to automatically show the price in other currencies, but he knew there must be a way. After all, Excel had never let him down to date. First though, he began to add to the spreadsheet. He added a column for the price in US dollars and one for the price in euros. Then he looked up the exchange rates and put those in the spreadsheet.

However, when he created the formula and then copied it, it did something a bit odd. He multiplied the cost per cup in GBP (the original cost per cup) by the dollar exchange rate and copied it to the other cells in the column to get the cost of chocolate and milk too. What on earth was this #VALUE! That popped up?

8					
9				1.22	1.17
10	**Ingredients**	**Total cost per ingredient**	**Cost per cup**	**Dollars**	**Euro**
11	Coffee Beans 1kg	26.00	0.18	0.22	
12	Chocolate 1kg	30.00	0.75	#VALUE!	
13	Milk 1L	0.44	0.07	0.02	
14					

Figure 116

Matt asks Lisa for help, and as he explains, Lisa is intrigued by his thoughts of expansion and knows that if they get it right, it could work smoothly.

Lisa explains about absolute cell references again. When setting up a formula to be copied, you must think hard about how you will use it. Which direction will it be copied in? Is it to be copied across columns or down every row? Or both?

When Matt started to copy this across and down, he found that the references were wrong. Lisa displays the formulas in the cells so that he can see.

	$	€
Cost per cup	**1.22**	**1.17**
=B11/$E2	=C11*D10	=D11*E10
=B12/$E3	=C12*D11	=D12*E11
=B13/$E4	=C13*D12	=D13*E12

Figure 117

Lisa also points out that Matt has the words *Dollars* and *Euro* underneath the exchange rates. She suggests to Matt that these words are removed and replaced with the symbols. Lisa also makes sure the exchange rates are below the symbols. When copying a formula using Autofill, Excel cannot handle text values. The text values had been included in the formula and were resulting in the #VALUE errors.

Now Matt can see what has happened. In the dollar column, the formula refers to C11*D10. C11 is correct as that is where the price in GBP is. D10 is also correct as that is where the dollar exchange rate is. As he copies it across the columns, it adjusts and seems to be correct. Matt then spots that in each column the formula is picking up the value in the previous column. It should be picking up the value in column C each time.

As Matt looks further, he notices that the rows are not reflecting the exchange rate either. They are adjusting and simply referring to the row above each time.

Matt needs each formula to refer to the value in column C in each column and the value in row 10 for each row.

Lisa explains that in some formulas, you only need part of the cell reference to be fixed. That is what is needed here.

The formula here would look like this: **=$C11*D$10**, and in the spreadsheet, it now looks like this.

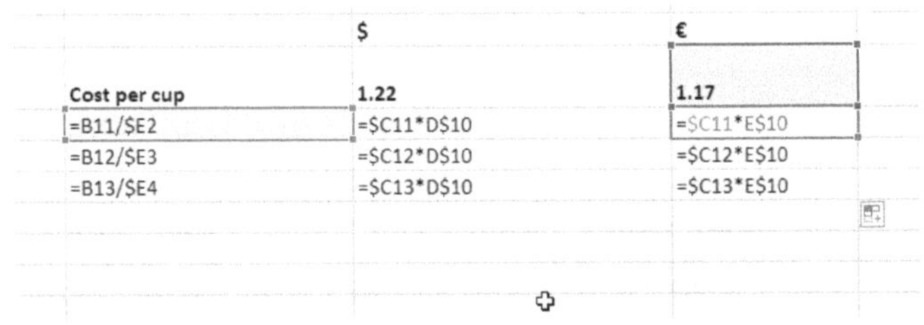

	$	€
Cost per cup	**1.22**	**1.17**
=B11/$E2	=$C11*D$10	=$C11*E$10
=B12/$E3	=$C12*D$10	=$C12*E$10
=B13/$E4	=$C13*D$10	=$C13*E$10

Figure 118

Lisa goes on to explain that the F4 key can be used to generate the $ sign in the place you want it to appear. See the table below.

Press once	Puts a dollar sign around both the column reference and the row reference, so fixes the whole cell and makes it absolute.
Press twice	Puts a dollar sign only on the row reference.
Press three times	Puts a dollar sign only on the column reference.
Press four times	Takes the dollar signs off altogether.

There are times when you will want to fix different parts of the formula, and now you know you can.

Working Out the Profit

Time to work out the profit on each cup. Matt needs to decide the retail price of each drink; then he can work it all out.

When Matt and Bob were doing their research, they took note of the prices in various coffee outlets.

Matt decided to start off charging £2.20 per cup of coffee and £2.50 per cup of hot chocolate (including VAT). He enters these prices into his spreadsheet.

He then needs to:

1. Exclude VAT as this is just tax he is collecting on behalf of the government and has already been ignored in the cost calculations. To do this, he needs to divide the price he is charging by 1.2.
2. Calculate the profit per cup sold, which is net sale price minus the cost price.
3. Calculate the mark-up on each cup sold, which is the sale price per cup divided by the cost price per cup.

In the spreadsheet, it looks like this:

	A	B	C	D	E	F	G	H
19				VAT Divider	1.2			
20								
21	**Coffee per cup**			Price to public inc VAT	Net Sale Price	Profit	Gross Profit	Markup
22	Coffee	0.18		2.2	1.83	1.58	86%	7.15
23	Milk	0.07						
24								
25		**0.25643**						
26								
27	**Hot Chocolate per cup**							
28	Hot Chocolate	0.75		2.5	2.08	1.26		
29	Milk	0.07						
30								
31		**0.82**						

Figure 119

With the formula showing, it looks like this:

	A	B	C	D	E	F	G	H
18								
19				VAT Divider	1.2			
20								
21	**Coffee per cup**			Price to public inc VAT	Net Sale Price	Profit	Gross Profit	Markup
22	Coffee	=C12		2.2	=D22/E19	=E22-B25	=F22/E22	=E22/B25
23	Milk	=C14						
24								
25		=SUM(B22:B24)						
26								
27	**Hot Chocolate per cup**							
28	Hot Chocolate	=C13		2.5	=D28/E19	=E28-B31		
29	Milk	=C14						
30								
31		=SUM(B28:B30)						

Figure 120

Looking at the numbers, Matt has a thought. He can see the profit margin on coffee is higher than on hot chocolate. He decides to play around with the numbers and work out how much he would need to sell hot chocolate for to make a bigger profit.

He wonders what a £3.00 price for hot chocolate will do. It increases the profit from 60% to 67% and the mark-up from 2.53 to 3.04.

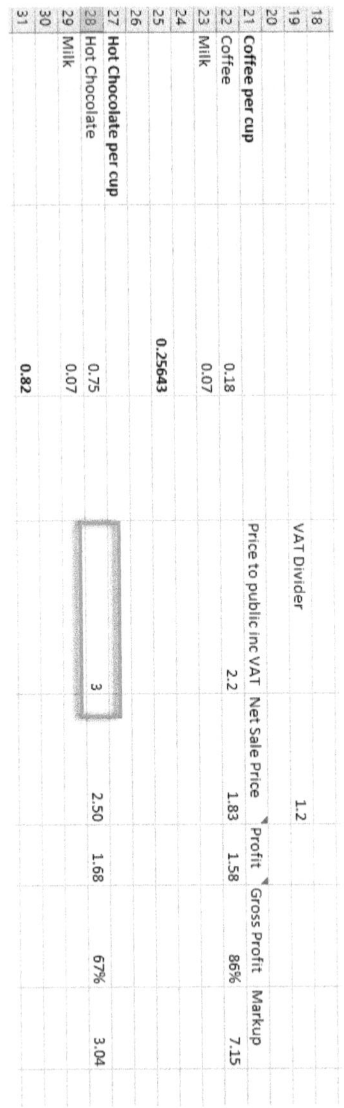

	A	B	C	D	E	F	G
18							
19			VAT Divider	1.2			
20							
21	**Coffee per cup**		Price to public inc VAT	Net Sale Price	Profit	Gross Profit	Markup
22	Coffee	0.18	2.2	1.83	1.58	86%	7.15
23	Milk	0.07					
24							
25		**0.25643**					
26							
27	**Hot Chocolate per cup**						
28	Hot Chocolate	0.75	3	2.50	1.68	67%	3.04
29	Milk	0.07					
30							
31		**0.82**					

Figure 121

Named Ranges

Whilst he's scrutinising this little spreadsheet, Matt has a thought. If you weren't the person who'd put it all together, would you be able to work out what was going on? Additionally, if you hadn't had the benefit of Lisa's tuition and had never heard of an absolute cell reference or created a formula with dollar signs, might you get really confused?

When he discusses these concerns with Lisa, she tells him about named ranges.

It is possible to name an individual cell – VAT for example – and use it in a formula. You can even name a range of cells such as a column or row.

When there is a whole range of data following the same structure, it too can be named. If you name whole columns or rows, the names will refer to the correct cell in the range when copying the formula down or across using Autofill.

Here is what the formula in Matt's spreadsheet say now:

=Net_Sale_Price-Cost_Price	This takes the value in the net sale price column on the row that the cursor is on and subtracts the cost price for that row.

=Profit/Net_Sale_Price	This takes the profit for the row the cursor is on and divides it by the corresponding net sale price.
=Net_Sale_Price/Cost_Price	This takes the net sale price for the row the cursor is on and divides it by the corresponding cost price.

Here is Matt's spreadsheet with the formula displayed:

	A	B	C	D	E	F	G	H
33			**VAT**	**1.2**				
34		**Cost Price**	**Sale Price**	**Net Sale Price**	**Profit**	**Gross Profit**	**Markup**	
35	**Coffee**	0.26	2.2	=Sale_Price/VAT	=Net_Sale_Price-Cost_Price	=Profit/Net_Sale_Price	=Net_Sale_Price/Cost_Price	
36	**Hot Chocolate**	0.82	3	=Sale_Price/VAT	=Net_Sale_Price-Cost_Price	=Profit/Net_Sale_Price	=Net_Sale_Price/Cost_Price	
37	**Cola**	0.35	1	=Sale_Price/VAT	=Net_Sale_Price-Cost_Price	=Profit/Net_Sale_Price	=Net_Sale_Price/Cost_Price	
38	**Orange Juice**	0.4	1.2	=Sale_Price/VAT	=Net_Sale_Price-Cost_Price	=Profit/Net_Sale_Price	=Net_Sale_Price/Cost_Price	
39	**Apple Juice**	0.4	1.5	=Sale_Price/VAT	=Net_Sale_Price-Cost_Price	=Profit/Net_Sale_Price	=Net_Sale_Price/Cost_Price	
40								

Figure 122

Koffee Says:

When naming a range in Excel and then using that range name in a formula, Excel will always refer to the correct cell reference.

When naming a single cell, it is an absolute cell reference, meaning it can refer only to that cell. Instead of referencing the cell D1 for example, once named, it has the name *VAT* instead.

Here is what the results look like:

D4 =Sale_Price/VAT

	A	B	C	D	E	F	G
1							
2			VAT	1.2			
3		Cost Price	Sale Price	Net Sale Price	Profit	Gross Profit	Markup
4	Coffee	0.26	2.2	1.83	1.57	0.86	7.05
5	Hot Chocolate	0.82	3	2.50	1.68	0.67	3.05
6	Cola	0.35	1	0.83	0.48	0.58	2.38
7	Orange Juice	0.4	1.2	1.00	0.60	0.60	2.50
8	Apple Juice	0.4	1.5	1.25	0.85	0.68	3.13

Figure 123

We are looking at the formula in Cell D4. The formula in the Formula Bar reads *=Sale_Price/VAT*. It is referring to C4 and dividing it by D2 but is using the names.

This means that on each row, Matt can now see what is involved.

Lisa first shows Matt how to name an individual cell and then a whole range of them, finishing up with using the names in the calculations.

Naming a Cell

We need to name the cell with 1.2 as VAT.

Here are the steps:

1. Click on the cell.
2. Click into the Name Box.
3. Type the name.
4. Press *Enter.*

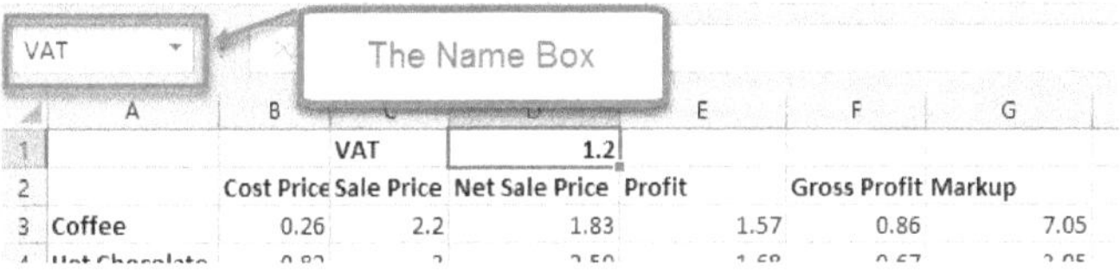

Figure 124

Name a Range

Select the cells to name. Once they are selected, click on the *Formula* ribbon, then choose *Create from Selection* in the *Defined Names* group.

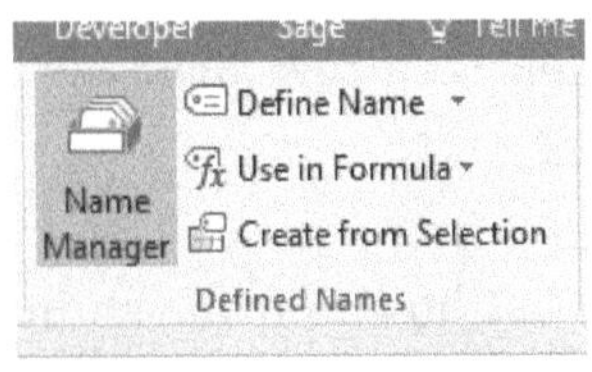

Figure 125

Excel looks at the data and recognises which part are the numbers and which are the text labels for each column or row. In the dialogue box that pops up, Matt needs to select the location of the labels for each range.

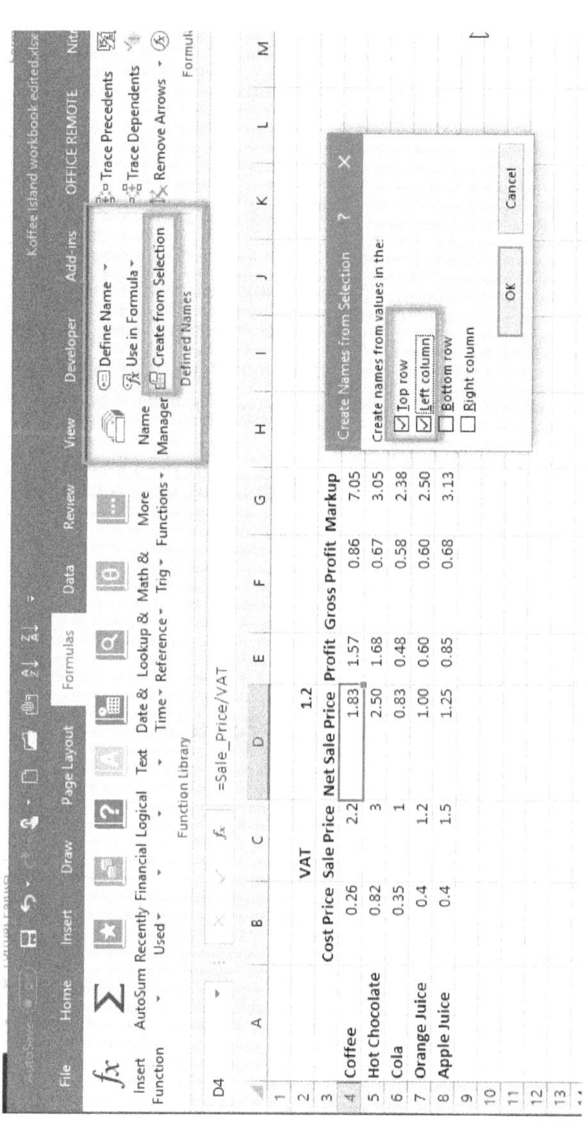
Koffee Island workbook edited.xlsx
File
Home
Insert
Draw
Page Layout
Formulas
Data
Review
View
Developer
Add-ins
OFFICE REMOTE
Insert Function
AutoSum
Recently Used
Financial
Logical
Text
Date & Time
Lookup & Reference
Math & Trig
More Functions
Function Library
Name Manager
Define Name
Use in Formula
Create from Selection
Defined Names
Trace Precedents
Trace Dependents
Remove Arrows
D4
=Sale_Price/VAT
VAT
1.2
Cost Price
Sale Price
Net Sale Price
Profit
Gross Profit
Markup
Coffee
Hot Chocolate
Cola
Orange Juice
Apple Juice
Create Names from Selection
Create names from values in the:
Top row
Left column
Bottom row
Right column
OK
Cancel

Figure 126

After clicking *OK*, Excel creates all the names. Matt can see them in the Name Box drop-down.

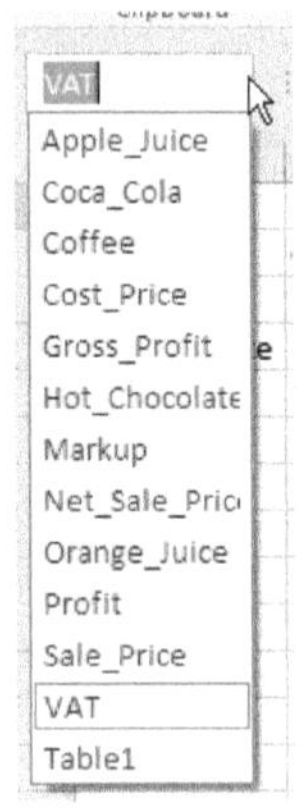

Koffee Says:

The names made up of two words do **not** have spaces in between, rather Excel has added an underscore.

When creating names, there are no spaces.

Figure 127

Use Names in Formula

Now to use the names in the formula.

	A	B	C	D	E	F	G	H
1								
2			VAT	1.2				
3		Cost Price	Sale Price	Net Sale Price	Profit	Gross Profit	Markup	
4	Coffee	0.26	2.2	=Sale_Price/VAT		0.86	7.05	
5	Hot Chocolate	0.82	3	2.50	1.68	0.67	3.05	
6	Cola	0.35	1	0.83	0.48	0.58	2.38	
7	Orange Juice	0.4	1.2	1.00	0.60	0.60	2.50	
8	Apple Juice	0.4	1.5	1.25	0.85	0.68	3.13	
9								
10								

Figure 128

In cell D4, Matt types =*Sale_Price/VAT*. Note that Excel highlights the column called *Sale Price*. However, it will use the number in the corresponding row, i.e. C4, in the calculation.

Having pressed *Enter* to accept, Matt copies that formula to the rest of column D.

Here is the result:

D7 | =Sale_Price/VAT

	A	B	C	D	E	F	G	H	I
1									
2			VAT	1.2					
3		Cost Price	Sale Price	Net Sale Price	Profit	Gross Profit	Markup		
4	Coffee	0.26	2.2	1.83	1.57	0.86	7.05		
5	Hot Chocolate	0.82	3	2.50	1.68	0.67	3.05		
6	Cola	0.35	1	0.83	0.48	0.58	2.38		
7	Orange Juice	0.4	1.2	1.00	0.60	0.60	2.50		
8	Apple Juice	0.4	1.5	1.25	0.85	0.68	3.13		
9									
10									

Figure 129

Having clicked on cell D7, he can see the same calculation. The amount is a result of the numbers in C7/D2.

Matt can now complete the whole list with names.

E7 | =Net_Sale_Price-Cost_Price

	A	B	C	D	E	F	G	H
1								
2			VAT	1.2				
3		Cost Price	Sale Price	Net Sale Price	Profit	Gross Profit	Markup	
4	Coffee	0.26	2.2	1.83	1.57	0.86	7.05	
5	Hot Chocolate	0.82	3	2.50	1.68	0.67	3.05	
6	Cola	0.35	1	0.83	0.48	0.58	2.38	
7	Orange Juice	0.4	1.2	1.00	0.60	0.60	2.50	
8	Apple Juice	0.4	1.5	1.25	0.85	0.68	3.13	
9								
10								
11								

Figure 130

The numbers are the same as before. However, when he clicks on E7, he can see the names rather than the cell references in the Formula Bar.

Fixed Costs

When setting up and running Koffee Island, Matt needs to consider all sorts of other expenses. Some of these will be recurring like rent, electricity, and wages, whereas others may be one-off or infrequent expenses.

Thinking about this, Matt sits down with his laptop and a cup of his favourite cappuccino, expertly made by Bob, and starts to make a new list.

- Rent
- Fixtures and fittings
- Heat
- Light
- Machines
- Staff wages
- Cleaning materials

Once Matt knows what his expenses are, he can start to work out how many coffees he needs to sell to cover the running costs and make a profit.

Matt lists everything in a spreadsheet to get an idea of the total expenses.

	A	B	C	D	E	F	G	H
1	Items	January	February	March	April		Grand Total Costs	
2	Rent	£25,000.00	£25,000.00	£25,000.00	£25,000.00			
3	Electricity	£500.00	£600.00	£500.00	£500.00			
4	Wifi	£100.00	£100.00	£100.00	£100.00			
5	Cleaning Materials	£150.00	£100.00	£200.00	£100.00			
6	Marketing	£200.00	£200.00	£200.00	£200.00			
7	Stationery	£50.00	£50.00	£50.00	£50.00			
8	Fixtures and Fittings	£700.00	£700.00	£700.00	£700.00			
9	Machine Servicing	£100.00	£100.00	£100.00	£100.00			
10	Salaries	£3,000.00	£2,444.00	£2,444.00	£2,444.00			
11								
12	**Total**	**£29,800.00**	**£29,294.00**	**£29,294.00**	**£29,194.00**		**£117,582.00**	
13								

Figure 131

Koffee Says:

What did Matt have to do to create this spreadsheet? Think about what Matt has learnt throughout the book and list the features he has used.

How Many Coffees Does Matt Need to Sell?

Now Matt knows his expenses are around £30,000.00 per month, he can work out how many drinks he needs to sell to break even and make a profit.

On a very simplistic level, Matt will divide the total expenses by the sales price of coffee, and that will give him a number. He needs to remember to use the net sale price.

Matt creates a small sample spreadsheet to test the idea.

Function Library

D2 fx =C2/B2

	A	B	C	D	E
1		Sales Price	Monthly Expenses	Number of Coffees	
2	**Coffee**	1.83	30000	16363.64	
3	**Hot Chocolate**	2.50	30000	12000.00	
4	**Cola**	0.83	30000	36000.00	
5	**Orange Juice**	1.00	30000	30000.00	
6	**Apple Juice**	1.25	30000	24000.00	
7					

Figure 132

In the first instance, Matt works out how many of each drink he would need to sell to make the £30,000.00 per month.

Once he knows how many he would need to sell if he only sold one type of drink, he can play with the numbers. Matt creates another working area to test this out.

J	K	L	M	N
	Number to Sell	Net Sales Price	Total	
Coffee	15000	1.83	27500	
Hot Chocolate	2000	2.50	5000	
Cola	1521	0.83	1267.5	
Orange Juice	900	1.00	900	
Apple Juice	950	1.25	1187.5	
			35855	

Figure 133

Now Matt can play with the numbers and see at what point he breaks even or even makes a profit.

Matt decides he will need to keep an eye on sales to begin with. Once he sees what the trends are, the pricing may need to be adjusted.

Analysing Sales

Matt needs to track which of Koffee Island's offerings are selling well and which aren't. He needs to know:

- The best-selling drinks
- The worst-selling drinks
- Which is taking more money – food or drink?
- What the total sales figures are

The data will come from the till, downloaded at the end of each day, and Lisa shows Matt how to set up a list in Excel, bearing in mind that a list has no blank columns or rows. It can have the occasional blank cell, but not a complete blank column or row.

	A	B	C	D	E	F	G
1	Date	Type	Category	Item	Cost per Item	Number Sold	Sales
2	01/11/2016	Beverage	Hot	Americano	1.9	20	£ 38.00
3	01/11/2016	Food	Cake	Apple Cake	3.5	750	£ 2,625.00
4	01/11/2016	Beverage	Cold	Apple Juice	1.5	600	£ 900.00
5	01/11/2016	Food	Cake	Brownie	3	23	£ 69.00
6	01/11/2016	Beverage	Hot	Cappuccino	1.9	650	£ 1,235.00
7	01/11/2016	Food	Cake	Carrot Cake	3.5	35	£ 122.50
8	01/11/2016	Food	Cake	Cheesecake	3.75	500	£ 1,875.00
9	01/11/2016	Beverage	Milkshake	Chocolate	3.5	250	£ 875.00
10	01/11/2016	Beverage	Milkshake	Cola	1	350	£ 350.00
11	01/11/2016	Food	Cake	Coffee Cake	3	54	£ 162.00
12	01/11/2016	Food	Cake	Cupcake	1.75	50	£ 87.50
13	01/11/2016	Food	Cake	Cupcake	1.75	23	£ 40.25
14	01/11/2016	Food	Sandwich	Egg	2.5	650	£ 1,625.00
15	01/11/2016	Beverage	Hot	Flat White	1.9	400	£ 760.00
16	01/11/2016	Food	Salad	Greek Salad	4.5	700	£ 3,150.00
17	01/11/2016	Beverage	Hot	Hot Chocolate	3	250	£ 750.00
18	01/11/2016	Beverage	Hot	Latte	1.9	350	£ 665.00
19	01/11/2016	Beverage	Hot	Macchiato	1.9	52	£ 98.80
20	01/11/2016	Beverage	Cold	Orange Juice	1.2	20	£ 24.00
21	01/11/2016	Food	Salad	Quinoa	4.75	4	£ 19.00
22	01/11/2016	Food	Sandwich	Smoked Salmon	4.75	654	£ 3,106.50
23	01/11/2016	Beverage	Milkshake	Strawberry	3.5	25	£ 87.50
24	01/11/2016	Food	Sandwich	Toasted Cheese	3.75	20	£ 75.00
25	02/11/2016	Beverage	Hot	Americano	1.9	250	£ 475.00
26	02/11/2016	Food	Cake	Apple Cake	3.5	65	£ 227.50
27	02/11/2016	Beverage	Cold	Apple Juice	1.5	898	£ 1,347.00
28	02/11/2016	Food	Cake	Brownie	3	444	£ 1,332.00
29	02/11/2016	Beverage	Hot	Cappuccino	1.9	485	£ 921.50
30	02/11/2016	Food	Cake	Carrot Cake	3.5	60	£ 210.00
31	02/11/2016	Food	Cake	Cheesecake	3.75	55	£ 206.25
32	02/11/2016	Beverage	Milkshake	Chocolate	3.5	450	£ 1,575.00
33	02/11/2016	Beverage	Milkshake	Cola	1	50	£ 50.00
34	02/11/2016	Food	Cake	Coffee Cake	3	45	£ 135.00
35	02/11/2016	Food	Cake	Coffee Cake	3	56	£ 168.00
36	02/11/2016	Food	Cake	Cupcake	1.75	55	£ 96.25
37	02/11/2016	Food	Cake	Cupcake	1.75	85	£ 148.75
38	02/11/2016	Food	Sandwich	Egg	2.5	54	£ 135.00

Figure 134

The header row has been formatted differently to the rest of the cells. The list is a summary of the total number of each type of item sold at Koffee Island.

Lisa makes a list of the functionality Matt will need so he can analyse this data in different ways.

- Sorting – both simple and custom sorting
- Filtering – pulling out certain data to focus on
- Subtotals – how many cups of cappuccino or latte sold
- Format the data as a table – this has added automatic functionality and looks nice too
- Pivot tables – arrange data swiftly in a way that both sorts and filters

Sorting

Data displayed in a list is not always sorted; it just gets added or, in this case, downloaded. As Matt now knows more about Excel, he wants to explore if there are other options for sorting the data as he already knows the basics.

Sorting options are:

A-Z – sorting either alphabetically from A to Z or numerically from smallest to largest.
Z-A – sorting either alphabetically from Z to A or numerically from largest to smallest.

For dates, this means earliest to latest or latest to earliest.

Sorting options can be found in several places in Excel.

Right-click

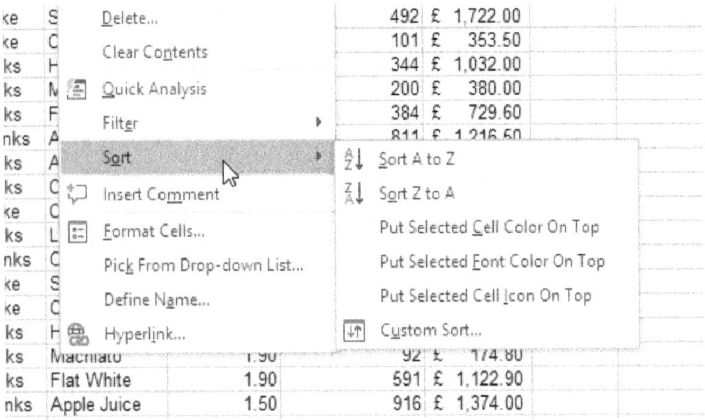

Figure 135

Sort & Filter on the *Home* ribbon

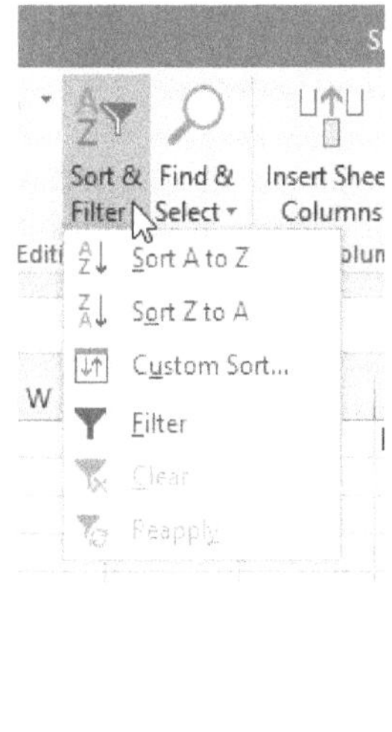

Figure 136

Sort and *Filter* on the *Data* ribbon

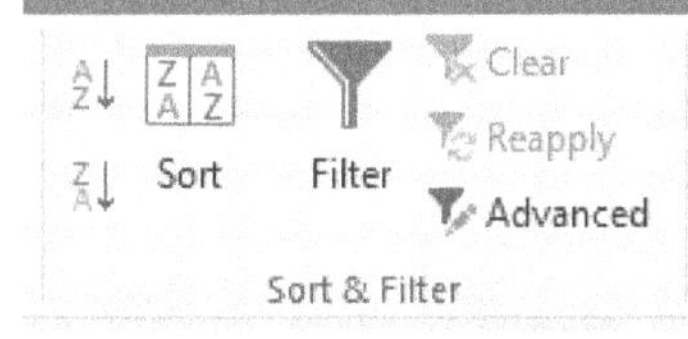

Figure 137

There is one other option. The sort icons can be placed on the Quick Access Toolbar.

As Matt has been busy learning about Excel functionality, Lisa realises she hasn't yet shown him the Quick Access Toolbar or its benefits. Time to rectify that.

The Quick Access Toolbar

The Quick Access Toolbar sits at the top of the Excel window and can have a customised list of icons ready for use. As it is displayed at the top of the Excel window, it is always visible. Icons that are used on a regular basis can be placed here and be readily accessed without having to remember which ribbon tab they come from.

Here is the Quick Access toolbar on Lisa's screen.

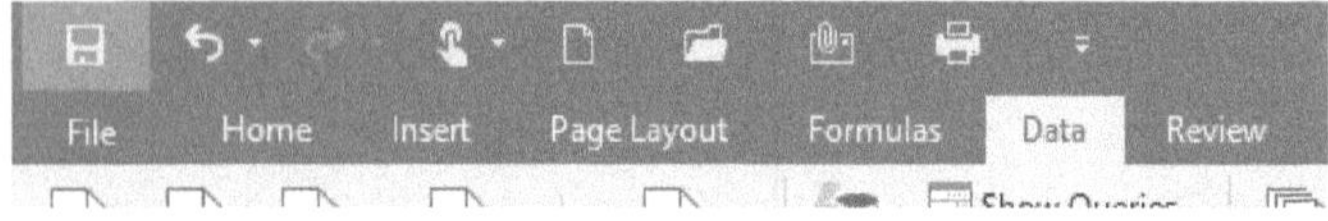

Figure 138

Lisa has various icons there. When Matt downloaded his copy of Excel, it only came with four icons in the Quick Access Toolbar.

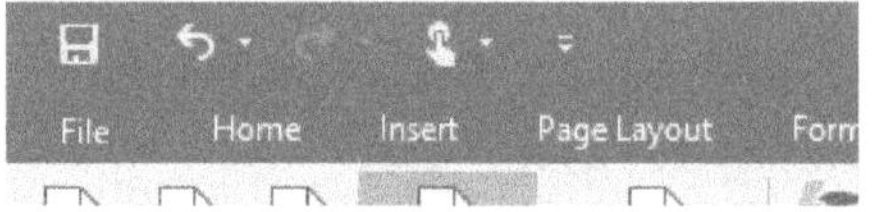

Figure 139

Lisa points out the drop-down arrow at the right-hand side of the Quick Access Toolbar and shows Matt how to add a few shortcuts that appear on the drop-down list. He can add the icons listed here or go to *More Commands* and find other icons that may not be shown here.

The Quick Access Toolbar can be shown below the ribbon too, giving you more space to add icons to fit the width of the

Excel workspace. This option means Matt is not restricted to a few icons at the top of the screen but can have a whole Quick Access Toolbar spanning the screen.

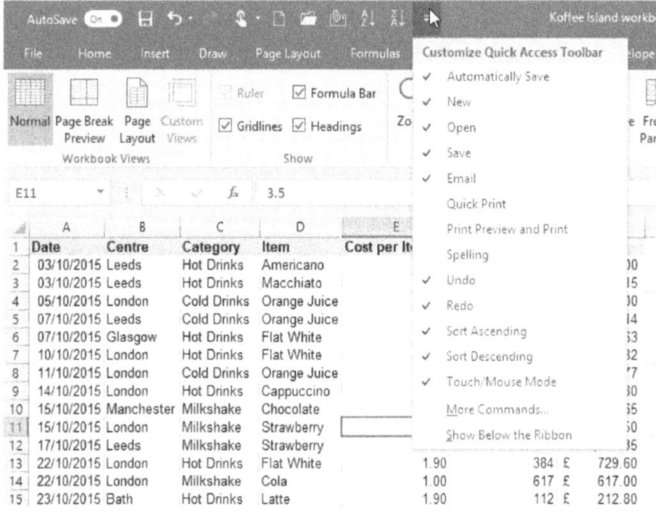

Figure 140

More Commands

Here, Matt can find popular commands or commands that are not on the ribbon. Select the icon on the left, click *Add* in the middle, and it moves across.

The icons on the Quick Access Toolbar can be moved around too. Click on an icon, and then use the up and down arrows on the right to reposition it.

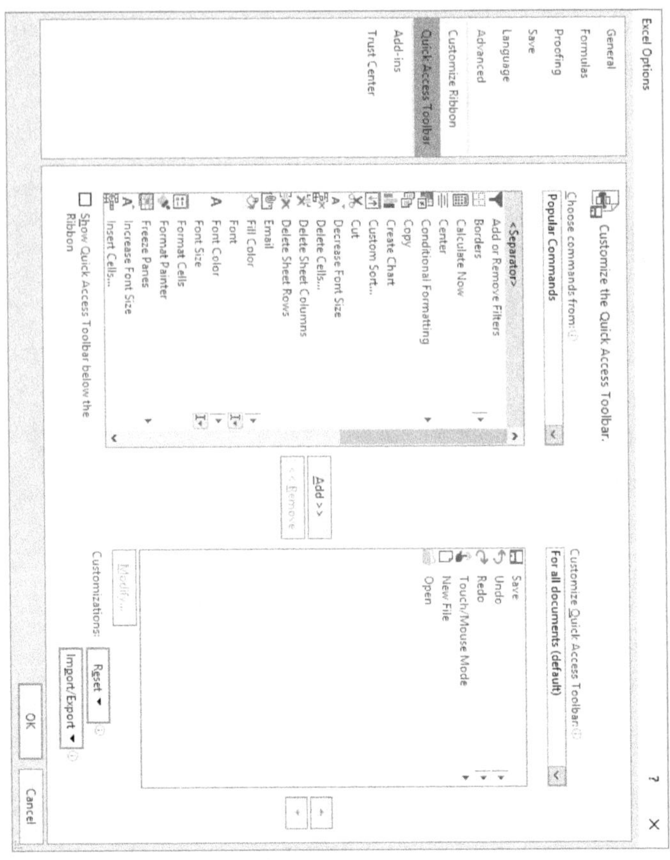

Figure 141

Right-Click

Icons can also be added by using the right-click. Find the icon you use all the time and right-click to *Add to Quick Access Toolbar*. In this picture, Matt adds the A-Z sort icon to his Quick Access Toolbar.

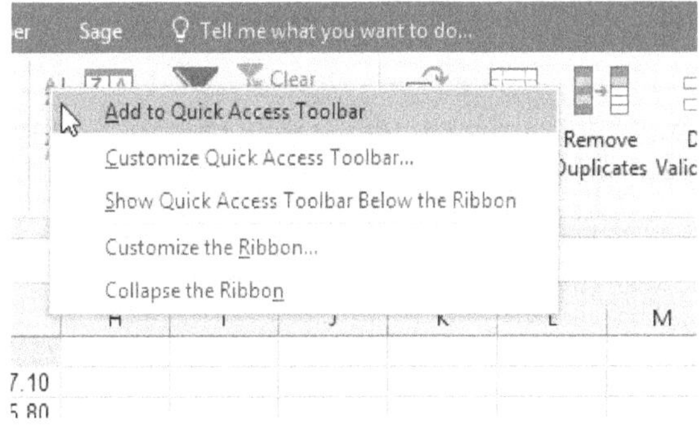

Figure 142

Remove from Quick Access Toolbar

Right-click the icon on the Quick Access Toolbar and select *Remove from Quick Access Toolbar.*

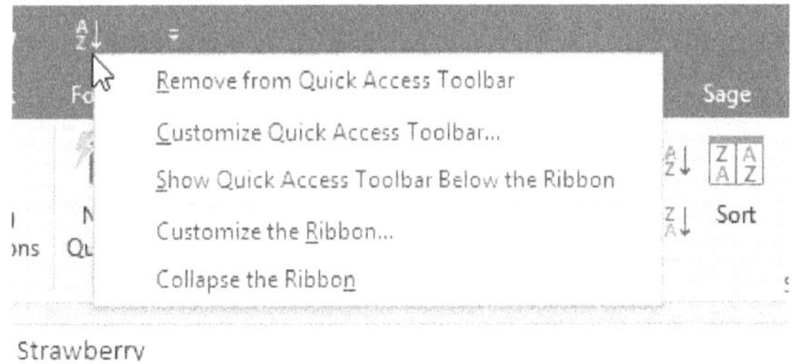

Figure 143

The Alt Key

If you prefer to use the keyboard rather than the mouse, then the *Alt* key will become your best friend. When pressed, the *Alt* key puts visual hints on the ribbon and icons to help you learn the keyboard shortcut combinations.

Here, Matt has pressed the *Alt* key.

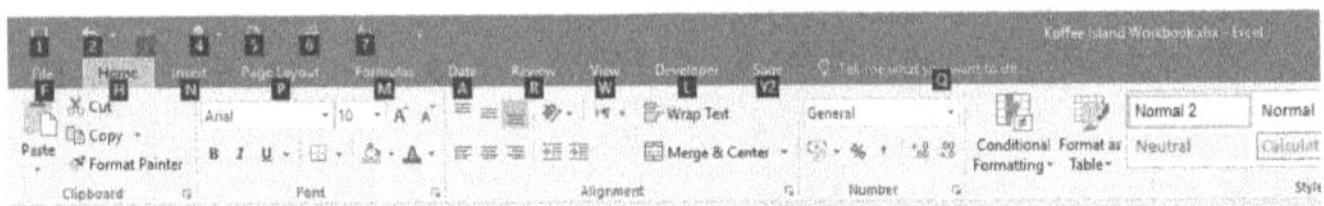

Figure 144

Notice the black letters that have appeared on each ribbon tab. These are the letters you press to get to the corresponding ribbon.

To get to the *Page Layout* ribbon, Matt will need to press the letter *P*.

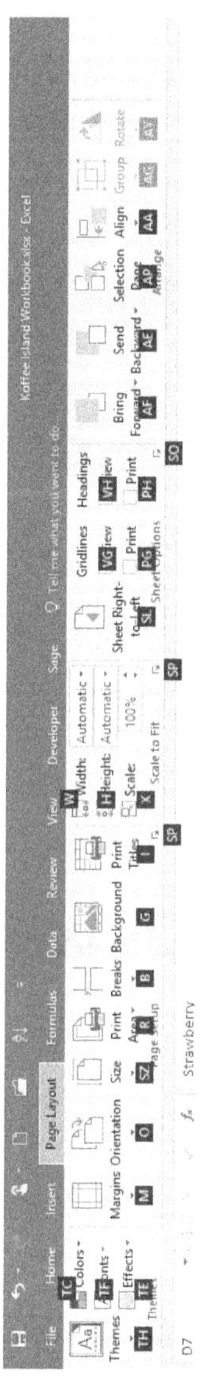
Koffee Island Workbook.xlsx - Excel
File
Home
Insert
Page Layout
Formulas
Data
Review
View
Developer
Sage
Tell me what you want to do...
Themes
Colors
Fonts
Effects
Margins
Orientation
Size
Print Area
Breaks
Background
Print Titles
Page Setup
Width:
Height:
Scale:
Automatic
Automatic
100%
Scale to Fit
Sheet Right-to-Left
Gridlines
Headings
View
View
Print
Print
Sheet Options
Bring Forward
Send Backward
Selection Pane
Align
Group
Rotate
Arrange
D7
Strawberry

Figure 145

Now he is on the *Page Layout* ribbon, there are more letters in black. To change the orientation, Matt needs to press the letter *O* and then use the arrow keys to move to the desired orientation.

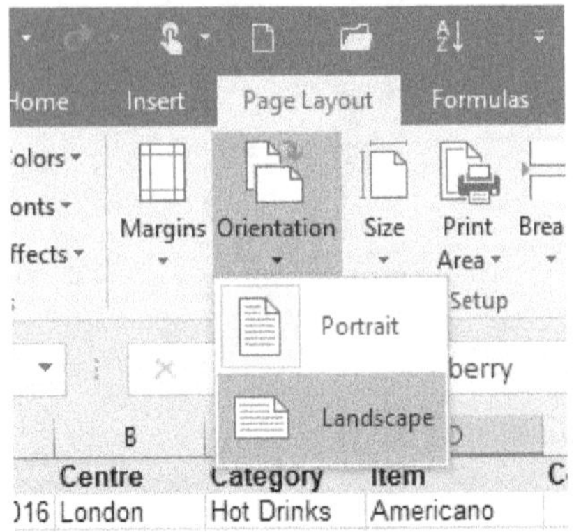

Figure 146

The Alt Key and Quick Access Toolbar

When Matt presses the *Alt* key, he notices the icons on the Quick Access Toolbar have numbers on them. This makes them very short shortcuts. Two keys instead of three or sometimes four.

To make the sort icon Alt + 3, he can move it around on the list. To do this, he chooses *More Commands* from the drop-down list and uses the arrows on the far right to move the icon up to third position.

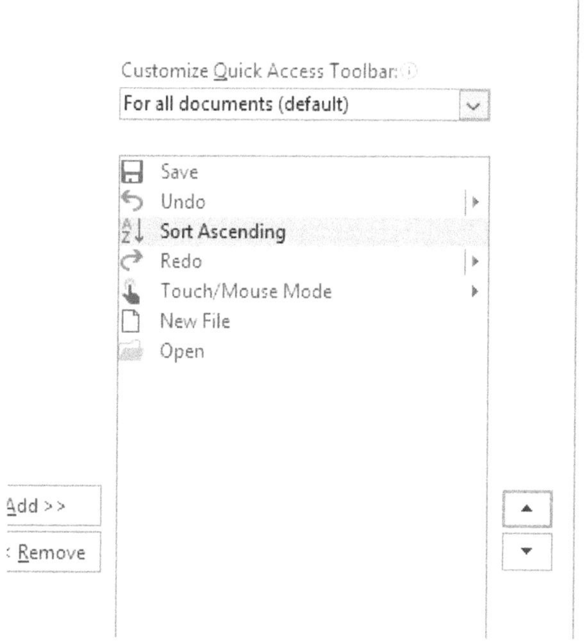

Figure 147

Now Matt just needs to press *Alt* and *3* to sort data.

After that detour, it's time to learn about sorting data.

Sort Using the Icon

The fastest way to sort data is to click into the column to sort and then click on the *Sort A to Z* or *Sort Z to A* icon. Like this:

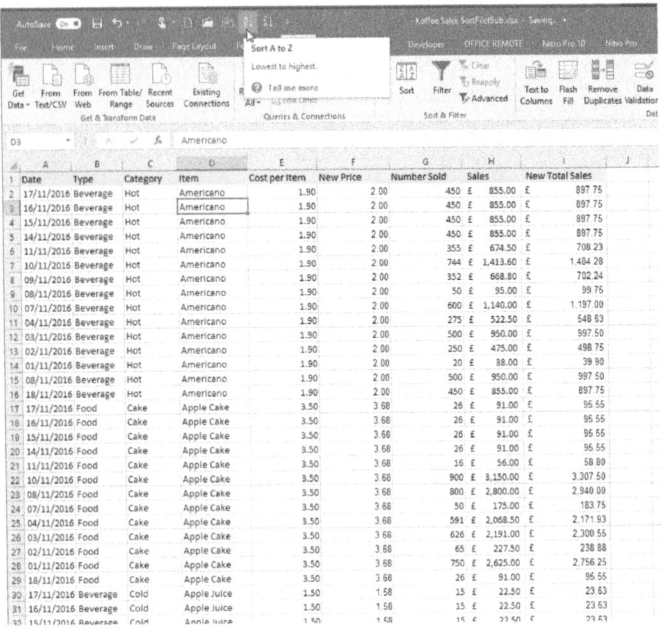

Figure 148

Now the item column is in alphabetical order.

Everything has gone with the item. The price, number sold, and date are all sorted by the item column.

Matt could have used any of the options to sort: right-click, the *Home* ribbon, *Data* ribbon, or Quick Access Toolbar.

Sorting Numbers

Matt just sorted the item column, which is full of text values. Now he wants to sort the sales column to see the amounts in numerical order. He wants the largest number at the top of the list so will choose *Z-A*.

	A	B	C	D	E	F	G	H	I
1	Date	Type	Category	Item	Cost per Item	New Price	Number Sold	Sales	New Total Sales
2	08/11/2016	Food	Sandwich	Smoked Salmon	4.75	4.99	2595	£ 12,326.25	£ 12,942.56
3	11/11/2016	Food	Cake	Cheesecake	3.75	3.94	2459	£ 9,221.25	£ 9,682.31
4	10/11/2016	Beverage	Hot	Hot Chocolate	3.00	3.15	2871	£ 8,613.00	£ 9,043.65
5	10/11/2016	Food	Cake	Cheesecake	3.75	3.94	1966	£ 7,372.50	£ 7,741.13
6	03/11/2016	Food	Sandwich	Smoked Salmon	4.75	4.99	800	£ 3,800.00	£ 3,990.00
7	07/11/2016	Food	Sandwich	Smoked Salmon	4.75	4.99	755	£ 3,586.25	£ 3,765.56
8	04/11/2016	Food	Salad	Greek Salad	4.50	4.73	750	£ 3,375.00	£ 3,543.75
9	03/11/2016	Food	Salad	Greek Salad	4.50	4.73	705	£ 3,172.50	£ 3,331.13
10	10/11/2016	Food	Cake	Apple Cake	3.50	3.68	900	£ 3,150.00	£ 3,307.50
11	07/11/2016	Beverage	Milkshake	Chocolate	3.50	3.68	900	£ 3,150.00	£ 3,307.50
12	01/11/2016	Food	Salad	Greek Salad	4.50	4.73	700	£ 3,150.00	£ 3,307.50
13	01/11/2016	Food	Sandwich	Smoked Salmon	4.75	4.99	654	£ 3,106.50	£ 3,261.83
14	10/11/2016	Food	Cake	Carrot Cake	3.50	3.68	842	£ 2,947.00	£ 3,094.35
15	07/11/2016	Food	Salad	Quinoa	4.75	4.99	600	£ 2,850.00	£ 2,992.50
16	07/11/2016	Food	Sandwich	Toasted Cheese	3.75	3.94	750	£ 2,812.50	£ 2,953.13
17	08/11/2016	Food	Cake	Apple Cake	3.50	3.68	800	£ 2,800.00	£ 2,940.00
18	08/11/2016	Beverage	Milkshake	Strawberry	3.50	3.68	800	£ 2,800.00	£ 2,940.00
19	11/11/2016	Food	Sandwich	Smoked Salmon	4.75	4.99	565	£ 2,683.75	£ 2,817.94
20	01/11/2016	Food	Cake	Apple Cake	3.50	3.68	750	£ 2,625.00	£ 2,756.25
21	11/11/2016	Beverage	Milkshake	Strawberry	3.50	3.68	750	£ 2,625.00	£ 2,756.25
22	02/11/2016	Food	Sandwich	Toasted Cheese	3.75	3.94	699	£ 2,621.25	£ 2,752.31
23	11/11/2016	Food	Cake	Carrot Cake	3.50	3.68	741	£ 2,593.50	£ 2,723.18
24	03/11/2016	Food	Sandwich	Toasted Cheese	3.75	3.94	682	£ 2,557.50	£ 2,685.38
25	07/11/2016	Beverage	Milkshake	Strawberry	3.50	3.68	704	£ 2,464.00	£ 2,587.20
26	08/11/2016	Food	Sandwich	Toasted Cheese	3.75	3.94	652	£ 2,445.00	£ 2,567.25
27	07/11/2016	Food	Cake	Brownie	3.00	3.15	800	£ 2,400.00	£ 2,520.00
28	09/11/2016	Food	Cake	Carrot Cake	3.50	3.68	680	£ 2,380.00	£ 2,499.00
29	04/11/2016	Food	Cake	Cheesecake	3.75	3.94	615	£ 2,306.25	£ 2,421.56
30	04/11/2016	Food	Cake	Brownie	3.00	3.15	750	£ 2,250.00	£ 2,362.50
31	08/11/2016	Food	Cake	Cheesecake	3.75	3.94	598	£ 2,242.50	£ 2,354.63
32	03/11/2016	Food	Cake	Apple Cake	3.50	3.68	626	£ 2,191.00	£ 2,300.55

Figure 149

The sales figures are now listed with the largest number at the top of the list.

Sort by Date

Next, Matt wants to see the information in date order. He clicks into the date column and again chooses *A-Z*.

	A	B	C	D	E	F	G
1	Date	Type	Category	Item	Cost per Item	Number Sold	Sales
2	01/11/2016	Food	Salad	Greek Salad	4.5	700	£ 3,150.00
3	01/11/2016	Food	Sandwich	Smoked Salmon	4.75	654	£ 3,106.50
4	01/11/2016	Food	Cake	Apple Cake	3.5	750	£ 2,625.00
5	01/11/2016	Food	Cake	Cheesecake	3.75	500	£ 1,875.00
6	01/11/2016	Food	Sandwich	Egg	2.5	650	£ 1,625.00
7	01/11/2016	Beverage	Hot	Cappuccino	1.9	650	£ 1,235.00
8	01/11/2016	Beverage	Cold	Apple Juice	1.5	600	£ 900.00
9	01/11/2016	Beverage	Milkshake	Chocolate	3.5	250	£ 875.00
10	01/11/2016	Beverage	Hot	Flat White	1.9	400	£ 760.00
11	01/11/2016	Beverage	Hot	Hot Chocolate	3	250	£ 750.00
12	01/11/2016	Beverage	Hot	Latte	1.9	350	£ 665.00
13	01/11/2016	Beverage	Milkshake	Cola	1	350	£ 350.00
14	01/11/2016	Food	Cake	Coffee Cake	3	54	£ 162.00
15	01/11/2016	Food	Cake	Carrot Cake	3.5	35	£ 122.50
16	01/11/2016	Beverage	Hot	Macchiato	1.9	52	£ 98.80
17	01/11/2016	Food	Cake	Cupcake	1.75	50	£ 87.50
18	01/11/2016	Beverage	Milkshake	Strawberry	3.5	25	£ 87.50
19	01/11/2016	Food	Sandwich	Toasted Cheese	3.75	20	£ 75.00
20	01/11/2016	Food	Cake	Brownie	3	23	£ 69.00
21	01/11/2016	Food	Cake	Cupcake	1.75	23	£ 40.25
22	01/11/2016	Beverage	Hot	Americano	1.9	20	£ 38.00
23	01/11/2016	Beverage	Cold	Orange Juice	1.2	20	£ 24.00
24	01/11/2016	Food	Salad	Quinoa	4.75	4	£ 19.00
25	02/11/2016	Food	Sandwich	Toasted Cheese	3.75	699	£ 2,621.25
26	02/11/2016	Beverage	Milkshake	Chocolate	3.5	450	£ 1,575.00
27	02/11/2016	Beverage	Cold	Apple Juice	1.5	898	£ 1,347.00
28	02/11/2016	Food	Cake	Brownie	3	444	£ 1,332.00
29	02/11/2016	Beverage	Hot	Flat White	1.9	500	£ 950.00
30	02/11/2016	Beverage	Hot	Cappuccino	1.9	485	£ 921.50
31	02/11/2016	Beverage	Hot	Americano	1.9	250	£ 475.00
32	02/11/2016	Food	Salad	Quinoa	4.75	56	£ 266.00
33	02/11/2016	Food	Cake	Apple Cake	3.5	65	£ 227.50

Figure 150

Custom Sort

When sorting on more than one field, a custom sort is used. There is a large icon which is labelled *Sort* on the *Data* ribbon, and this is used to perform a custom sort. Matt would like to see the data sorted by type and then item so he has *Beverage* first with items in alphabetical order, and then *Food* with items in alphabetical order.

The steps:

1. Click inside the data.
2. Click on the large custom sort icon.
3. In the first level that appears, choose *Type* and then *Values* and order *A to Z.*
4. Then click *Add Level* and sort by *Item*, *Values,* and *A to Z.*
5. Click *OK.*

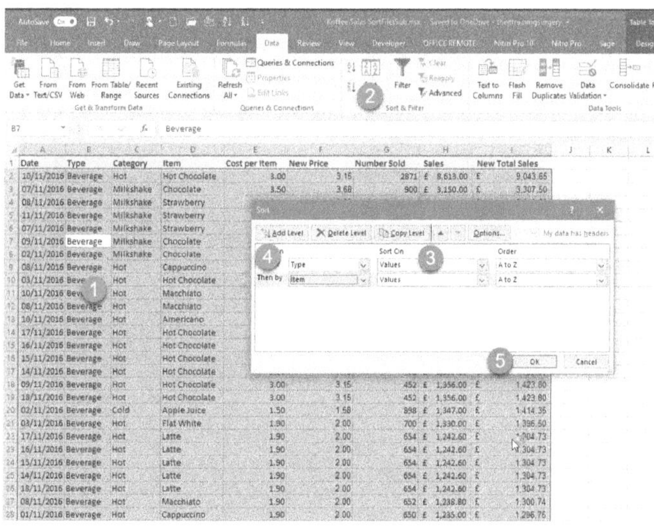

Figure 151

In the resulting data, Matt can see that all the entries for beverage are now listed together, and within the entries for beverage, the items are in alphabetical order.

	A	B	C	D	E	F	G	H
79	14/11/2016	Beverage	Hot	Latte	1.90	654	£ 1,242.60	
80	01/11/2016	Beverage	Hot	Macchiato	1.90	52	£ 98.80	
81	02/11/2016	Beverage	Hot	Macchiato	1.90	54	£ 102.60	
82	03/11/2016	Beverage	Hot	Macchiato	1.90	250	£ 475.00	
83	04/11/2016	Beverage	Hot	Macchiato	1.90	32	£ 60.80	
84	07/11/2016	Beverage	Hot	Macchiato	1.90	200	£ 380.00	
85	08/11/2016	Beverage	Hot	Macchiato	1.90	652	£ 1,238.80	
86	10/11/2016	Beverage	Hot	Macchiato	1.90	761	£ 1,445.40	
87	11/11/2016	Beverage	Hot	Macchiato	1.90	15	£ 28.50	
88	14/11/2016	Beverage	Hot	Macchiato	1.90	256	£ 486.40	
89	01/11/2016	Beverage	Cold	Orange Juice	1.20	20	£ 24.00	
90	02/11/2016	Beverage	Cold	Orange Juice	1.20	60	£ 72.00	
91	03/11/2016	Beverage	Cold	Orange Juice	1.20	50	£ 60.00	
92	04/11/2016	Beverage	Cold	Orange Juice	1.20	800	£ 960.00	
93	07/11/2016	Beverage	Cold	Orange Juice	1.20	30	£ 36.00	
94	08/11/2016	Beverage	Cold	Orange Juice	1.20	435	£ 522.00	
95	09/11/2016	Beverage	Cold	Orange Juice	1.20	13	£ 15.60	
96	10/11/2016	Beverage	Cold	Orange Juice	1.20	251	£ 301.20	
97	11/11/2016	Beverage	Cold	Orange Juice	1.20	17	£ 20.40	
98	01/11/2016	Beverage	Milkshake	Strawberry	3.50	25	£ 87.50	
99	02/11/2016	Beverage	Milkshake	Strawberry	3.50	25	£ 87.50	
100	03/11/2016	Beverage	Milkshake	Strawberry	3.50	150	£ 525.00	
101	04/11/2016	Beverage	Milkshake	Strawberry	3.50	45	£ 157.50	
102	07/11/2016	Beverage	Milkshake	Strawberry	3.50	704	£ 2,464.00	
103	08/11/2016	Beverage	Milkshake	Strawberry	3.50	800	£ 2,800.00	
104	09/11/2016	Beverage	Milkshake	Strawberry	3.50	25	£ 87.50	
105	10/11/2016	Beverage	Milkshake	Strawberry	3.50	50	£ 175.00	
106	11/11/2016	Beverage	Milkshake	Strawberry	3.50	750	£ 2,625.00	
107	14/11/2016	Beverage	Milkshake	Strawberry	3.50	60	£ 210.00	
108	01/11/2016	Food	Cake	Apple Cake	3.50	750	£ 2,625.00	
109	02/11/2016	Food	Cake	Apple C[illegible]e	3.50	65	£ 227.50	
110	03/11/2016	Food	Cake	Apple Cake	3.50	626	£ 2,191.00	
111	04/11/2016	Food	Cake	Apple Cake	3.50	591	£ 2,068.50	
112	07/11/2016	Food	Cake	Apple Cake	3.50	50	£ 175.00	
113	08/11/2016	Food	Cake	Apple Cake	3.50	800	£ 2,800.00	
114	10/11/2016	Food	Cake	Apple Cake	3.50	2241	£ 7,842.42	
115	11/11/2016	Food	Cake	Apple Cake	3.50	16	£ 56.00	
116	14/11/2016	Food	Cake	Apple Cake	3.50	26	£ 91.00	
117	01/11/2016	Food	Cake	Brownie	3.00	23	£ 69.00	
118	02/11/2016	Food	Cake	Brownie	3.00	444	£ 1,332.00	
119	03/11/2016	Food	Cake	Brownie	3.00	50	£ 150.00	
120	04/11/2016	Food	Cake	Brownie	3.00	750	£ 2,250.00	
121	07/11/2016	Food	Cake	Brownie	3.00	800	£ 2,400.00	
122	08/11/2016	Food	Cake	Brownie	3.00	580	£ 1,740.00	

Figure 152

Filtering

Now Matt has seen how to sort his data, he starts to think about other ways of seeing what's going on. What if he only wants to focus on one type of beverage? Perhaps he just wants to see sales of cappuccino? Or maybe cappuccino and chocolate cake?

Filtering allows you to pull out and focus on precisely the data you wish to see.

Where to Find the Filter Icon

Sort & Filter on the *Home* ribbon	*Filter* on the *Data* ribbon
 Figure 153	 Figure 154

Right-click

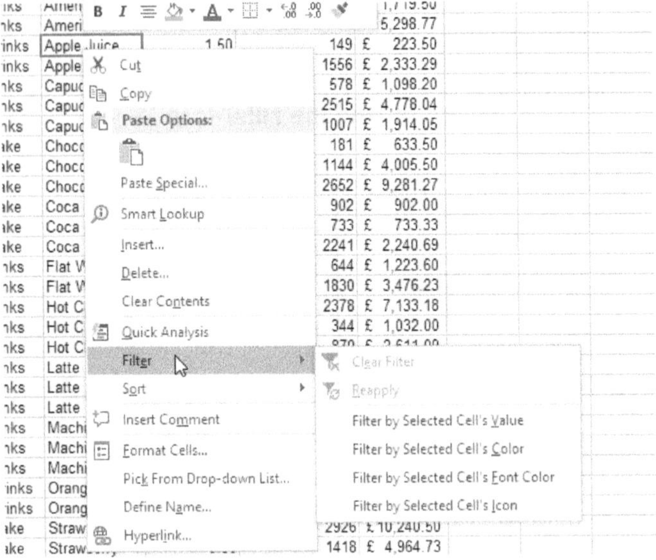

Figure 155

Matt decides to use the large filter icon on the *Data* ribbon.

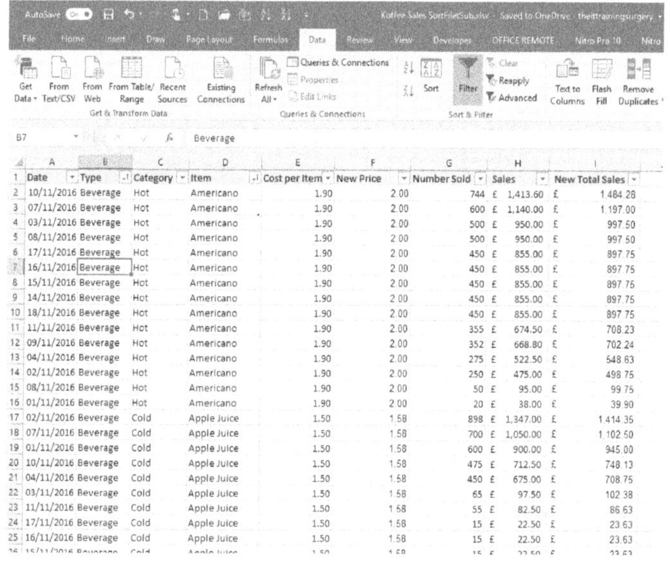

	Date	Type	Category	Item	Cost per Item	New Price	Number Sold	Sales	New Total Sales
2	10/11/2016	Beverage	Hot	Americano	1.90	2.00	744	£ 1,413.60	£ 1,484.28
3	07/11/2016	Beverage	Hot	Americano	1.90	2.00	600	£ 1,140.00	£ 1,197.00
4	03/11/2016	Beverage	Hot	Americano	1.90	2.00	500	£ 950.00	£ 997.50
5	08/11/2016	Beverage	Hot	Americano	1.90	2.00	500	£ 950.00	£ 997.50
6	17/11/2016	Beverage	Hot	Americano	1.90	2.00	450	£ 855.00	£ 897.75
7	16/11/2016	Beverage	Hot	Americano	1.90	2.00	450	£ 855.00	£ 897.75
8	15/11/2016	Beverage	Hot	Americano	1.90	2.00	450	£ 855.00	£ 897.75
9	14/11/2016	Beverage	Hot	Americano	1.90	2.00	450	£ 855.00	£ 897.75
10	18/11/2016	Beverage	Hot	Americano	1.90	2.00	450	£ 855.00	£ 897.75
11	11/11/2016	Beverage	Hot	Americano	1.90	2.00	355	£ 674.50	£ 708.23
12	09/11/2016	Beverage	Hot	Americano	1.90	2.00	352	£ 668.80	£ 702.24
13	04/11/2016	Beverage	Hot	Americano	1.90	2.00	275	£ 522.50	£ 548.63
14	02/11/2016	Beverage	Hot	Americano	1.90	2.00	250	£ 475.00	£ 498.75
15	08/11/2016	Beverage	Hot	Americano	1.90	2.00	50	£ 95.00	£ 99.75
16	01/11/2016	Beverage	Hot	Americano	1.90	2.00	20	£ 38.00	£ 39.90
17	02/11/2016	Beverage	Cold	Apple Juice	1.50	1.58	898	£ 1,347.00	£ 1,414.35
18	07/11/2016	Beverage	Cold	Apple Juice	1.50	1.58	700	£ 1,050.00	£ 1,102.50
19	01/11/2016	Beverage	Cold	Apple Juice	1.50	1.58	600	£ 900.00	£ 945.00
20	10/11/2016	Beverage	Cold	Apple Juice	1.50	1.58	475	£ 712.50	£ 748.13
21	04/11/2016	Beverage	Cold	Apple Juice	1.50	1.58	450	£ 675.00	£ 708.75
22	03/11/2016	Beverage	Cold	Apple Juice	1.50	1.58	65	£ 97.50	£ 102.38
23	11/11/2016	Beverage	Cold	Apple Juice	1.50	1.58	55	£ 82.50	£ 86.63
24	17/11/2016	Beverage	Cold	Apple Juice	1.50	1.58	15	£ 22.50	£ 23.63
25	16/11/2016	Beverage	Cold	Apple Juice	1.50	1.58	15	£ 22.50	£ 23.63

Figure 156

The *Filter* icon now looks as if it is switched on, and small AutoFilter icons have appeared at the top of each column.

Apply a Filter

Click the drop-down arrow on the column to filter by and choose your options. Matt is going to look for all rows that have cappuccino in them to begin with so he can get the hang of filtering.

1. Click the drop-down arrow next to *Item.*
2. Uncheck the box next to *Select All.*
3. Check the box next to *Cappuccino.*

4. The list is filtered.

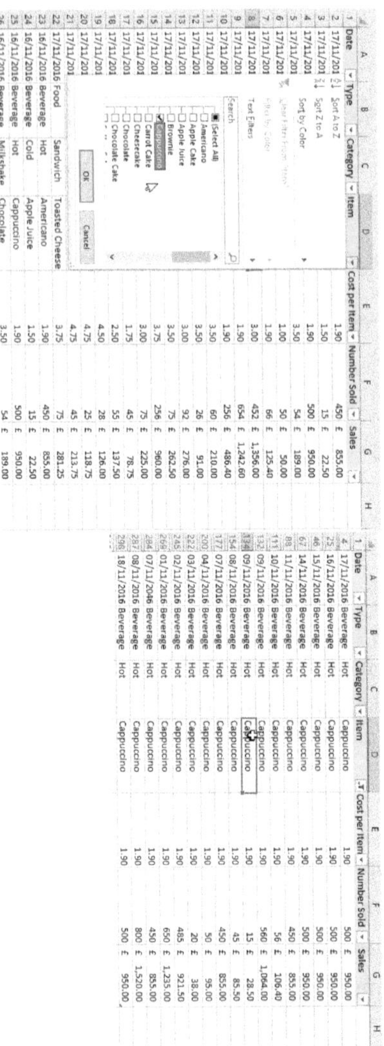

Figure 157

Cappuccino and Chocolate Cake Sales – What Does This Look Like?

Matt clicks on the drop-down arrow on the *Item* column and unchecks *Select All*. Then he ticks both *Cappuccino* and *Chocolate Cake*.

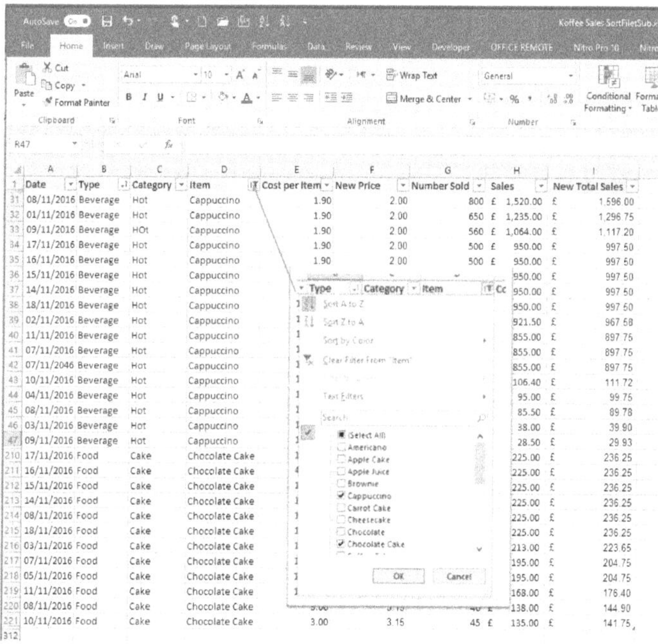

Figure 158

Sales of Cappuccino in the First Week of November 2016

Matt wants to see the sales of cappuccino in the first week of November 2016. This was his first full week of trading. Well, almost full week. November 1st in 2016 was a Tuesday!

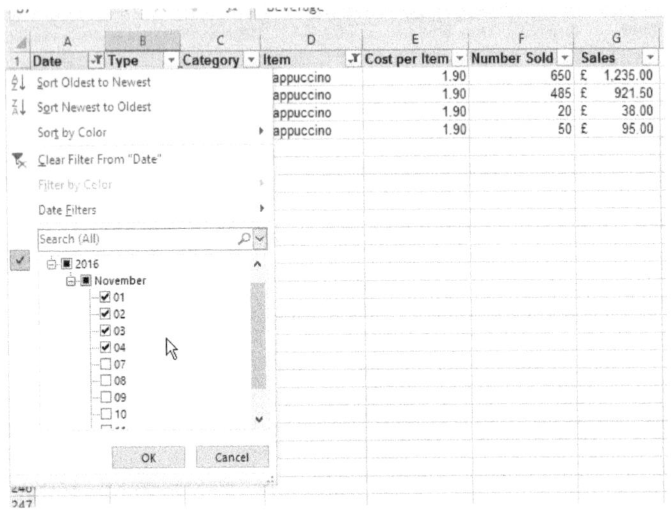

Figure 159

Find All Sales in a Date Range

There is a list of date filters with many options to choose from.

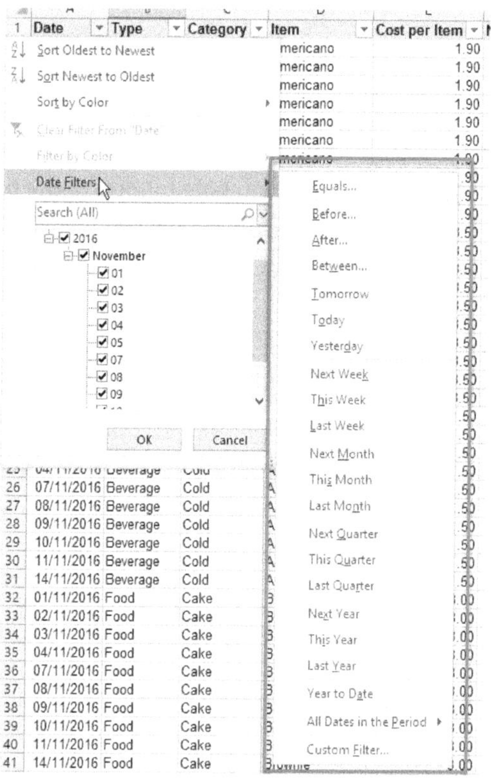

Figure 160

Koffee Says:

To get a date range, Matt needs to pick *Between* and fill in the first and last dates of the range.

Similar filters exist for numbers: *Greater Than* and *Less Than* instead of *Before* or *After*. *Between* still finds a range.

The Power of Data

Matt is now seeing the power of the data. By keeping sales records, he can start to analyse the data and see what works and what doesn't. This data can help him drive the business forward. He needs to keep on top of it and is really excited about analysing data in a way he never was before!

Matt has more questions for Lisa though. How can he see which type of drink is his best-selling or worst-selling? Is there a way of seeing all this in one place without having to apply new filters all the time?

There are several ways of finding this information.

- The subtotals function
- Format as a table
- Create a pivot table

Lisa starts by showing Matt the subtotals command. The subtotals command combines sorting and filtering with a calculation. He can get the subtotals for each item sold or for the type of item: beverage and food.

For the subtotal command to work, he needs to clear any filters and switch off the AutoFilter.

Before applying a subtotal, the data needs to be sorted. To find the subtotal of sales for each type of item sold, the data must be sorted by item first.

Clear a Filter

There are two ways to clear the filter. Click *Clear* in the *Sort & Filter* group on the *Data* ribbon, or click the drop-down arrow on the column filtered, and select *Clear Filter*. It is also possible to tick *Select All* on the column filtered to get all the data back.

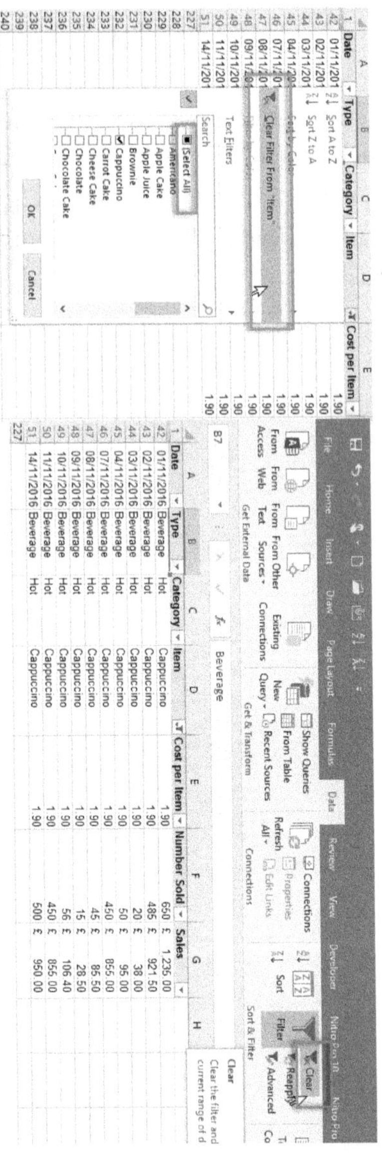

Figure 161

Turn Off the Filter

Click on the big filter button on the *Data* ribbon. This will remove all applied filters and turn off the AutoFilter drop-down arrows.

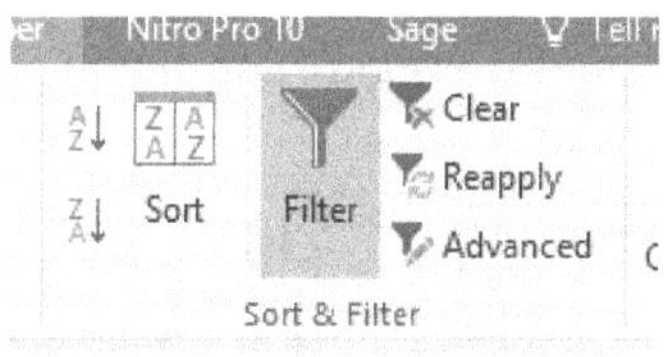

Figure 162

Subtotals

Before applying subtotals, the data must first be sorted by the column Matt wants to analyse. To see the subtotals for items, first sort the data by the item column. Then go to the *Data* ribbon where the *Subtotal* command can be found.

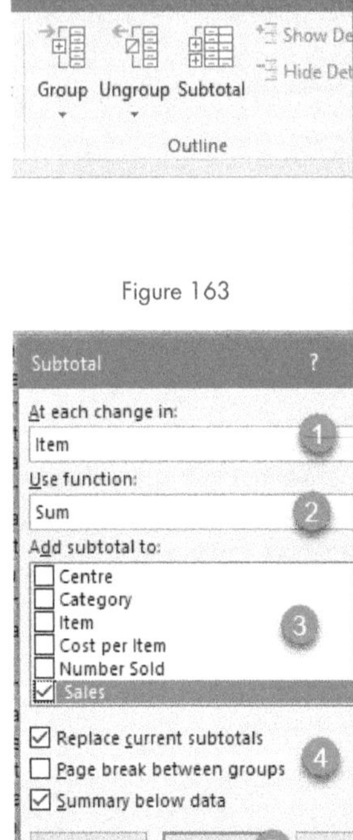

Figure 163

Figure 164

1. Choose the heading you want to subtotal. In this case, it is *Item* –that's where each type of drink is listed.
2. Decide which function to use. We are going to use *Sum.*
3. Choose which columns to total. We will focus on the *Sales* column as that holds the total sales for each row.
4. Extra choices:
    a. *Replace current subtotals* – when you perform the subtotal command again, Excel will replace the one you just did. So if you had done a sum and then you perform an average, you will only see the average. Unchecking this box will display both the sum and the average on separate rows.
    b. *Page break between groups* – will print each group on a separate page.
    c. *Summary below data* – places the subtotals beneath each group of data.
5. Click *OK* when done.

Excel adds subtotals to the worksheet and adds in some extra visuals to help with focus.

	Date	Type	Category	Item	Cost per Item	Number Sold	Sales
2	17/11/2016	Beverage	Hot	Americano	1.90	450	£ 855.00
3	16/11/2016	Beverage	Hot	Americano	1.90	450	£ 855.00
4	15/11/2016	Beverage	Hot	Americano	1.90	450	£ 855.00
5	14/11/2016	Beverage	Hot	Americano	1.90	450	£ 855.00
6	11/11/2016	Beverage	Hot	Americano	1.90	355	£ 674.50
7	10/11/2016	Beverage	Hot	Americano	1.90	744	£ 1,413.60
8	09/11/2016	Beverage	Hot	Americano	1.90	352	£ 668.80
9	08/11/2016	Beverage	Hot	Americano	1.90	50	£ 95.00
10	07/11/2016	Beverage	Hot	Americano	1.90	600	£ 1,140.00
11	04/11/2016	Beverage	Hot	Americano	1.90	275	£ 522.50
12	03/11/2016	Beverage	Hot	Americano	1.90	500	£ 950.00
13	02/11/2016	Beverage	Hot	Americano	1.90	250	£ 475.00
14	01/11/2016	Beverage	Hot	Americano	1.90	20	£ 38.00
15	08/11/2016	Beverage	Hot	Americano	1.90	500	£ 950.00
16	18/11/2016	Beverage	Hot	Americano	1.90	[illegible]	£ 855.00
17				**Americano Total**			£ 11,202.40
18	17/11/2016	Food	Cake	Apple Cake	3.50	[illegible]	£ 91.00
19	16/11/2016	Food	Cake	Apple Cake	3.50	26	£ 91.00
20	15/11/2016	Food	Cake	Apple Cake	3.50	26	£ 91.00
21	14/11/2016	Food	Cake	Apple Cake	3.50	26	£ 91.00
22	11/11/2016	Food	Cake	Apple Cake	3.50	16	£ 56.00
23	10/11/2016	Food	Cake	Apple Cake	3.50	900	£ 3,150.00
24	08/11/2016	Food	Cake	Apple Cake	3.50	800	£ 2,800.00
25	07/11/2016	Food	Cake	Apple Cake	3.50	50	£ 175.00
26	04/11/2016	Food	Cake	Apple Cake	3.50	591	£ 2,068.50
27	03/11/2016	Food	Cake	Apple Cake	3.50	626	£ 2,191.00
28	02/11/2016	Food	Cake	Apple Cake	3.50	65	£ 227.50
29	01/11/2016	Food	Cake	Apple Cake	3.50	750	£ 2,625.00
30	18/11/2016	Food	Cake	Apple Cake	3.50	26	£ 91.00
31				**Apple Cake Total**			£ 13,748.00
32	17/11/2016	Beverage	Cold	Apple Juice	1.50	15	£ 22.50
33	16/11/2016	Beverage	Cold	Apple Juice	1.50	15	£ 22.50
34	15/11/2016	Beverage	Cold	Apple Juice	1.50	15	£ 22.50
35	14/11/2016	Beverage	Cold	Apple Juice	1.50	15	£ 22.50
36	11/11/2016	Beverage	Cold	Apple Juice	1.50	55	£ 82.50
37	10/11/2016	Beverage	Cold	Apple Juice	1.50	475	£ 712.50
38	09/11/2016	Beverage	Cold	Apple Juice	1.50	3	£ 4.50

Figure 165

1. Numbers that allow you to collapse the headings to show grand total only, subtotals, or everything.
2. + or – signs so you can collapse a group of data.
3. Excel adds a new row and places the subtotal of each group there.

To see the various subtotals, click on the numbers in the top left of the screen.

Clicking on the number *1* will show just the grand total.

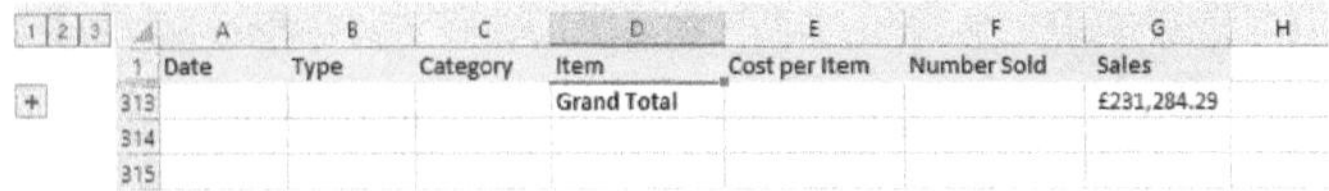

	A	B	C	D	E	F	G	H
1	Date	Type	Category	Item	Cost per Item	Number Sold	Sales	
313				Grand Total			£231,284.29	
314								
315								

Figure 166

Clicking on the number *2* will show the subtotal of each group.

	A	B	C	D	E	F	G	H
1	Date	Type	Category	Item	Cost per Item	Number Sold	Sales	
15				Americano Total			£ 9,397.40	
29				Apple Cake Total			£ 20,309.42	
43				Apple Juice Total			£ 4,981.50	
57				Brownie Total			£ 12,441.00	
71				Cappuccino Total			£ 8,019.90	
85				Carrot Cake Total			£ 10,692.35	
99				Cheesecake Total			£ 28,584.64	
113				Chocolate Total			£ 9,506.00	
125				Chocolate Cake Total			£ 2,169.00	
134				Coffee Cake Total			£ 1,320.00	
148				Cola Total			£ 1,941.00	
162				Cupcake Total			£ 1,225.00	
176				Egg Total			£ 4,822.50	
190				Flat White Total			£ 4,770.90	
204				Greek Salad Total			£ 15,443.65	
218				Hot Chocolate Total			£ 18,165.13	
232				Latte Total			£ 9,211.20	
246				Macchiato Total			£ 5,783.10	
256				Orange Juice Total			£ 2,011.20	
270				Quinoa Total			£ 6,944.50	
284				Smoked Salmon Total			£ 29,217.15	
298				Strawberry Total			£ 9,849.00	
312				Toasted Cheese Total			£ 14,478.75	
313				Grand Total			£231,284.29	
314								
315								

Figure 167

Clicking on the number *3* will bring the whole list back into view, including the subtotals.

To change what is being subtotalled, first remove the current subtotals, then re-sort the data on the new column to subtotal, and then apply subtotals again.

Remove Current Subtotals

Click on the *Subtotals* icon again, and from the dialogue box, select *Remove All*, and you will be back with no subtotals showing.

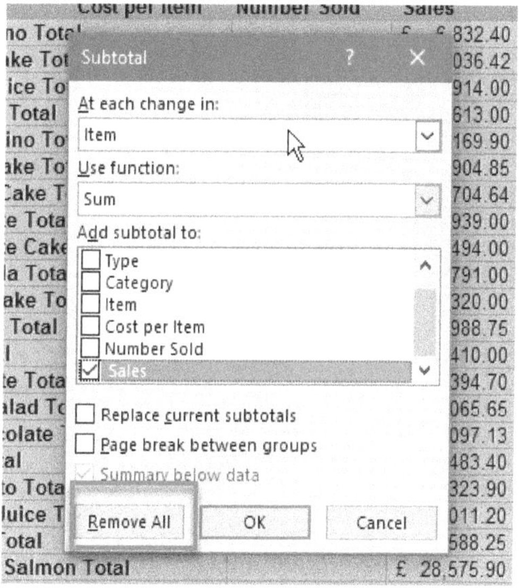

Figure 168

Re-Sort and Apply Subtotals

To see the subtotals for *Type*, Matt needs to re-sort the spreadsheet. He sorts the type column A-Z, which puts it in alphabetical order, beverage first then food.

He can now use subtotals again, telling Excel to subtotal at each change in type.

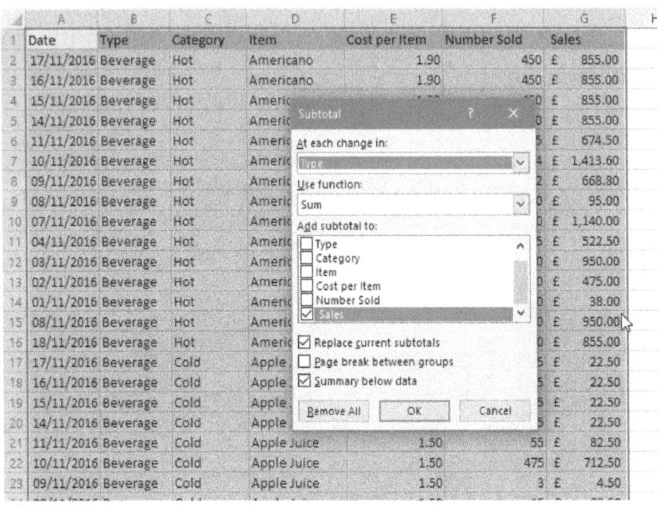

Figure 169

Now Matt can see the breakdown by food or beverage.

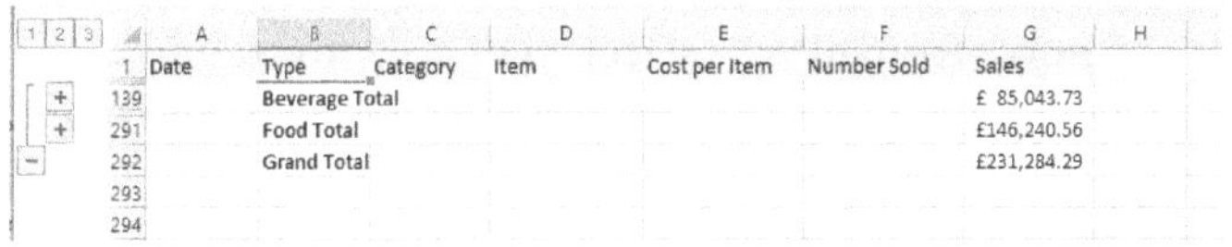

	A	B	C	D	E	F	G	H
1	Date	Type	Category	Item	Cost per Item	Number Sold	Sales	
139		Beverage Total					£ 85,043.73	
291		Food Total					£146,240.56	
292		Grand Total					£231,284.29	
293								
294								

Figure 170

Format as Table

To get even more information from the data, Lisa shows Matt how to use the *Format as Table* command. Matt's seen this before, but now it's time to see it work in more detail. Here is a list of things that *Format as Table* can do:

- Apply fancy formatting to make data more presentable and easy to read
- Add automatic functionality so formatting continues if more rows and columns are added
- Automatic calculation – enables a whole column to be completed in one go without having to use Autofill
- Add totals to the data – with the totals adjusting based on sorting and filtering
- Use slicers to filter the data
- Summarise with a pivot table – if basing a pivot table on a formatted table, it makes updating the pivot table much simpler when adding data to the list

To allow the formatting to work, it is best to remove any formatting already on the spreadsheet.

To remove formatting, select the cells to remove the formatting from, and use the *Clear* icon on the *Home* ribbon.

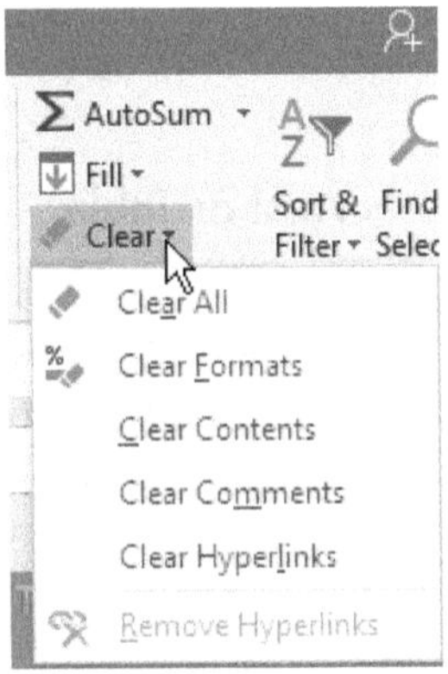

Figure 171

Then follow the steps outlined here to format your table.

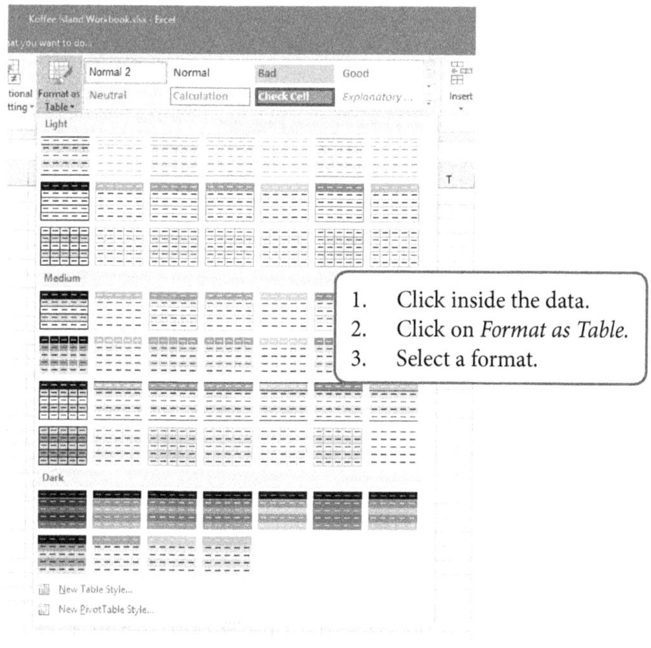

Figure 172

Koffee Says:

The keyboard shortcut to create a table is CTRL+T.

Hold down the *Control* key and the letter *T* together to get the insert table dialogue box.

A dialogue box pops up, checking the correct data has been selected and making sure that the data has headers. This is important as the header needs to be formatted differently to the rest of the data so the AutoFilter can be applied.

Figure 173

Once you click *OK*, the new formatting is applied.

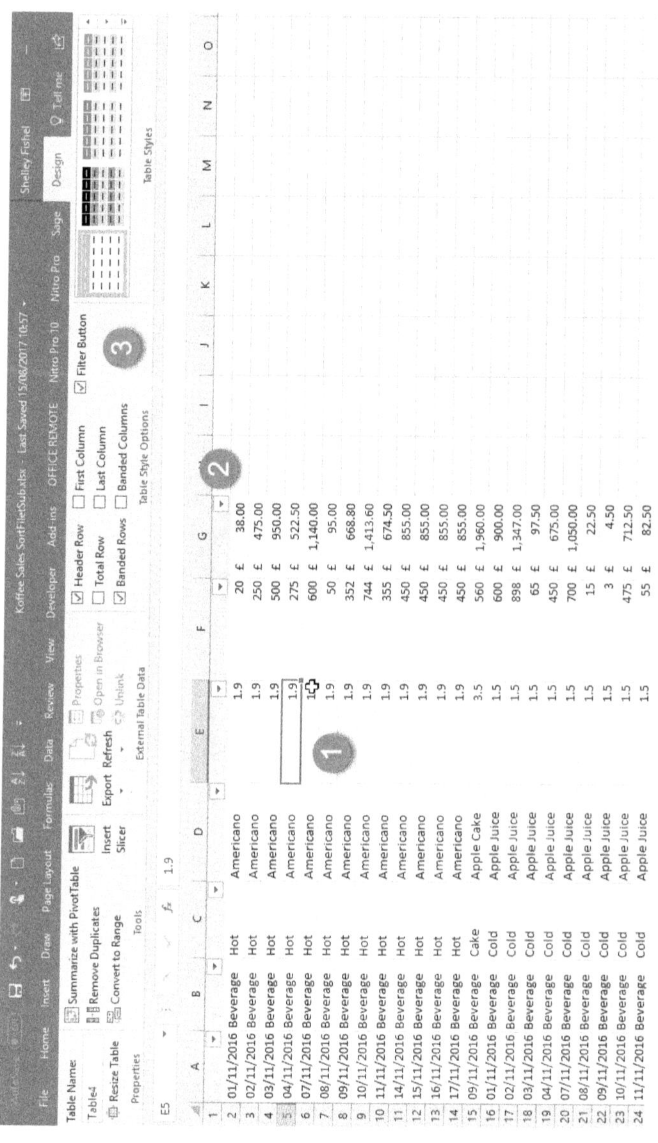

Figure 174

1. Formatting applied.
2. AutoFilter applied.
3. *Table Tools Design* ribbon appears.

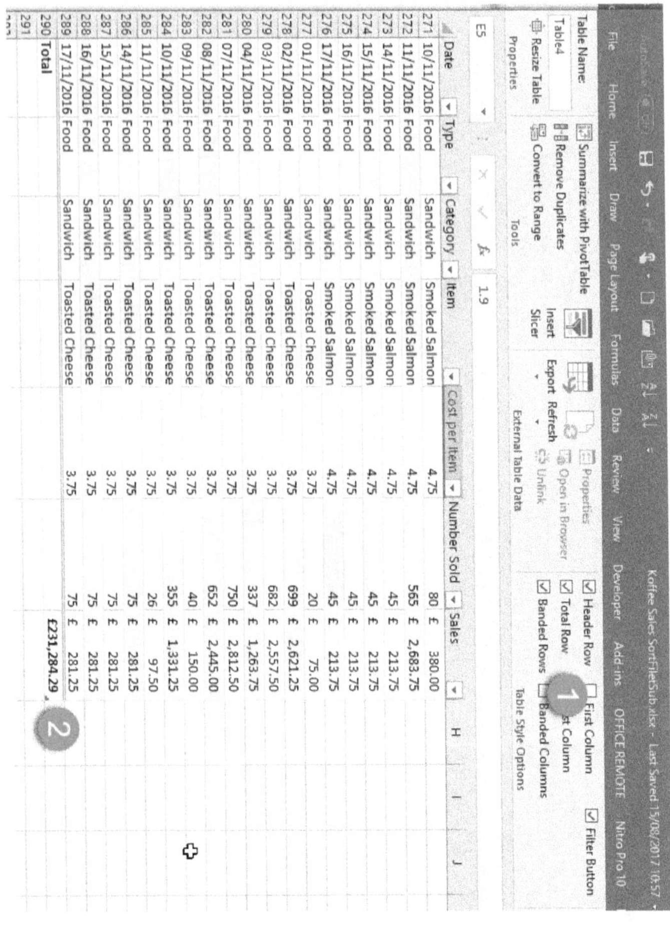

	Date	Type	Category	Item	Cost per Item	Number Sold	Sales
271	10/11/2016	Food	Sandwich	Smoked Salmon	4.75	80	£ 380.00
272	11/11/2016	Food	Sandwich	Smoked Salmon	4.75	565	£ 2,683.75
273	14/11/2016	Food	Sandwich	Smoked Salmon	4.75	45	£ 213.75
274	15/11/2016	Food	Sandwich	Smoked Salmon	4.75	45	£ 213.75
275	16/11/2016	Food	Sandwich	Smoked Salmon	4.75	45	£ 213.75
276	17/11/2016	Food	Sandwich	Smoked Salmon	4.75	45	£ 213.75
277	01/11/2016	Food	Sandwich	Toasted Cheese	3.75	20	£ 75.00
278	02/11/2016	Food	Sandwich	Toasted Cheese	3.75	699	£ 2,621.25
279	03/11/2016	Food	Sandwich	Toasted Cheese	3.75	682	£ 2,557.50
280	04/11/2016	Food	Sandwich	Toasted Cheese	3.75	337	£ 1,263.75
281	07/11/2016	Food	Sandwich	Toasted Cheese	3.75	750	£ 2,812.50
282	08/11/2016	Food	Sandwich	Toasted Cheese	3.75	652	£ 2,445.00
283	09/11/2016	Food	Sandwich	Toasted Cheese	3.75	40	£ 150.00
284	10/11/2016	Food	Sandwich	Toasted Cheese	3.75	355	£ 1,331.25
285	11/11/2016	Food	Sandwich	Toasted Cheese	3.75	26	£ 97.50
286	14/11/2016	Food	Sandwich	Toasted Cheese	3.75	75	£ 281.25
287	15/11/2016	Food	Sandwich	Toasted Cheese	3.75	75	£ 281.25
288	16/11/2016	Food	Sandwich	Toasted Cheese	3.75	75	£ 281.25
289	17/11/2016	Food	Sandwich	Toasted Cheese	3.75	75	£ 281.25
290	Total						£231,284.29

Figure 175

To have a total row appear, tick *Total Row* (1) on the *Table Tools Design* ribbon, and a new row is added to the bottom of the data (2). It has the word *Total* on the left, and at the bottom of the sales column, there is now a grand total of the whole column.

Lisa tells Matt to get ready for magic to happen. Remember the subtotals by item earlier? First sort, then apply subtotals and tell Excel which ones. Then collapse the list to see just the subtotals. Well, *Format as Table* does all of that!

To test this out, Matt applies a filter to the item column and checks only *Cappuccino*.

Now the data is filtered, and the total is auto-magically updated to show just the cappuccino total.

	A	B	C	D	E	F	G	H
1								
29	01/11/2016	Beverage	Hot	Cappuccino	1.9	650	£ 1,235.00	
30	02/11/2016	Beverage	Hot	Cappuccino	1.9	485	£ 921.50	
31	03/11/2016	Beverage	Hot	Cappuccino	1.9	20	£ 38.00	
32	04/11/2016	Beverage	Hot	Cappuccino	1.9	50	£ 95.00	
33	07/11/2016	Beverage	Hot	Cappuccino	1.9	450	£ 855.00	
34	08/11/2016	Beverage	Hot	Cappuccino	1.9	45	£ 85.50	
35	09/11/2016	Beverage	Hot	Cappuccino	1.9	15	£ 28.50	
36	10/11/2016	Beverage	Hot	Cappuccino	1.9	56	£ 106.40	
37	11/11/2016	Beverage	Hot	Cappuccino	1.9	450	£ 855.00	
38	14/11/2016	Beverage	Hot	Cappuccino	1.9	500	£ 950.00	
39	15/11/2016	Beverage	Hot	Cappuccino	1.9	500	£ 950.00	
40	16/11/2016	Beverage	Hot	Cappuccino	1.9	500	£ 950.00	
41	17/11/2016	Beverage	Hot	Cappuccino	1.9	500	£ 950.00	
290	**Total**						**£ 8,019.90**	
291								

Figure 176

To see the sales of cappuccino on the first four days of November, Matt can apply a filter to show just the cappuccino rows on the 1st, 2nd, 3rd and 4th of November, which would be Tuesday 1st to Friday 4th. Note that the data changes along with the total.

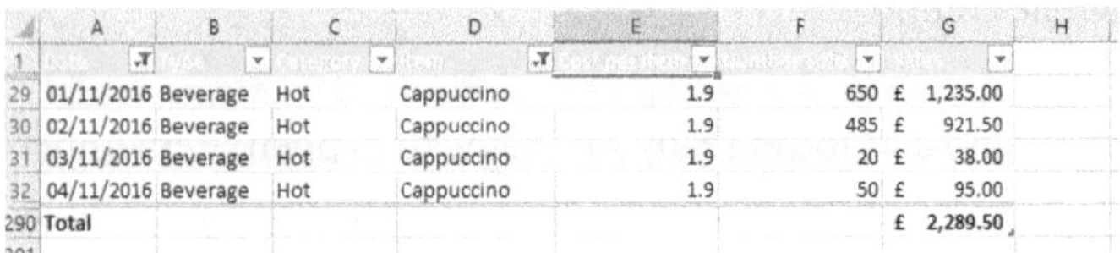

	A	B	C	D	E	F	G	H
1	Date	Type	Category	Item	Cost per item	Number sold	Sales	
29	01/11/2016	Beverage	Hot	Cappuccino	1.9	650	£ 1,235.00	
30	02/11/2016	Beverage	Hot	Cappuccino	1.9	485	£ 921.50	
31	03/11/2016	Beverage	Hot	Cappuccino	1.9	20	£ 38.00	
32	04/11/2016	Beverage	Hot	Cappuccino	1.9	50	£ 95.00	
290	Total						£ 2,289.50	

Figure 177

Finally, he can use a slicer to apply a filter. A slicer is a way of adding some buttons to the spreadsheet to allow you to filter by that criteria.

Add Slicers

Click inside the data, and on the *Table Tools* ribbon, click *Insert Slicer* (1). Tick the checkbox corresponding to the column you want to filter on (2) and click *OK* (3). The slicer will appear on the worksheet (4).

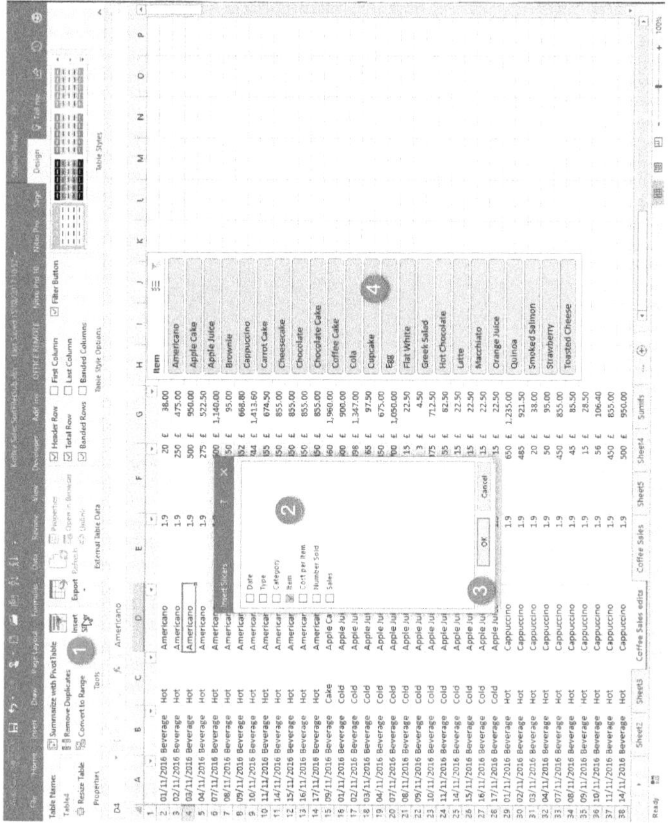

Figure 178

To use the slicer, click on the item to filter. In the example below, we are looking at sales of cappuccino. The only button showing blue now is the *Cappuccino* one, showing that this is the filter applied. To remove the filter, Matt needs to click on the clear filter icon at the top right of the slicer.

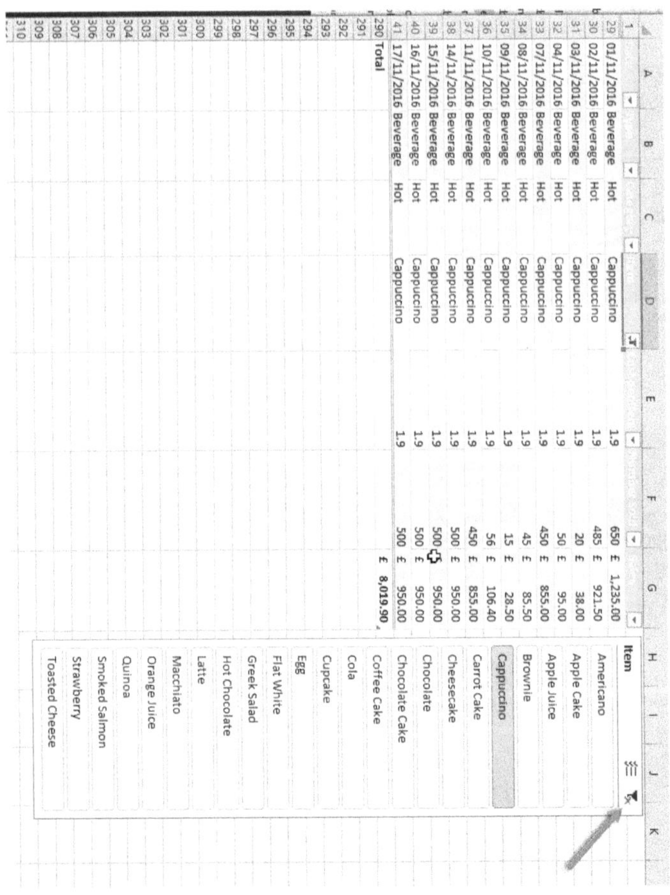

Figure 179

Add a Second Slicer

To have more than one slicer on the worksheet, simply repeat the process and select a different column. Here, Matt has added a slicer to filter on category as well as item. When he added the slicer, it was also blue. To change the colour, Matt clicked on the style he wanted to apply from the *Slicer Styles* gallery.

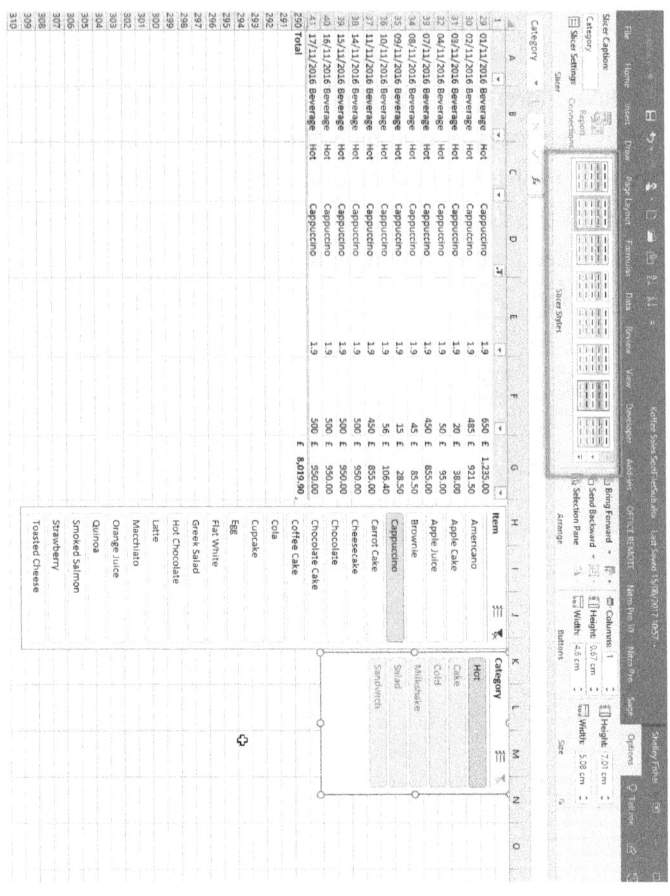

Figure 180

Filter on More Than One Item Using a Slicer

Click on the multiple select icon in the top right and select the filters you want to apply. If you have an earlier version of Excel, you may not see the multiple select icon on the slicer.

In this case, you can hold down the *Control* key to select multiple options.

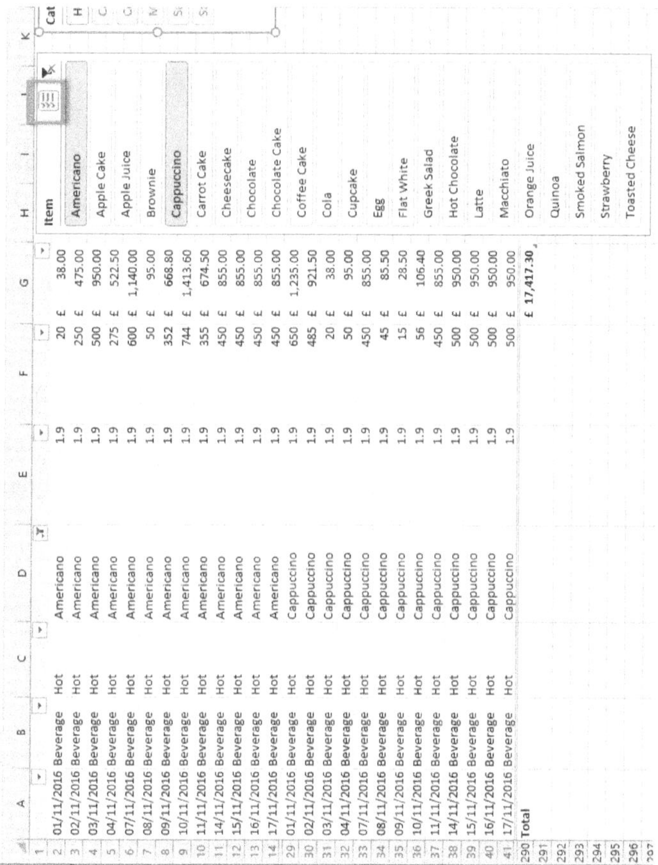

	A	B	C	D	E	F	G
1							
2	01/11/2016	Beverage	Hot	Americano	1.9	20	£ 38.00
3	02/11/2016	Beverage	Hot	Americano	1.9	250	£ 475.00
4	03/11/2016	Beverage	Hot	Americano	1.9	500	£ 950.00
5	04/11/2016	Beverage	Hot	Americano	1.9	275	£ 522.50
6	07/11/2016	Beverage	Hot	Americano	1.9	600	£ 1,140.00
7	08/11/2016	Beverage	Hot	Americano	1.9	50	£ 95.00
8	09/11/2016	Beverage	Hot	Americano	1.9	352	£ 668.80
9	10/11/2016	Beverage	Hot	Americano	1.9	744	£ 1,413.60
10	11/11/2016	Beverage	Hot	Americano	1.9	355	£ 674.50
11	14/11/2016	Beverage	Hot	Americano	1.9	450	£ 855.00
12	15/11/2016	Beverage	Hot	Americano	1.9	450	£ 855.00
13	16/11/2016	Beverage	Hot	Americano	1.9	450	£ 855.00
14	17/11/2016	Beverage	Hot	Americano	1.9	450	£ 855.00
29	01/11/2016	Beverage	Hot	Cappuccino	1.9	650	£ 1,235.00
30	02/11/2016	Beverage	Hot	Cappuccino	1.9	485	£ 921.50
31	03/11/2016	Beverage	Hot	Cappuccino	1.9	20	£ 38.00
32	04/11/2016	Beverage	Hot	Cappuccino	1.9	50	£ 95.00
33	07/11/2016	Beverage	Hot	Cappuccino	1.9	450	£ 855.00
34	08/11/2016	Beverage	Hot	Cappuccino	1.9	45	£ 85.50
35	09/11/2016	Beverage	Hot	Cappuccino	1.9	15	£ 28.50
36	10/11/2016	Beverage	Hot	Cappuccino	1.9	56	£ 106.40
37	11/11/2016	Beverage	Hot	Cappuccino	1.9	450	£ 855.00
38	14/11/2016	Beverage	Hot	Cappuccino	1.9	500	£ 950.00
39	15/11/2016	Beverage	Hot	Cappuccino	1.9	500	£ 950.00
40	16/11/2016	Beverage	Hot	Cappuccino	1.9	500	£ 950.00
41	17/11/2016	Beverage	Hot	Cappuccino	1.9	500	£ 950.00
290	Total						£ 17,417.30
291							
292							
293							
294							
295							
296							

Figure 181

Delete a Slicer

When the slicer is no longer needed, click on it and press the *Delete* key. It will be gone!

Summarise with a Pivot Table

A pivot table combines sorting, filtering, and subtotals along with more powerful ways of arranging the data. With a pivot table, Matt can rearrange the data without having to re-sort it each time. He can also decide what to summarise and what type of function to use.

One of the benefits of formatting the data as a table is that the option to *Summarise with PivotTable* is right there on the ribbon. When clicked, it will start creating a pivot table, which we will see in greater detail shortly.

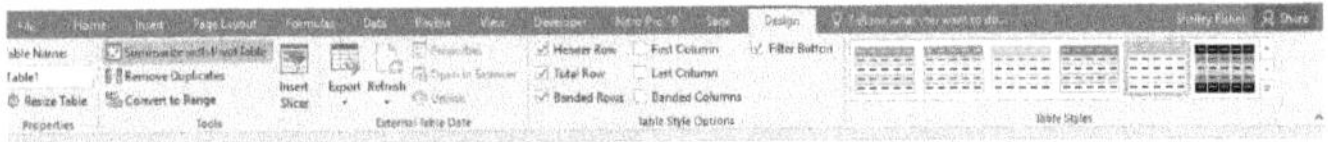

Figure 182

First, Excel checks that the table is the range you wish to use.

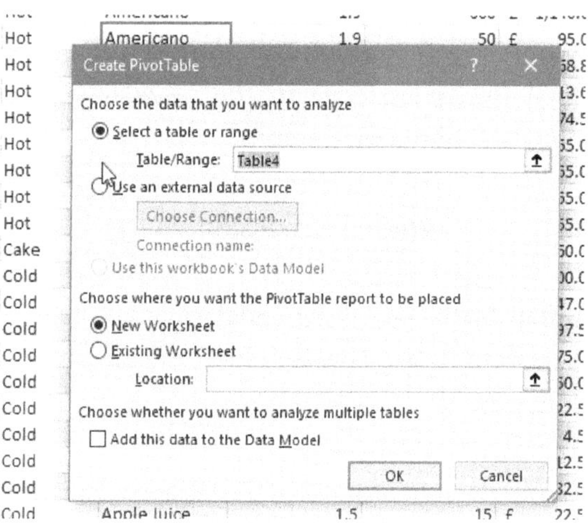

Figure 183

Then you are offered the tools to build the pivot table from scratch. We'll see this on page 222.

Automatic Table Features

Earlier we saw that by adding a total row to the table, Excel automatically calculates a total. There are a couple of other great features of automatic tables.

Automatic Formatting

When you add a new heading in the next column of the table, the formatting you chose will be applied to that whole new column. Equally, the formatting will also be applied to any new rows of data.

It does not stop there, however. Any calculation that is performed in the first cell in the new column will be replicated throughout the column.

Automatic Calculations

Before Matt learns any more about what automatic tables can do, he wants to see how automatic calculations can save him time.

Matt wants to find out what his sales would be if he increased the price of each item by just 5%. In an automatic table, the calculation will be applied to the entire *New Total Sales* column. Note that in Fig 184, there is a new column to work out the new price (1), a multiplier of 1.05 in cell M1 (2), and a new column for the new total sales (3).

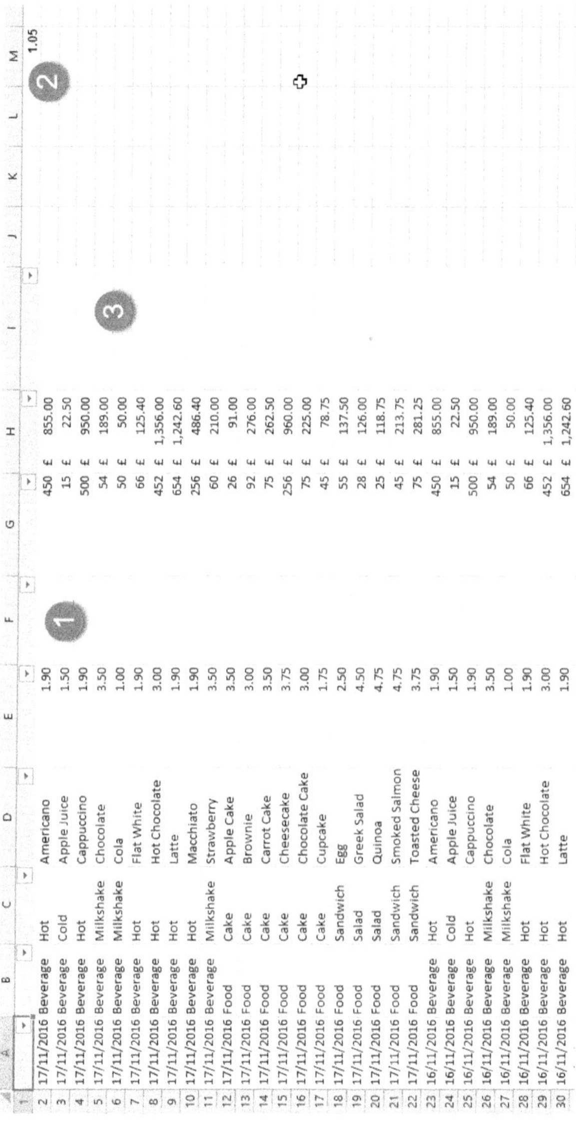

	A	B	C	D	E	F	G	H	I	J	K	L	M
1													1.05
2	17/11/2016	Beverage	Hot	Americano	1.90		450	£ 855.00					
3	17/11/2016	Beverage	Cold	Apple Juice	1.50		15	£ 22.50					
4	17/11/2016	Beverage	Hot	Cappuccino	1.90		500	£ 950.00					
5	17/11/2016	Beverage	Milkshake	Chocolate	3.50		54	£ 189.00					
6	17/11/2016	Beverage	Milkshake	Cola	1.00		50	£ 50.00					
7	17/11/2016	Beverage	Hot	Flat White	1.90		66	£ 125.40					
8	17/11/2016	Beverage	Hot	Hot Chocolate	3.00		452	£ 1,356.00					
9	17/11/2016	Beverage	Hot	Latte	1.90		654	£ 1,242.60					
10	17/11/2016	Beverage	Hot	Macchiato	1.90		256	£ 486.40					
11	17/11/2016	Beverage	Milkshake	Strawberry	3.50		60	£ 210.00					
12	17/11/2016	Food	Cake	Apple Cake	3.50		26	£ 91.00					
13	17/11/2016	Food	Cake	Brownie	3.00		92	£ 276.00					
14	17/11/2016	Food	Cake	Carrot Cake	3.50		75	£ 262.50					
15	17/11/2016	Food	Cake	Cheesecake	3.75		256	£ 960.00					
16	17/11/2016	Food	Cake	Chocolate Cake	3.00		75	£ 225.00					
17	17/11/2016	Food	Cake	Cupcake	1.75		45	£ 78.75					
18	17/11/2016	Food	Sandwich	Egg	2.50		55	£ 137.50					
19	17/11/2016	Food	Salad	Greek Salad	4.50		28	£ 126.00					
20	17/11/2016	Food	Salad	Quinoa	4.75		25	£ 118.75					
21	17/11/2016	Food	Sandwich	Smoked Salmon	4.75		45	£ 213.75					
22	17/11/2016	Food	Sandwich	Toasted Cheese	3.75		75	£ 281.25					
23	16/11/2016	Beverage	Hot	Americano	1.90		450	£ 855.00					
24	16/11/2016	Beverage	Cold	Apple Juice	1.50		15	£ 22.50					
25	16/11/2016	Beverage	Hot	Cappuccino	1.90		500	£ 950.00					
26	16/11/2016	Beverage	Milkshake	Chocolate	3.50		54	£ 189.00					
27	16/11/2016	Beverage	Milkshake	Cola	1.00		50	£ 50.00					
28	16/11/2016	Beverage	Hot	Flat White	1.90		66	£ 125.40					
29	16/11/2016	Beverage	Hot	Hot Chocolate	3.00		452	£ 1,356.00					
30	16/11/2016	Beverage	Hot	Latte	1.90		654	£ 1,242.60					

Figure 184

To perform the calculation, Matt will multiply the price by the increase to get a new price. He only needs to perform this in the first cell in the *New Price* column. Excel will do the rest as soon as he presses the *Enter* key.

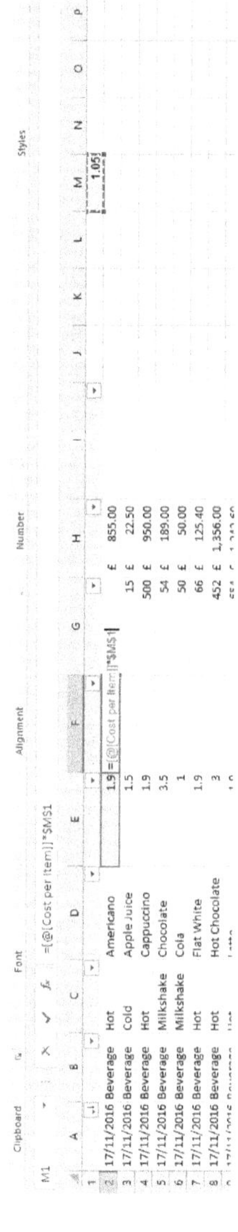

Clipboard
Font
Alignment
Number
Styles
M1
=[@[Cost per Item]]*$M$1
1.05
17/11/2016 Beverage
Hot
Cold
Milkshake
Americano
Apple Juice
Cappuccino
Chocolate
Cola
Flat White
Hot Chocolate

Figure 185

Note that Matt has fixed the reference to M1, and the calculation reads as follows:

=[@[Cost per Item]]*$M$1

The = sign tells Excel we will calculate, then in square brackets we have *@[Cost per Item]*, which is the name of the column, the @ signifying that it is in a table. Then we multiply it by $M$1, which is absolute because we need to copy this down the whole column.

When Matt presses the *Enter* key, the whole column will be populated.

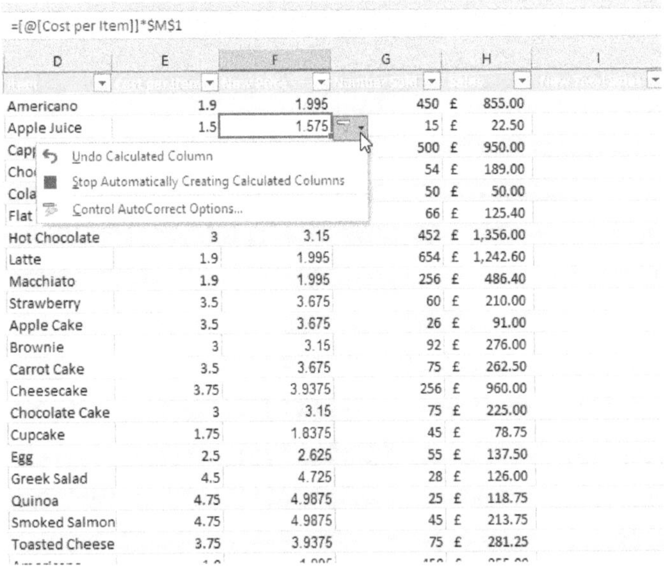

=[@[Cost per Item]]*$M$1

D	E	F	G	H
Americano	1.9	1.995	450	£ 855.00
Apple Juice	1.5	1.575	15	£ 22.50
Capp			500	£ 950.00
Cho			54	£ 189.00
Cola			50	£ 50.00
Flat			66	£ 125.40
Hot Chocolate	3	3.15	452	£ 1,356.00
Latte	1.9	1.995	654	£ 1,242.60
Macchiato	1.9	1.995	256	£ 486.40
Strawberry	3.5	3.675	60	£ 210.00
Apple Cake	3.5	3.675	26	£ 91.00
Brownie	3	3.15	92	£ 276.00
Carrot Cake	3.5	3.675	75	£ 262.50
Cheesecake	3.75	3.9375	256	£ 960.00
Chocolate Cake	3	3.15	75	£ 225.00
Cupcake	1.75	1.8375	45	£ 78.75
Egg	2.5	2.625	55	£ 137.50
Greek Salad	4.5	4.725	28	£ 126.00
Quinoa	4.75	4.9875	25	£ 118.75
Smoked Salmon	4.75	4.9875	45	£ 213.75
Toasted Cheese	3.75	3.9375	75	£ 281.25

Undo Calculated Column
Stop Automatically Creating Calculated Columns
Control AutoCorrect Options...

Figure 186

Note the smart tag that appears. It shows you that you can switch off the automatic calculation if you wish.

Next, Matt is going to see what his new total sales would be with a 5% increase in the price. Again, he will let Excel do the heavy lifting.

=[@[New Price]]*[@[Number Sold]]

D	E	F	G	H	I	J	K
Americano	1.90	2.00	450	£ 855.00	=[@[New Price]]*[@[Number Sold]]		
Apple Juice	1.50	1.58	15	£ 22.50			
Cappuccino	1.90	2.00	500	£ 950.00			
Chocolate	3.50	3.68	54	£ 189.00			
Cola	1.00	1.05	50	£ 50.00			
Flat White	1.90	2.00	66	£ 125.40			
Hot Chocolate	3.00	3.15	452	£ 1,356.00			
Latte	1.90	2.00	654	£ 1,242.60			
Macchiato	1.90	2.00	256	£ 486.40			
Strawberry	3.50	3.68	60	£ 210.00			
Apple Cake	3.50	3.68	26	£ 91.00			
Brownie	3.00	3.15	92	£ 276.00			
Carrot Cake	3.50	3.68	75	£ 262.50			
Cheesecake	3.75	3.94	256	£ 960.00			
Chocolate Cake	3.00	3.15	75	£ 225.00			

Figure 187

Once Matt presses *Enter*, away Excel goes! He now has a new total sales column, and by adding a total row and doing a bit of formatting, he can now compare the two figures. This can help Matt decide on the price of individual items.

	Date	Type	Category	Item	Cost per Item	New Price	Number Sold	Sales	New Total Sales
265	02/11/2016	Food	Sandwich	Smoked Salmon	4.75	4.99	45	£ 213.75	£ 224.44
266	02/11/2016	Food	Sandwich	Toasted Cheese	3.75	3.94	699	£ 2,621.25	£ 2,752.31
267	01/11/2016	Beverage	Hot	Americano	1.90	2.00	20	£ 38.00	£ 39.90
268	01/11/2016	Beverage	Cold	Apple Juice	1.50	1.58	600	£ 900.00	£ 945.00
269	01/11/2016	Beverage	Hot	Cappuccino	1.90	2.00	650	£ 1,235.00	£ 1,296.75
270	01/11/2016	Beverage	Milkshake	Chocolate	3.50	3.68	250	£ 875.00	£ 918.75
271	01/11/2016	Beverage	Milkshake	Cola	1.00	1.05	350	£ 350.00	£ 367.50
272	01/11/2016	Beverage	Hot	Flat White	1.90	2.00	400	£ 760.00	£ 798.00
273	01/11/2016	Beverage	Hot	Hot Chocolate	3.00	3.15	250	£ 750.00	£ 787.50
274	01/11/2016	Beverage	Hot	Latte	1.90	2.00	350	£ 665.00	£ 698.25
275	01/11/2016	Beverage	Hot	Macchiato	1.90	2.00	52	£ [illegible]80	£ 103.74
276	01/11/2016	Beverage	Cold	Orange Juice	1.20	1.26	20	£ 24.00	£ 25.20
277	01/11/2016	Beverage	Milkshake	Strawberry	3.50	3.68	25	£ 87.50	£ 91.88
278	01/11/2016	Food	Cake	Apple Cake	3.50	3.68	750	£ 2,625.00	£ 2,756.25
279	01/11/2016	Food	Cake	Brownie	3.00	3.15	23	£ 69.00	£ 72.45
280	01/11/2016	Food	Cake	Carrot Cake	3.50	3.68	35	£ 122.50	£ 128.63
281	01/11/2016	Food	Cake	Cheesecake	3.75	3.94	500	£ 1,875.00	£ 1,968.75
282	01/11/2016	Food	Cake	Coffee Cake	3.00	3.15	54	£ 162.00	£ 170.10
283	01/11/2016	Food	Cake	Cupcake	1.75	1.84	50	£ 87.50	£ 91.88
284	01/11/2016	Food	Cake	Cupcake	1.75	1.84	23	£ 40.25	£ 42.26
285	01/11/2016	Food	Sandwich	Egg	2.50	2.63	650	£ 1,625.00	£ 1,706.25
286	01/11/2016	Food	Salad	Greek Salad	4.50	4.73	700	£ 3,150.00	£ 3,307.50
287	01/11/2016	Food	Salad	Quinoa	4.75	4.99	4	£ 19.00	£ 19.95
288	01/11/2016	Food	Sandwich	Smoked Salmon	4.75	4.99	654	£ 3,106.50	£ 3,261.83
289	01/11/2016	Food	Sandwich	Toasted Cheese	3.75	3.94	20	£ 75.00	£ 78.75
290	**Total**							**£231,284.29**	**£ 242,848.51**

Figure 188

Pivot Tables

Now Matt is happy with automatic calculations, he's ready to learn more about pivot tables.

Pivot tables make analysing large amounts of data easy. They also help to present that data in a way that is easy to read. They are called pivot tables because the data can be pivoted and changed easily. One moment you can be looking at one scenario, then with the click of a button, you can see a different set of options.

Lisa shows Matt what she means. She starts by building a simple pivot table to see the sales of drink by item.

Create a Recommended Pivot Table

Before Lisa shows Matt how to build a pivot table from scratch, she first shows him how to create a recommended pivot table. For simple pivot tables, this is an extremely useful option, and if this is your first time building a pivot table, it's a great place to start.

From inside the data, click on *Insert* and *Recommended PivotTables.*

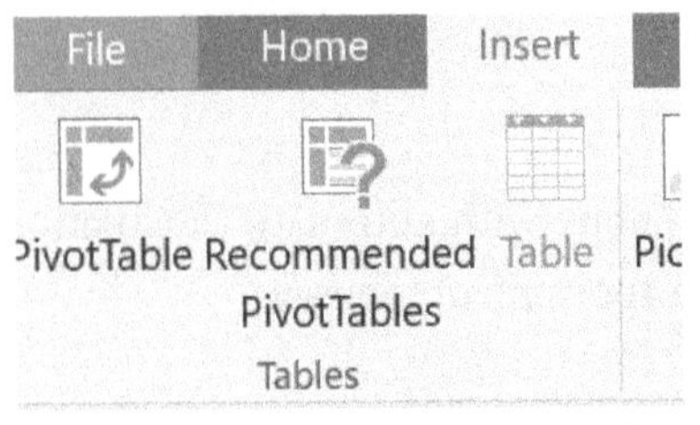

Figure 189

Now Excel will recommend a selection of options, and you can pick the one that matches what you need or at least one that comes close.

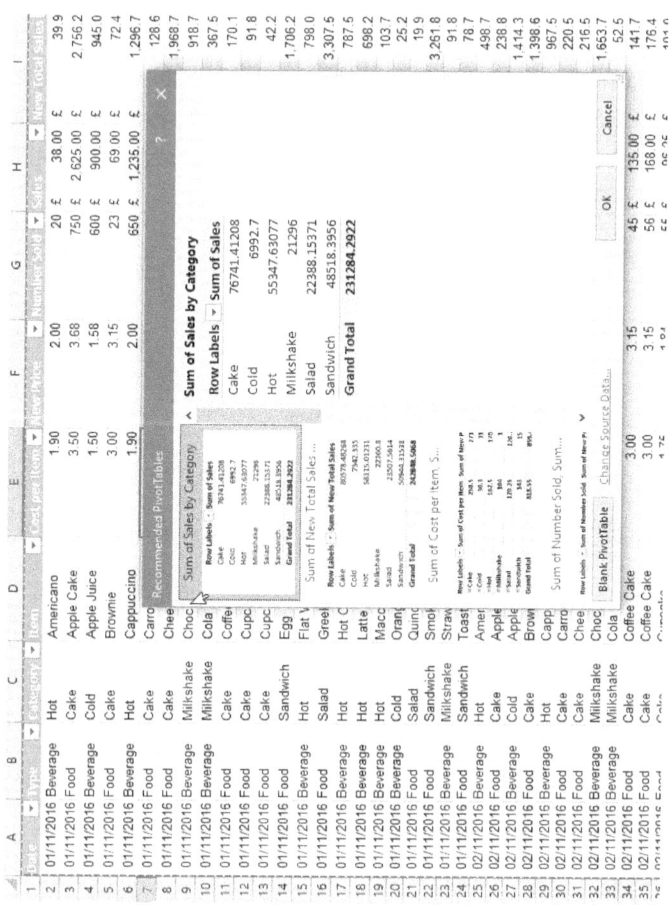

Figure 190

Here is a pivot table showing the total sales by category.

Select it and click *OK*.

A new pivot table is added (1) with the field list and the areas that are used to build the pivot table showing in the task pane on the right of the screen (2). To move the fields around, drag them between the different areas in the field area (3).

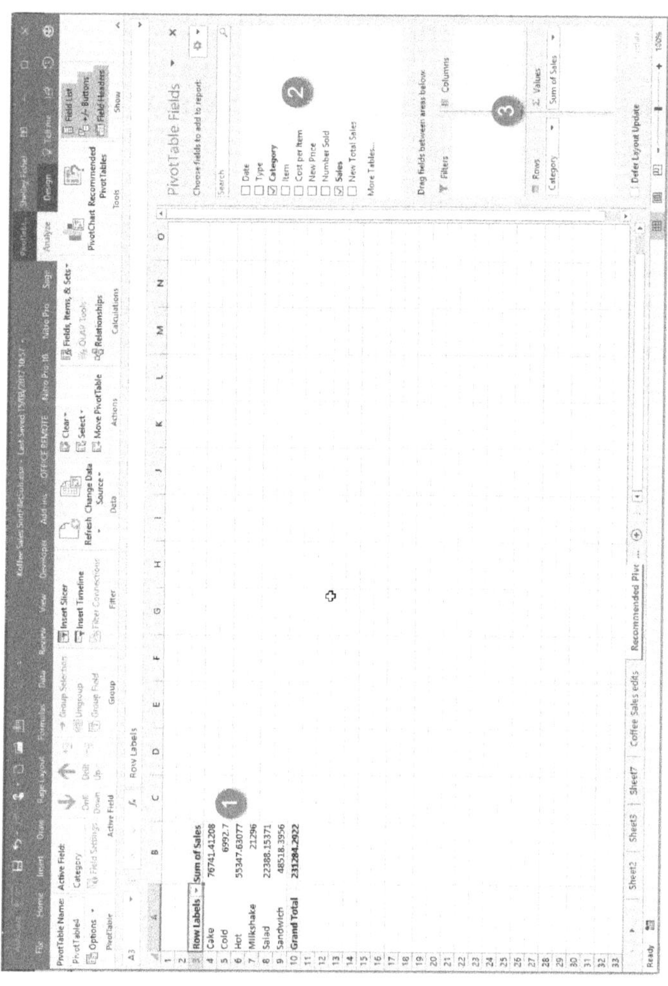
Row Labels
Sum of Sales
Cake
76741.41208
Cold
6992.7
Hot
55347.63077
Milkshake
21296
Salad
22388.15371
Sandwich
48518.3956
Grand Total
231284.2922
1
PivotTable Fields
Choose fields to add to report:
Date
Type
Category
Item
Cost per Item
New Price
Number Sold
Sales
New Total Sales
More Tables...
2
Drag fields between areas below:
Filters
Columns
Rows
Category
Values
Sum of Sales
3
Defer Layout Update

Figure 191

Build a Pivot Table from Scratch

Time to build a pivot table from scratch without using the recommended options.

Remember the data is still formatted as a table, and this is a good thing as it allows Matt to add data at the end of the table and refresh the pivot table easily. It is more complex to update the pivot table to include new rows when you base it on data that has not been formatted as a table.

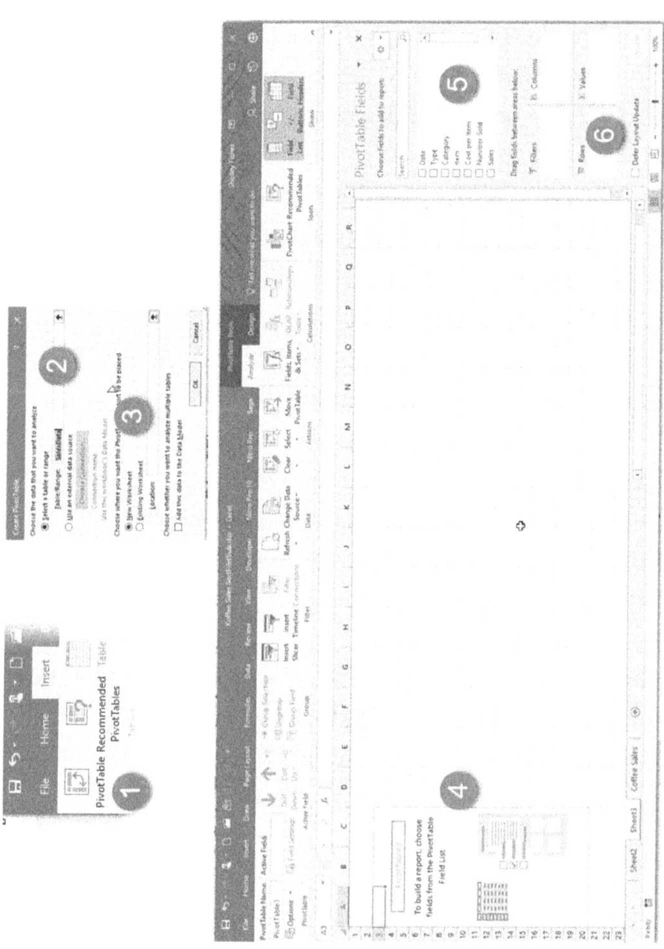

Figure 192

1. Click on the insert *PivotTable* icon.
2. In the select data dialogue, it shows that *SalesData* (the table) is the area selected.
3. Choose where to place the pivot table. *New Worksheet*

is the default, although a pivot table can be placed on the worksheet next to the data.

4. The area on the blank worksheet where the pivot table will be built.
5. The list of column headings or fields to select from.
6. The pivot table quadrants, *Filters*, *Columns*, *Rows*, *Values* – this is where the fields will go to determine the structure of the pivot table.

The first pivot table will be a list of the items with their sales totals.

Tick the *Item* checkbox and the *Sales* checkbox. Notice how the field headings appear in the quadrants: *Items* in *Rows* and *Sales* in *Values*.

The spreadsheet shows the list of items with the total sales for each item (1), the fields that are checked (2), and the quadrants governing how the data is arranged (3).

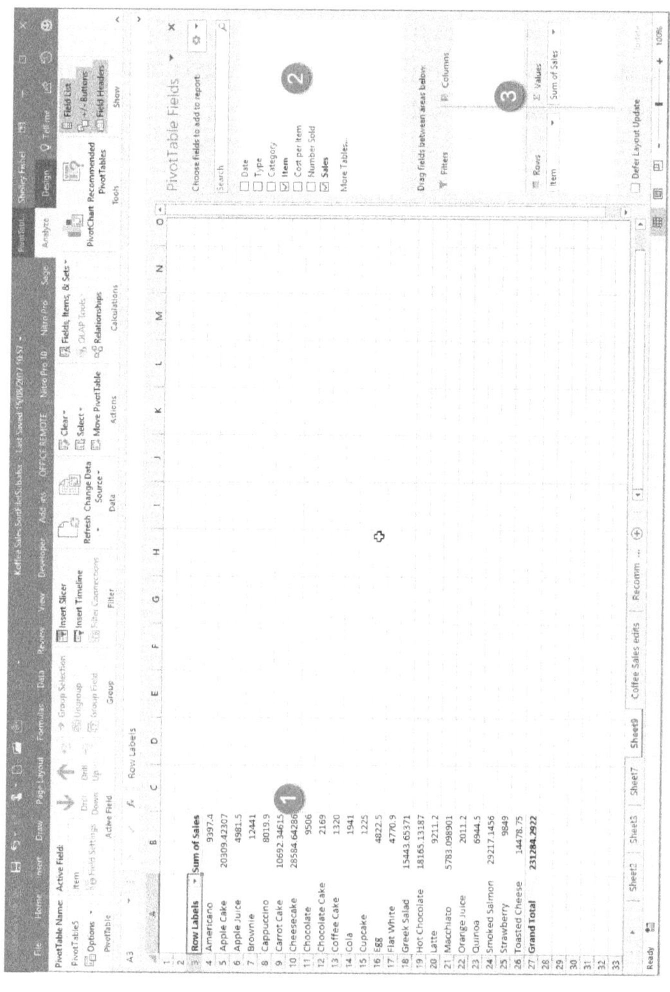

Figure 193

Immediately, Matt can see the totals of each type of item sold. To change what he sees, Matt can uncheck a field and check a different one.

Instead of seeing the totals of each item, Matt would like to see the totals by category. Easy to accomplish. Simply uncheck *Item* and check *Category*.

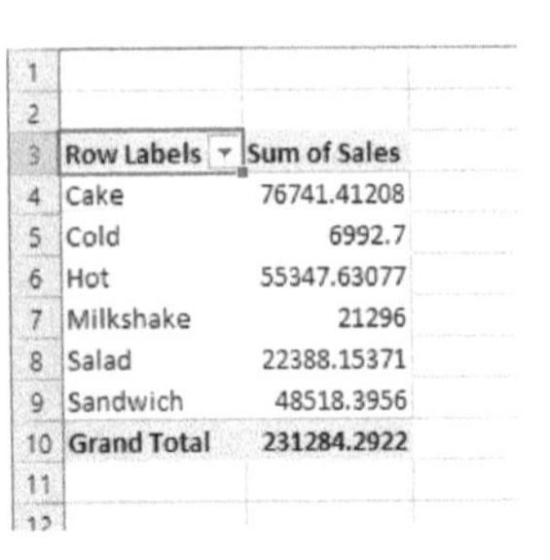

Row Labels	Sum of Sales
Cake	76741.41208
Cold	6992.7
Hot	55347.63077
Milkshake	21296
Salad	22388.15371
Sandwich	48518.3956
Grand Total	**231284.2922**

Figure 194

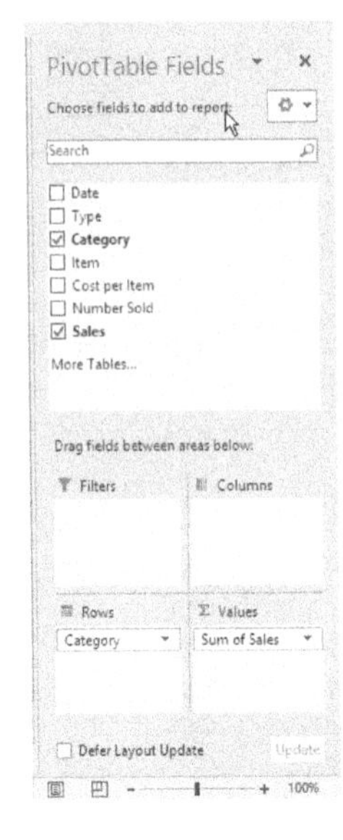

Figure 195

To see the values of category and item at the same time, Matt unticks everything and ticks the relevant fields.

This is what he sees:

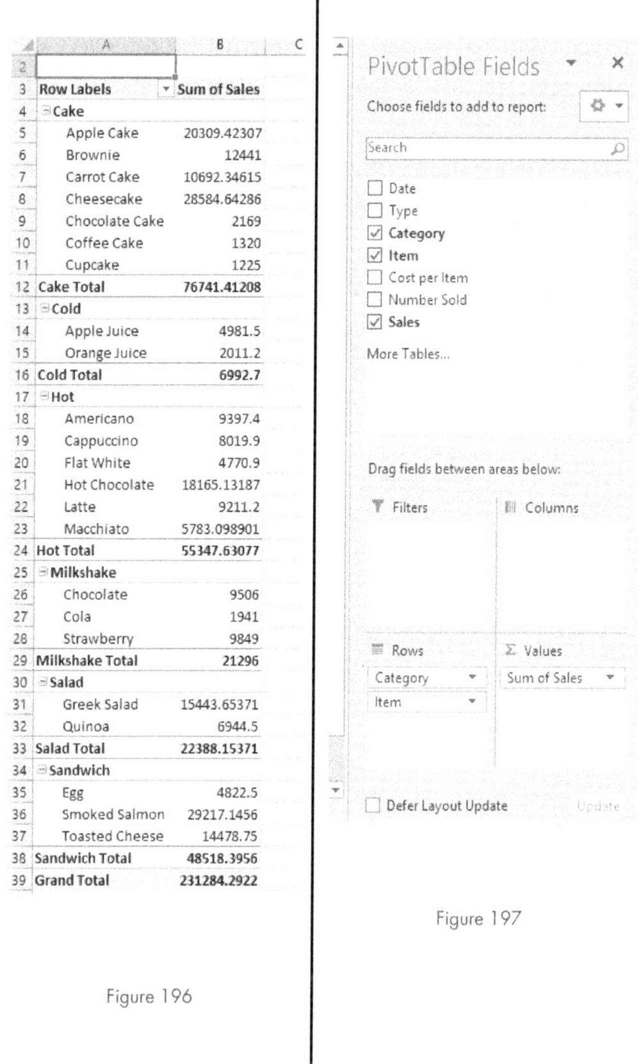

Row Labels	Sum of Sales
Cake	
Apple Cake	20309.42307
Brownie	12441
Carrot Cake	10692.34615
Cheesecake	28584.64286
Chocolate Cake	2169
Coffee Cake	1320
Cupcake	1225
Cake Total	**76741.41208**
Cold	
Apple Juice	4981.5
Orange Juice	2011.2
Cold Total	**6992.7**
Hot	
Americano	9397.4
Cappuccino	8019.9
Flat White	4770.9
Hot Chocolate	18165.13187
Latte	9211.2
Macchiato	5783.098901
Hot Total	**55347.63077**
Milkshake	
Chocolate	9506
Cola	1941
Strawberry	9849
Milkshake Total	**21296**
Salad	
Greek Salad	15443.65371
Quinoa	6944.5
Salad Total	**22388.15371**
Sandwich	
Egg	4822.5
Smoked Salmon	29217.1456
Toasted Cheese	14478.75
Sandwich Total	**48518.3956**
Grand Total	**231284.2922**

Figure 196

Figure 197

The items are now totalled and appear under each category. The category appears in the row area first as it was ticked first.

In effect, Matt has sorted the whole list by category, and within each category, by item, and he has subtotals of each.

This is all very exciting stuff. Again, Matt is impressed by the amount of information he can glean from his daily takings.

By changing the fields in the different areas of the pivot table, Matt can see the data in different ways. Here, Matt had dragged *Category* to the *Columns* area and left *Items* in the *Rows.*

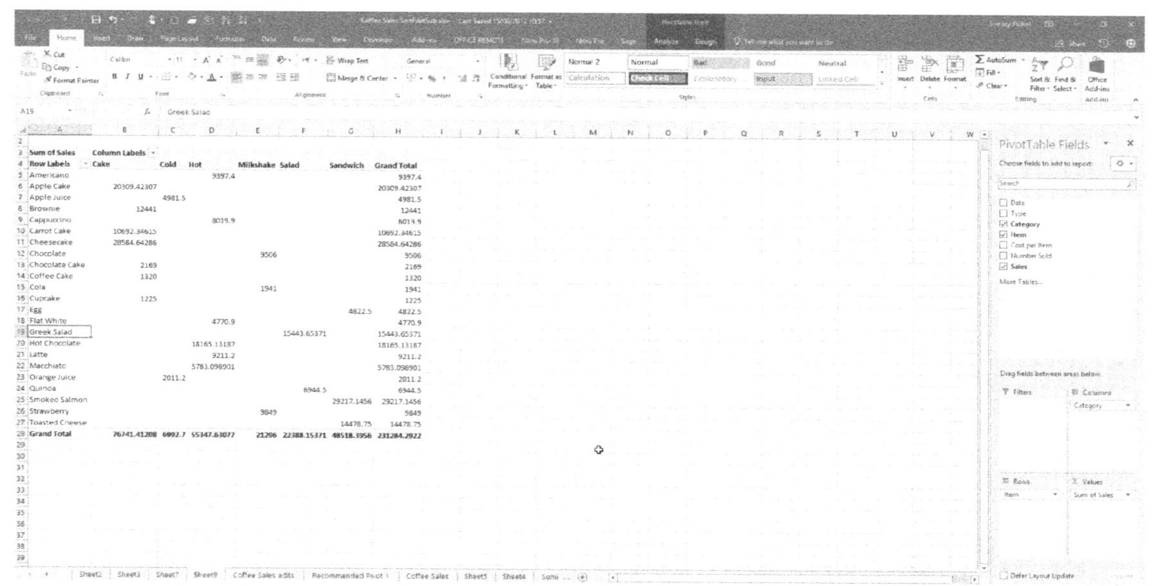
A19 Greek Salad
Sum of Sales Column Labels
Row Labels Cake Cold Hot Milkshake Salad Sandwich Grand Total
Americano 9397.4 9397.4
Apple Cake 20309.42307 20309.42307
Apple Juice 4981.5 4981.5
Brownie 12441 12441
Cappuccino 8019.9 8019.9
Carrot Cake 10692.34615 10692.34615
Cheesecake 28584.64286 28584.64286
Chocolate 9506 9506
Chocolate Cake 2169 2169
Coffee Cake 1320 1320
Cola 1941 1941
Cupcake 1225 1225
Egg 4822.5 4822.5
Flat White 4770.9 4770.9
Greek Salad 15443.65371 15443.65371
Hot Chocolate 18165.13187 18165.13187
Latte 9211.2 9211.2
Macchiato 5783.098901 5783.098901
Orange Juice 2011.2 2011.2
Quinoa 6944.5 6944.5
Smoked Salmon 29217.1456 29217.1456
Strawberry 9849 9849
Toasted Cheese 14478.75 14478.75
Grand Total 76741.41208 6992.7 55347.63077 21296 22388.15371 48518.3956 231284.2922
PivotTable Fields
Choose fields to add to report:
Date
Type
Category
Item
Cost per Item
Number Sold
Sales
More Tables...
Drag fields between areas below:
Filters
Columns
Category
Rows
Item
Values
Sum of Sales
Defer Layout Update
Sheet2 Sheet3 Sheet7 Sheet9 Coffee Sales edits Recommended Pivot 1 Coffee Sales Sheet5 Sheet4

Figure 198

When a pivot table is added to a worksheet, two new ribbon tabs appear under *PivotTable Tools. Analyze* and *Design.*

On the *Design* ribbon, a new format for the pivot table can be chosen. There are options to change how the totals behave as well as the look of the pivot table.

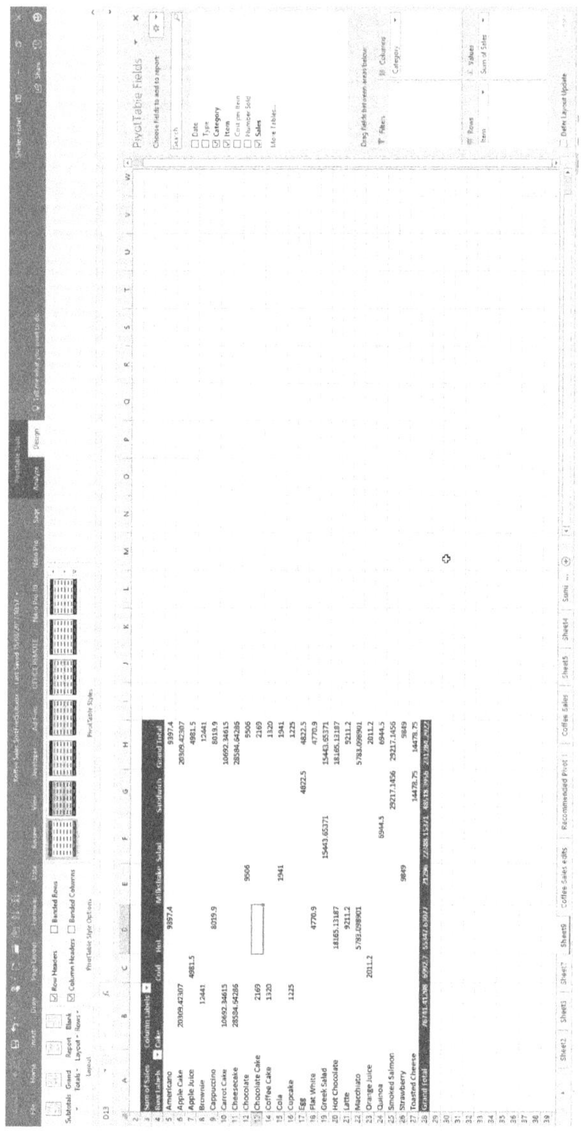

Figure 199

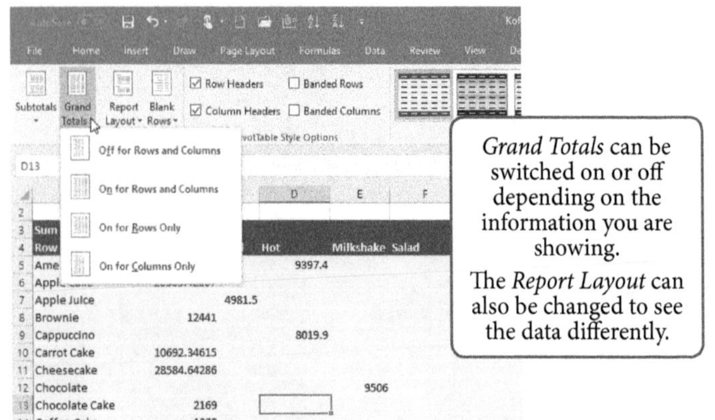
Subtotals
Grand Totals
Report Layout
Blank Rows
Row Headers
Banded Rows
Column Headers
Banded Columns
Off for Rows and Columns
On for Rows and Columns
On for Rows Only
On for Columns Only
Grand Totals can be switched on or off depending on the information you are showing.
The *Report Layout* can also be changed to see the data differently.

Figure 200

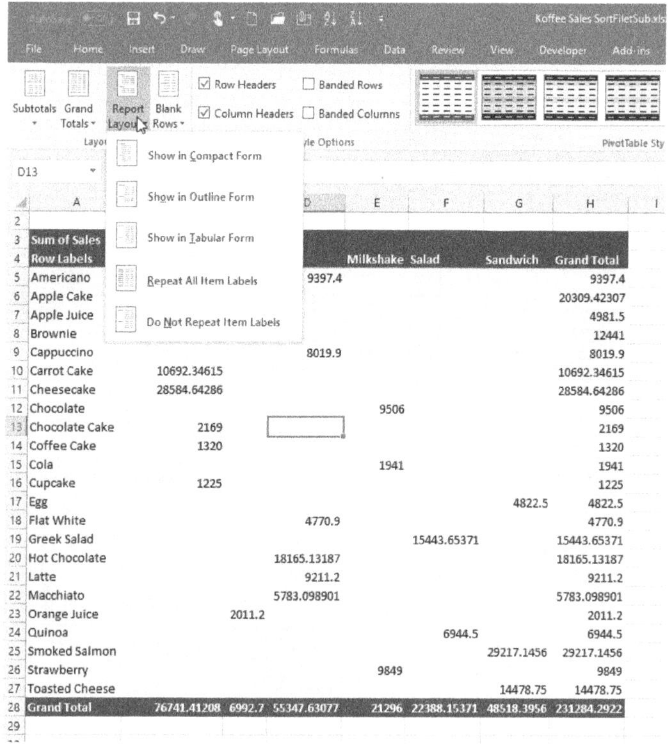

Figure 201

The Analyze Ribbon

Here, it is possible to add a slicer for the pivot table just like in the formatted table. The process is the same.

By adding a slicer, it makes filtering a pivot table simple. Here we can see only the items that are shown in blue on the slicer. Click on the items to display, and everything else is hidden.

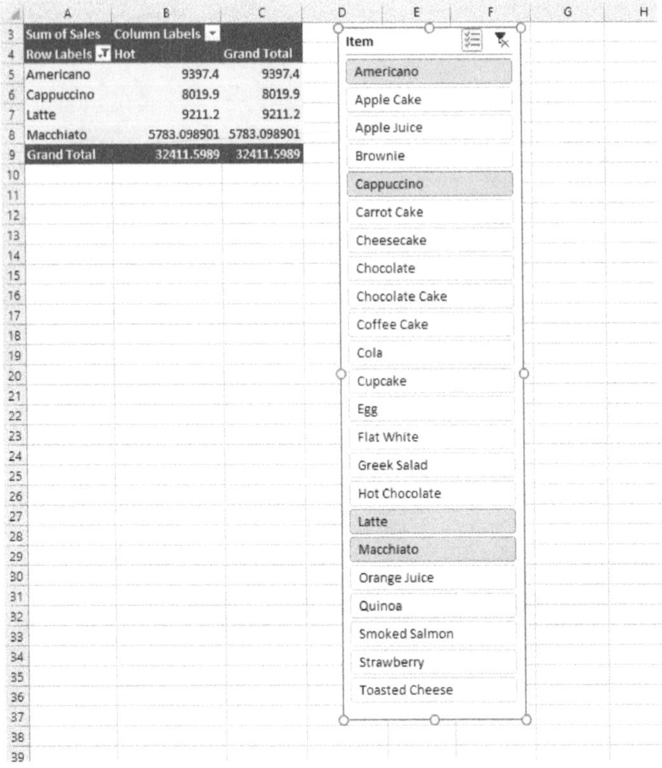

Sum of Sales	Column Labels	
Row Labels	Hot	Grand Total
Americano	9397.4	9397.4
Cappuccino	8019.9	8019.9
Latte	9211.2	9211.2
Macchiato	5783.098901	5783.098901
Grand Total	32411.5989	32411.5989

Figure 202

Filter a Pivot Table Without a Slicer

Note that at the top of each major column there is a filter icon. Click it to see the drop-down and use the AutoFilter features seen earlier.

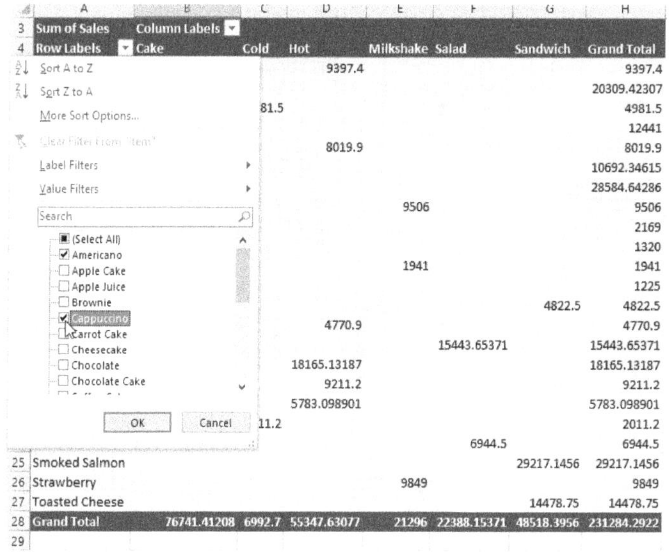

Figure 203

Adding Extra Data

The data in Matt's table is based on the daily takings for the first couple of weeks trading at Koffee Island. Now Matt has some more data to add, he will copy it into the worksheet with the table. It is for the next few days. There are quite a lot of extra rows, and Matt wants to avoid having to make lots of changes. He just wants an easy way to refresh the data. Luckily, he based the pivot table on an automatic table that he formatted earlier. So now all he needs to do is refresh the pivot table.

Here is some of the new data:

289	01/11/2016	Food	Cake	Cupcake	1.75	1.84	50	£	87.50	£	91.88
290	01/11/2016	Food	Cake	Cupcake	1.75	1.84	23	£	40.25	£	42.26
291	01/11/2016	Food	Sandwich	Egg	2.50	2.63	650	£	1,625.00	£	1,706.25
292	01/11/2016	Food	Salad	Greek Salad	4.50	4.73	700	£	3,150.00	£	3,307.50
293	01/11/2016	Food	Salad	Quinoa	4.75	4.99	4	£	19.00	£	19.95
294	01/11/2016	Food	Sandwich	Smoked Salmon	4.75	4.99	654	£	3,106.50	£	3,261.83
295	01/11/2016	Food	Sandwich	Toasted Cheese	3.75	3.94	20	£	75.00	£	78.75
296	18/11/2016	Beverage	Hot	Americano	1.90	2.00	450	£	855.00	£	897.75
297	18/11/2016	Beverage	Cold	Apple Juice	1.50	1.58	15	£	22.50	£	23.63
298	18/11/2016	Beverage	Hot	Cappuccino	1.90	2.00	500	£	950.00	£	997.50
299	18/11/2016	Beverage	Milkshake	Chocolate	3.50	3.68	54	£	189.00	£	198.45
300	18/11/2016	Beverage	Milkshake	Cola	1.00	1.05	50	£	50.00	£	52.50
301	18/11/2016	Beverage	Hot	Flat White	1.90	2.00	66	£	125.40	£	131.67
302	18/11/2016	Beverage	Hot	Hot Chocolate	3.00	3.15	452	£	1,356.00	£	1,423.80
303	18/11/2016	Beverage	Hot	Latte	1.90	2.00	654	£	1,242.60	£	1,304.73
304	18/11/2016	Beverage	Hot	Macchiato	1.90	2.00	256	£	486.40	£	510.72
305	18/11/2016	Beverage	Milkshake	Strawberry	3.50	3.68	60	£	210.00	£	220.50
306	18/11/2016	Food	Cake	Apple Cake	3.50	3.68	26	£	91.00	£	95.55
307	18/11/2016	Food	Cake	Brownie	3.00	3.15	92	£	276.00	£	289.80
308	18/11/2016	Food	Cake	Carrot Cake	3.50	3.68	75	£	262.50	£	275.63
309	18/11/2016	Food	Cake	Cheesecake	3.75	3.94	256	£	960.00	£	1,008.00
310	18/11/2016	Food	Cake	Chocolate Cake	3.00	3.15	75	£	225.00	£	236.25
311	18/11/2016	Food	Cake	Cupcake	1.75	1.84	45	£	78.75	£	82.69
312											
313											

Figure 204

Now to add this to the pivot table, click *Refresh All* on the *Analyze* ribbon.

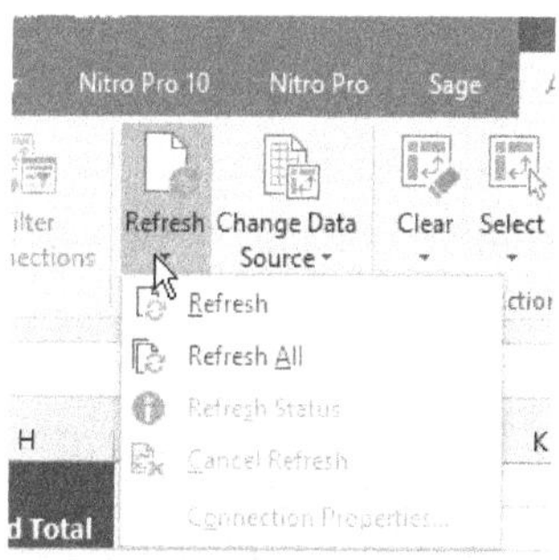

Figure 205

Now the pivot table has included the new data in the totals.

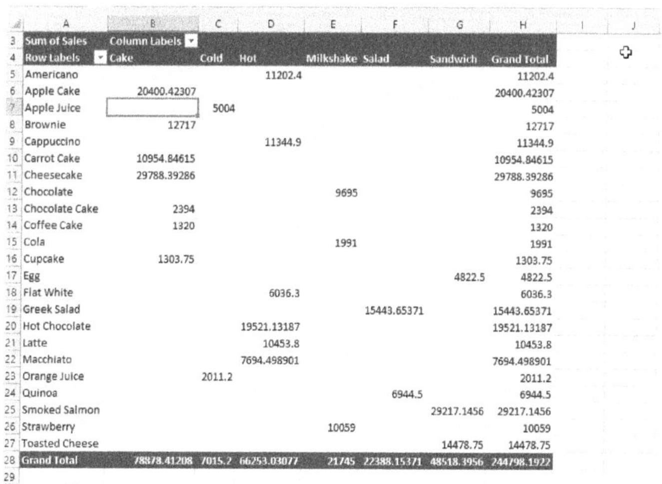

	A	B	C	D	E	F	G	H
3	Sum of Sales	Column Labels						
4	Row Labels	Cake	Cold	Hot	Milkshake	Salad	Sandwich	Grand Total
5	Americano			11202.4				11202.4
6	Apple Cake	20400.42307						20400.42307
7	Apple Juice		5004					5004
8	Brownie	12717						12717
9	Cappuccino			11344.9				11344.9
10	Carrot Cake	10954.84615						10954.84615
11	Cheesecake	29788.39286						29788.39286
12	Chocolate				9695			9695
13	Chocolate Cake	2394						2394
14	Coffee Cake	1320						1320
15	Cola				1991			1991
16	Cupcake	1303.75						1303.75
17	Egg						4822.5	4822.5
18	Flat White			6036.3				6036.3
19	Greek Salad					15443.65371		15443.65371
20	Hot Chocolate			19521.13187				19521.13187
21	Latte			10453.8				10453.8
22	Macchiato			7694.498901				7694.498901
23	Orange Juice		2011.2					2011.2
24	Quinoa					6944.5		6944.5
25	Smoked Salmon						29217.1456	29217.1456
26	Strawberry				10059			10059
27	Toasted Cheese						14478.75	14478.75
28	Grand Total	78878.41208	7015.2	66253.03077	21745	22388.15371	48518.3956	244798.1922
29								

Figure 206

Move the Pivot Table

To move the pivot table to a different location, simply click on the *Move PivotTable* icon and select where it needs to go.

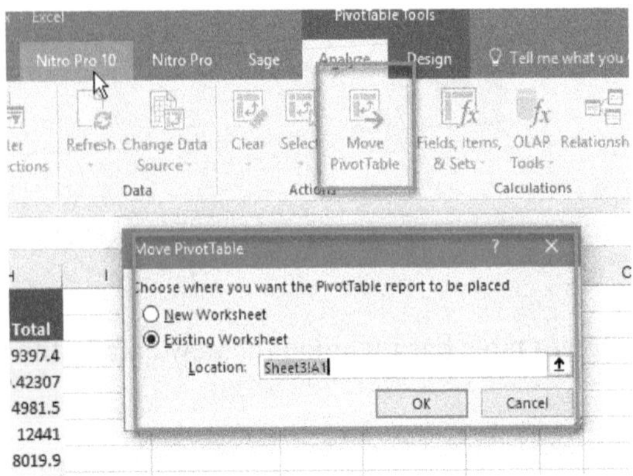

Figure 207

Change the Data Source

Sometimes you might want to change the range of data that the pivot table is drawing from. To do this, use the *Change Data Source* button. You might need to do this because you had not created a table, or you added so much extra information that it would be much simpler to change the range from scratch.

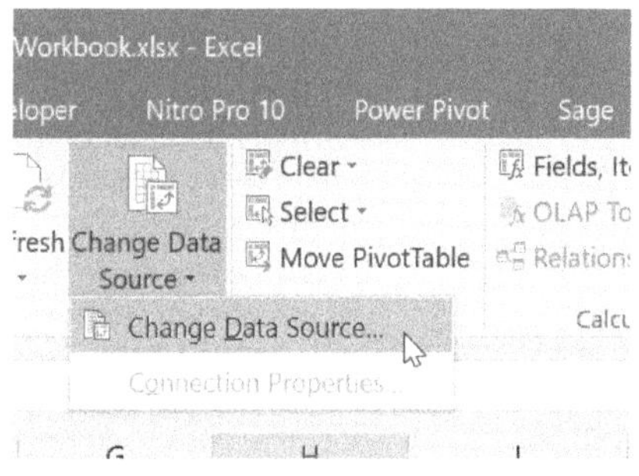

Figure 208

Pivot Table Arrangement

When a pivot table is first created, the pivot table fields show up in the task pane on the right of the screen. Sometimes the arrangement of the grid is different, and you may be wondering how to make it look as it does in our examples here.

Show/Hide Elements in the Pivot Table

Firstly, you can decide what to show in the pivot table and what not to show.

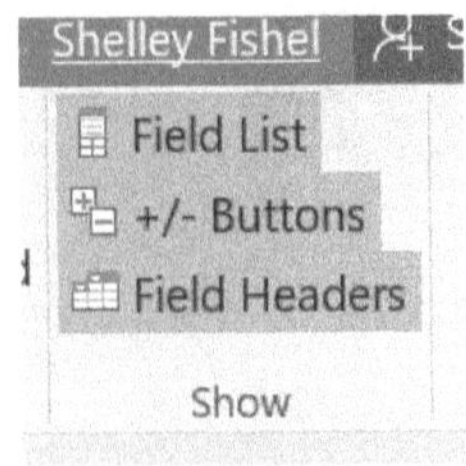

Field List – you can show or hide the field list.

+/- Buttons – these buttons allow you to collapse or expand items within the pivot table.

Field Headers – hide this if you do not want to filter on the row and column labels.

Figure 209

Change the Layout of the Task Pane

To make sure the layout of the task pane is how you want it, click the cog and select from the options on the drop-down list.

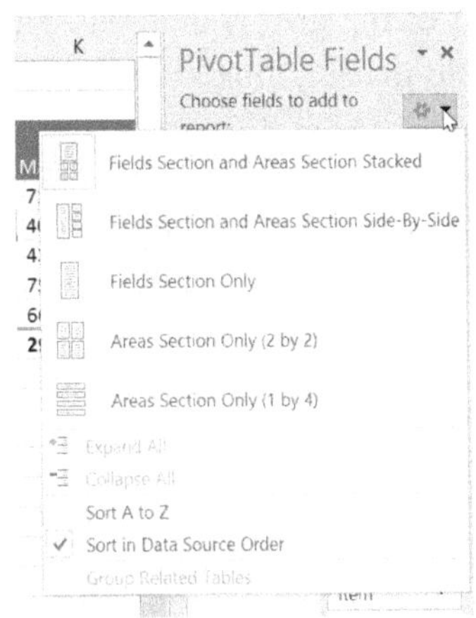

Figure 210

Fields Section and Areas Section Stacked	This is the standard layout where you can drag field headings between the areas.
Fields Section and Areas Section Side-By-Side	Still see all the same areas, just arranged side by side instead of above and below.
Fields Section Only	Shows only the field headings.
Areas Section Only (2 by 2)	Shows the quadrants arranged as 2 x 2.
Areas Section Only (1 by 4)	Puts all the areas in a line top to bottom.
Expand All and *Collapse All*	Allows you to expand or collapse all headings.
Sort A to Z or *Sort in Data Source Order*	Governs how data is sorted in the pivot table.

Insert a Timeline

A timeline is like a slicer but used for dates. By inserting a timeline, you can click on a button, and the pivot table will be filtered to show that range.

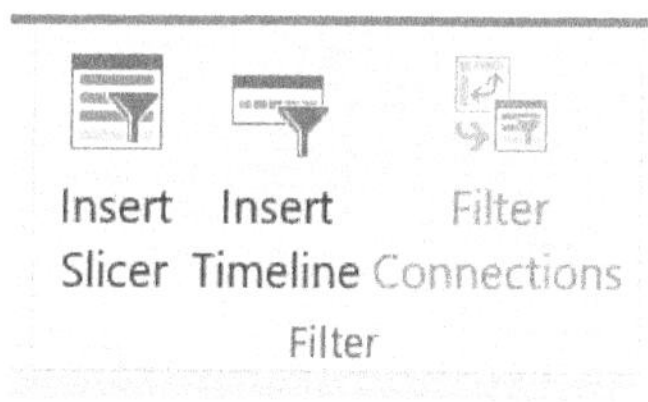

Figure 211

Figure 212

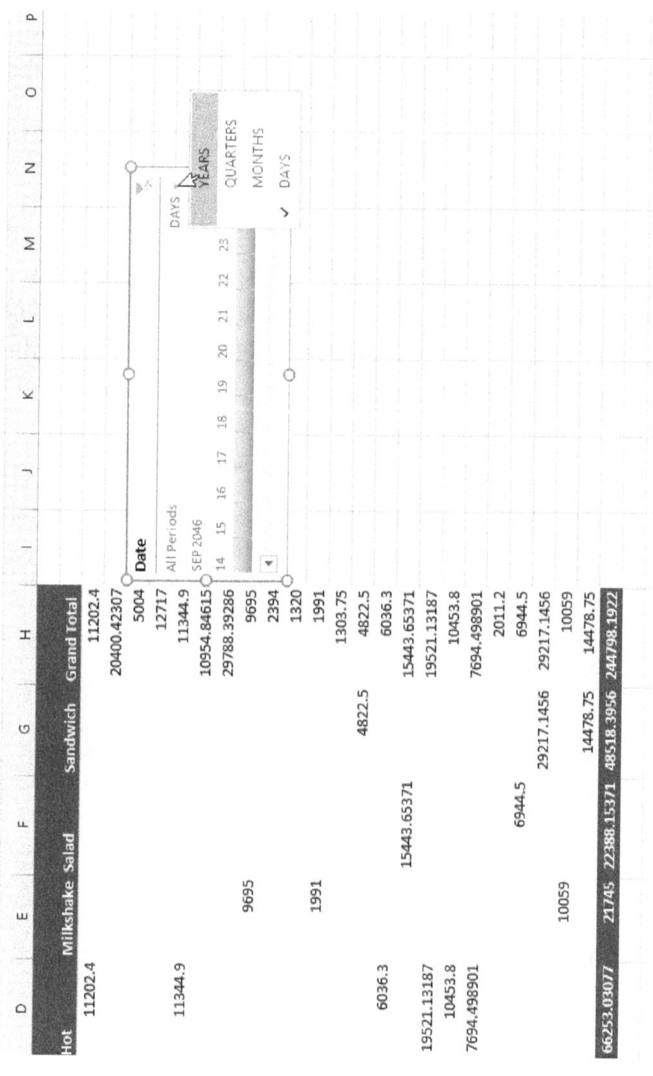

Hot	Milkshake	Salad	Sandwich	Grand Total
11202.4				11202.4
				20400.42307
				5004
				12717
11344.9				11344.9
				10954.84615
				29788.39286
	9695			9695
				2394
				1320
	1991			1991
				1303.75
			4822.5	4822.5
6036.3				6036.3
		15443.65371		15443.65371
19521.13187				19521.13187
10453.8				10453.8
7694.498901				7694.498901
				2011.2
		6944.5		6944.5
			29217.1456	29217.1456
	10059			10059
			14478.75	14478.75
66253.03077	21745	22388.15371	48518.3956	244798.1922

Figure 213

Matt's data is for days; there is not enough yet to show months' worth of data. Click the drop-down to change the time frame to *DAYS* instead of *YEARS, QUARTERS,* or *MONTHS.*

To see data for just one day, all Matt needs to do is click on the date he wants to see. To see more than one day, use the *Shift* key and click or *Control* key and click shortcuts. *Shift* and click selects everything between the first click and the last. *Control* and click selects each item clicked on whilst the *Control* key is pressed down.

To remove the filter, click on the remove filter icon in the top right of the timeline box. To delete the timeline altogether, simply click on it and press *Delete.*

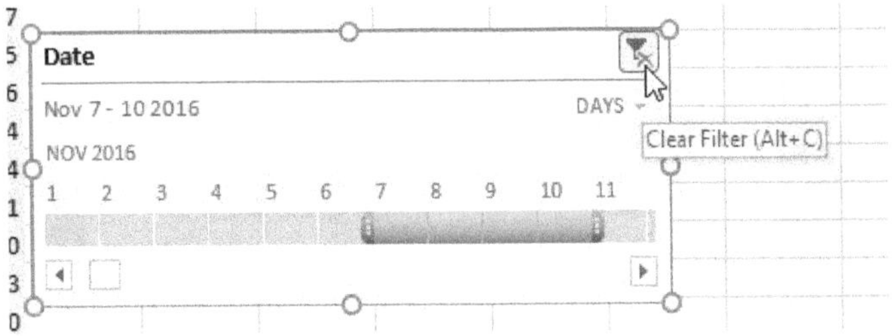

Figure 214

Matt is seriously impressed. All that data magic and how it can help him run his business is fantastic, and he's bowled over by Lisa's knowledge.

Pivot Charts

A pivot chart is a chart that can be filtered and pivoted just like the data in a pivot table.

Starting with a pivot table showing the total sales by item, Lisa shows Matt how to add a pivot chart.

1. Click the *PivotChart* icon – it is on the *Analyze* contextual ribbon.
2. Select a pivot chart style.
3. The chart is inserted next to data.
4. Filter the data using the filter buttons available on the chart.
5. See the new chart and the filtered data.

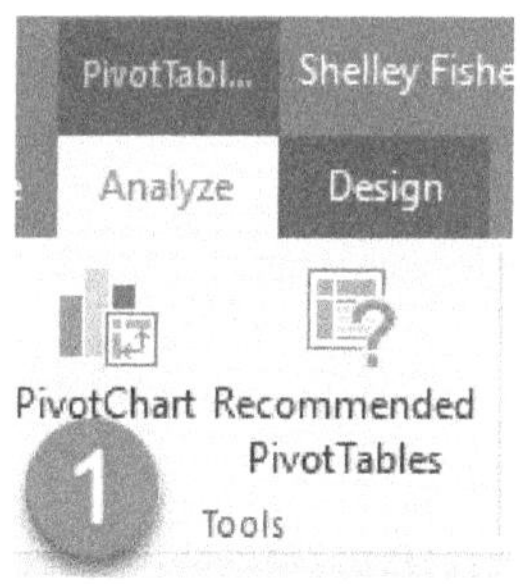

Figure 215

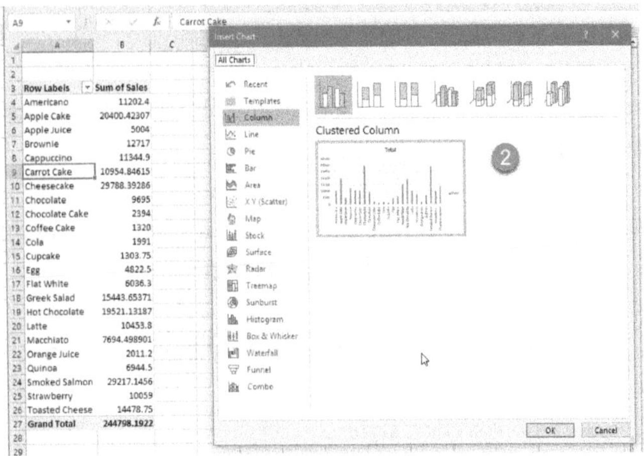

Figure 216

Figure 217

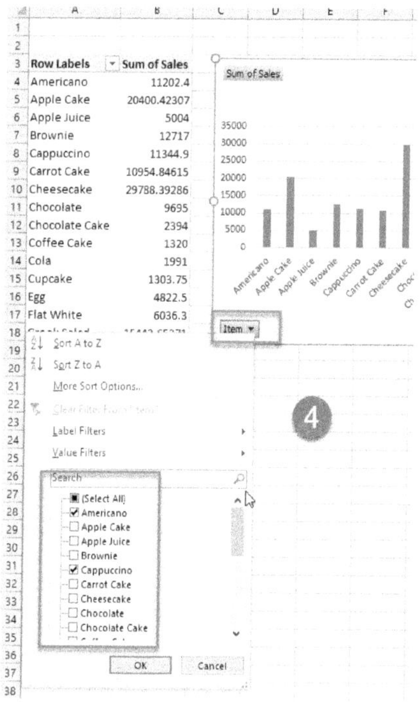

Figure 218

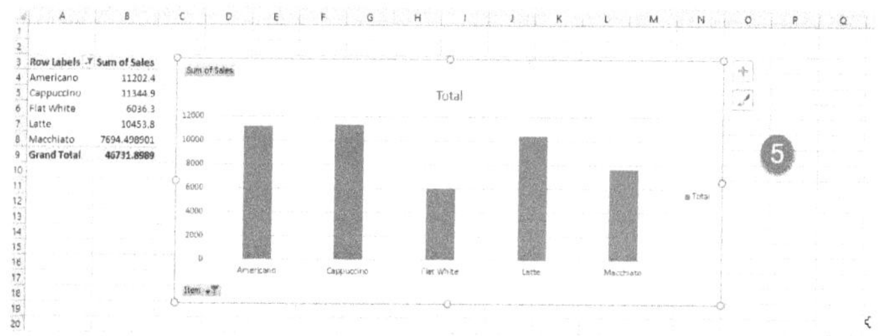

Figure 219

IF Statements – Working Out Overtime Pay

Matt needs to work out if staff need to receive overtime pay. He needs to add some columns to the staff payroll worksheet created earlier. This will enable him to add in the calculations for overtime and keep everything in one place.

He needs to add in columns for:

Overtime Rate	The amount they get paid for any hours of overtime worked.
Overtime Yes/No	To get Excel to put a *yes* if there is overtime and a *no* if there isn't.
Overtime	This is the overtime pay. If there is a *yes* in the *Overtime Yes/No* column, Excel will work out how much to pay based on the number of overtime hours worked.
Total Taxable	This is because staff will need to pay tax on the overtime pay, so it needs to be added to any taxable pay previously calculated.
Tax	This is the tax column, and we will recalculate it now using the new numbers.
Net	This is the total taxable minus the tax.

Here it is completed.

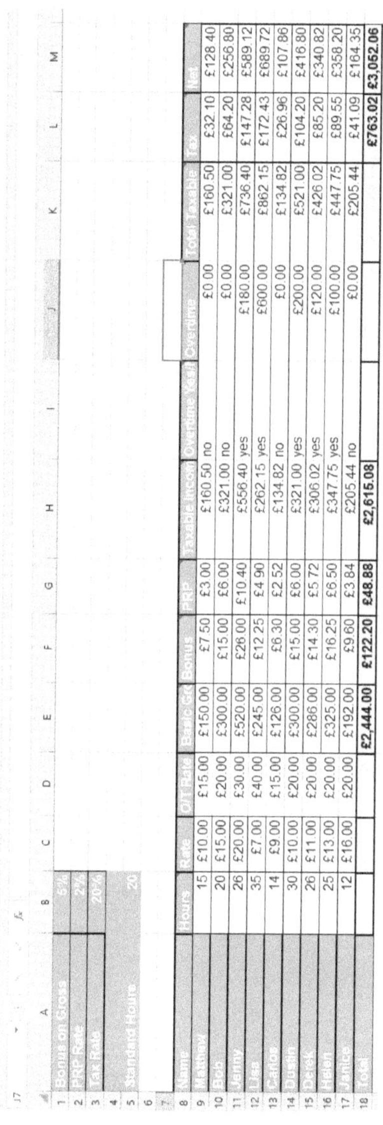

	A	B	C	D	E	F	G	H	I	J	K	L	M
1	Bonus on Gross	5%											
2	PRP Rate	2%											
3	Tax Rate	20%											
4													
5	Standard Hours	20											
6													
7													
8	Name	Hours	Rate	O/T Rate	Basic Gr	Bonus	PRP	Taxable Incom	Overtime Yes/	Overtime	Total Taxable	Tax	Net
9	Matthew	15	£10.00	£15.00	£150.00	£7.50	£3.00	£160.50	no	£0.00	£160.50	£32.10	£128.40
10	Bob	20	£15.00	£20.00	£300.00	£15.00	£6.00	£321.00	no	£0.00	£321.00	£64.20	£256.80
11	Jenny	26	£20.00	£30.00	£520.00	£26.00	£10.40	£556.40	yes	£180.00	£736.40	£147.28	£589.12
12	Lisa	35	£7.00	£40.00	£245.00	£12.25	£4.90	£262.15	yes	£600.00	£862.15	£172.43	£689.72
13	Carlos	14	£9.00	£15.00	£126.00	£6.30	£2.52	£134.82	no	£0.00	£134.82	£26.96	£107.86
14	Dustin	30	£10.00	£20.00	£300.00	£15.00	£6.00	£321.00	yes	£200.00	£521.00	£104.20	£416.80
15	Derek	26	£11.00	£20.00	£286.00	£14.30	£5.72	£306.02	yes	£120.00	£426.02	£85.20	£340.82
16	Helen	25	£13.00	£20.00	£325.00	£16.25	£6.50	£347.75	yes	£100.00	£447.75	£89.55	£358.20
17	Janice	12	£16.00	£20.00	£192.00	£9.60	£3.84	£205.44	no	£0.00	£205.44	£41.09	£164.35
18	Total				**£2,444.00**	**£122.20**	**£48.88**	**£2,615.08**				**£763.02**	**£3,052.06**

Figure 220

Let's break down each part.

Overtime Yes/No

This is a simple IF statement. An IF statement is built following this syntax or language.

=IF(Logical_Test,Answer_if_True,Answer_if_False)

In our case, the logical test for overtime yes/no is, are the hours worked greater than the standard hours? If the answer is yes (true), put a *yes* in the column, otherwise, put a *no* in the column.

It will read as follows:

=IF(**B9>$B$5**,"yes","no") Note that B5 has been fixed so that we can fill down the column.

Overtime

This column is working out the amount of overtime pay.

=IF(**I9="yes"**,**(B9-$B$5)*D9**,**0**)

If **the value in I9 is *yes***, do the following calculation. Hours worked minus standard hours, multiplied by the overtime rate. **If *no*, put 0.**

Total Taxable

=H9+J9

Add up the taxable income plus the overtime.

Tax

=K9*$B$3

Multiply the total taxable by the tax rate. The tax rate is fixed so it can be copied using Autofill.

Net

=K9-L9

Total taxable minus the tax.

Koffee Says:

When building complex formulas, there are no spaces. So after any double quotation marks or commas where you feel you should add a space, please don't!

Nested IF Statements – Working Out When to Reorder Stock

One of the things Matt knows he needs to do is keep on top of supplies so he never runs out of coffee beans, sugar, or syrup. Takeaway cups are another thing he can't afford to be without.

He knows the turnaround for ordering items is two days, so he devises a spreadsheet that is the responsibility of Bob to update. Every two days, Bob must check the storeroom and count up the current stock. When he puts the numbers into the spreadsheet, the spreadsheet will tell him whether he needs to reorder.

Here is the spreadsheet they created. Now all Bob needs to do is input the current number of items in stock every two days, and it will update. There is also a field where Bob can enter the current date, and Excel will work out when the next check is due. This is how they created this.

	A	B	C	D	E	F	G
1	When to Reorder Supplies						
2	Check every two days	Date Checked	02/01/2016				
3		Next Check Due	04/01/2016				
4							
5							
6		Current Stock	Reorder?	Min Number	Max Number		
7	Coffee	20	No	10	20		
8	Hot Chocolate	11	Watch	10	15		
9	Sugar	5	Reorder Now	10	15		
10	Syrup	15	No	6	15		
11	Takeaway Cups	1500	Reorder Now	1500	2000		
12	Dishwasher Powder	8	Watch	5	10		
13	Washing Up Liquid	4	Reorder Now	5	8		
14	Floor Cleaner	7	Reorder Now	10	20		
15							

Figure 221

Matt doesn't want to keep too much coffee in stock as it may go stale, so he has to order at the right time, making sure he's never in a situation where there's not enough coffee to get through two days.

Lisa shows Matt how to use an IF statement to work out when to reorder. He needs to know the minimum number and the maximum number.

The difference with this type of IF statement is that it has more than one condition.

=IF(B7>=E7,"No",IF(B7<=D7,"Reorder Now","Watch"))

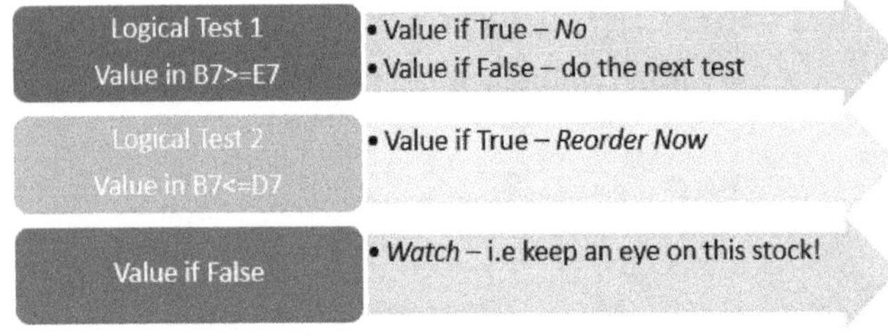

Figure 222

In English, it says:

If the value in B7 is greater than or equal to the maximum number, then *No*, I don't need to reorder, otherwise, go and check another if. If the value in B7 is less than or equal to the minimum number, then tell me to *Reorder Now*! If the number in B7 is greater than the minimum and less than the maximum, Matt wants Bob to *Watch* that particular item, keeping an eye on it as it may be nearly time to reorder.

Matt can continue to add IF statements if there are more things to test for. He can nest up to 64 conditions. The mind boggles!

VLOOKUP and HLOOKUP

These are two variations on the same function. One looks things up that are stored in a vertical list, and one looks things up that are stored in a horizontal list.

Matt uses the VLOOKUP and HLOOKUP functions to help him with room hire.

Meeting Room Hire – Booking Form

One of the brilliant things about Koffee Island is the availability of a couple of meeting rooms. Customers can hire them by the hour and order the refreshments they want.

When a customer asks to book a meeting room, there is a form to fill in. To avoid his staff making mistakes, and to make sure it takes as little time as possible, Matt and Lisa set about creating an order form that will do things automatically.

The Structure of the Booking Form

	A	B	C	D
1	Meeting Room Booking Form			
2				
3	Items	Quantity	Unit Price	Total
4	Cappuccino	12	£1.90	£22.80
5	Latte	4	£1.90	£7.60
6	Americano	2	£1.90	£3.80
7	Hot Chocolate	3	£2.10	£6.30
8	Macchiato	2	£1.90	£3.8
9	Chocolate Milkshake		£2.50	£0.
10	Vanilla Milkshake	2	£2.50	£5.
11	Strawberry Milkshake		£2.50	£0.
12	Tea		£1.50	£0.
13	Earl Grey Tea	2	£1.50	£3.
14	Selection of Fruit Teas	6	£1.50	£9.
15	Water - still	6	£1.00	£6.
16	Water - sparkling	5	£1.00	£5.
17	Croissant	4	£1.50	£6.
18	Danish	5	£1.50	£7.
19	Chocolate Cake	4	£1.25	£5.
20	Carrot Cake		£1.25	£0.
21	Salad with Salmon		£3.50	£0.
22	Salad with Cheese		£3.20	£0.
23	Salad	3	£3.00	£9.
24	Tropical Room 1 hr		£25.00	£0.
25	Sunshine Room 1 hr		£30.00	£0.0
26	Sand Room 1 hr	1	£25.00	£25.00
27	**Total Booking**			**£124.80**
28	**VAT @ 20%**	0.2		**£24.96**
29				
30	**Total inc VAT**			**£149.76**
31				
32				

Matt wants his staff to enter the quantity of each item ordered and for Excel to fill in the unit price and work out the total.

For this, Matt will use a VLOOKUP function to find the price of each item in the price list worksheet.

Figure 223

	A	B	C
1	Item	Price	
2	Cappuccino	£1.90	
3	Latte	£1.90	
4	Americano	£1.90	
5	Macchiato	£1.90	
6	Hot Chocolate	£2.10	
7	Chocolate Milkshake	£2.50	
8	Vanilla Milkshake	£2.50	
9	Strawberry Milkshake	£2.50	
10	Tea	£1.50	
11	Earl Grey Tea	£1.50	
12	Selection of Fruit Teas	£1.50	
13	Water - still	£1.00	
14	Water - sparkling	£1.00	
15	Croissant	£1.50	
16	Danish	£1.50	
17	Chocolate Cake	£1.25	
18	Carrot Cake	£1.25	
19	Salad with Salmon	£3.50	
20	Salad with Cheese	£3.20	
21	Salad	£3.00	
22	Tropical Room 1 hr	£25.00	
23	Sunshine Room 1 hr	£30.00	
24	Sand Room 1 hr	£25.00	
25			
26			
27			

The price list worksheet is simply a list of all the items and their prices arranged in a vertical table.

Figure 224

The VLOOKUP Function

The VLOOKUP function looks like this:

=VLOOKUP(A4,'Price list'!$A$2:$B$24,2,FALSE)

What it means:

=VLOOKUP(A4	• VLOOKUP – the function • A4 – the item you are looking for
'Price list'!$A$2:$B$24	Where to look for the value – the item Matt is looking for
2	The column to return the answer from – in our case, the price is in column 2
FALSE	This tells Excel to return an exact match

The first part tells the function what Matt needs to match. What value is the VLOOKUP looking for? In our example, the name of the item on the booking form.

Where should the VLOOKUP go to find this information? In our example, the worksheet called *Price list* and the range of cells to look in. As Matt only ever wants to do this once, Matt uses F4 to fix the region to look in as he wants to copy this formula down the whole column. (Note the*!* after *Price list*. This means it is a worksheet name.)

What should the VLOOKUP return when it finds the lookup value? In our example, the price, which is in the second column of the price list, so we have a 2 here.

Range lookup tells Excel if we are looking for an exact match or not. By default, Excel will look for the nearest value and drop back to the nearest range. When we need an exact match, as in this example a price, we need to put a *False* or a 0 in here. Then Excel will return an exact match or an error message if it is not found.

VLOOKUP =VLOOKUP(Items,'Price list'!$A$2:$B$24,2,FALSE)

Meeting Room Booking Form			
Items	Quantity	Unit Price	Total
Cappuccino	12	=VLOOKUP(Items,'Price list'!$A$2:$B$24,2,FALSE)	
Latte	4	VLOOKUP(lookup_value, table_array, col_index_num, [range_lookup])	
Americano	2	£1.90	£3.80
Hot Chocolate	3	£2.10	£6.30
Macchiato	2	£1.90	£3.80
Chocolate Milkshake		£2.50	£0.00
Vanilla Milkshake	2	£2.50	£5.00
Strawberry Milkshake		£2.50	£0.00

Figure 225

Koffee Says:

When building a VLOOKUP, the table where the information is stored can be anywhere on a spreadsheet. The name of the item we are looking for is in the first column, and the values we wish to see returned could be in any column from column 2 onwards.

When building the VLOOKUP function, the columns are always referenced as numbers in order from left to right. The first column which holds the label is column 1 and the next is column 2.

	1	2	3	D	E
1	Item	Price			
2	Cappuccino	£1.90			
3	Latte	£1.90			
4	Americano	£1.90			
5	Macchiato	£1.90			
6	Hot Chocolate	£2.10			
7	Chocolate Milkshake	£2.50			
8	Vanilla Milkshake	£2.50			
9	Strawberry Milkshake	£2.50			
10	Tea	£1.50			
11	Earl Grey Tea	£1.50			
12	Selection of Fruit Teas	£1.50			
13	Water - still	£1.00			
14	Water - sparkling	£1.00			
15	Croissant	£1.50			
16	Danish	£1.50			
17	Chocolate Cake	£1.25			
18	Carrot Cake	£1.25			
19	Salad with Salmon	£3.50			
20	Salad with Cheese	£3.20			
21	Salad	£3.00			
22	Tropical Room 1 hr	£25.00			
23	Sunshine Room 1 hr	£30.00			
24	Sand Room 1 hr	£25.00			

Figure 226

When building a function, you can type it in, or you can use the insert function option to help you construct the function.

Use the Insert Function with a VLOOKUP

Place the cursor where you want the first answer, and then click on the insert function button. Then either select the function from the recently used list which appears, or type it into the box, and click *Go* to search for it.

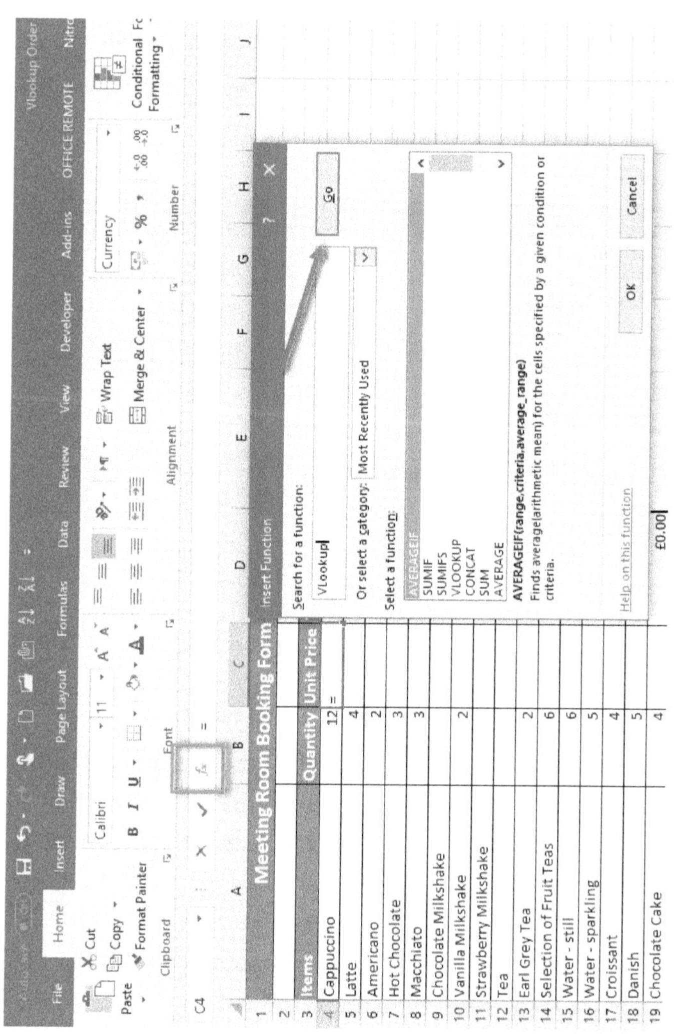

Meeting Room Booking Form
Items
Quantity
Unit Price
Cappuccino
Latte
Americano
Hot Chocolate
Macchiato
Chocolate Milkshake
Vanilla Milkshake
Strawberry Milkshake
Tea
Earl Grey Tea
Selection of Fruit Teas
Water - still
Water - sparkling
Croissant
Danish
Chocolate Cake
Insert Function
Search for a function:
VLookup
Go
Or select a category: Most Recently Used
Select a function:
AVERAGEIF
SUMIF
SUMIFS
VLOOKUP
CONCAT
SUM
AVERAGE
AVERAGEIF(range,criteria,average_range)
Finds average(arithmetic mean) for the cells specified by a given condition or criteria.
Help on this function
OK
Cancel

Figure 227

Once you have the function box open, you can fill in the fields. It sometimes makes it easier to see what you are doing.

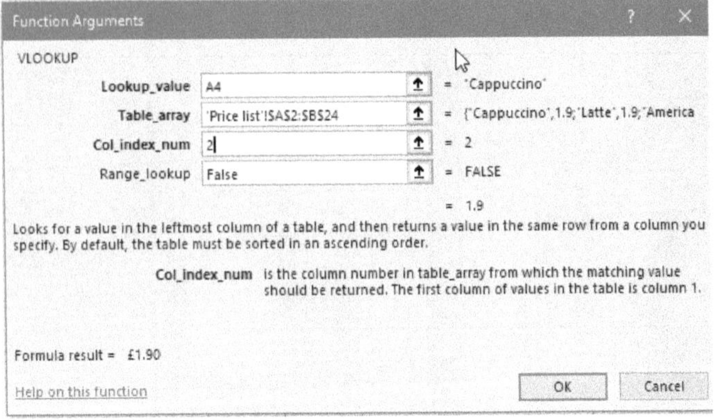

Figure 228

Once you have the answer in the first cell of the order form, it can be copied to all the other rows using Autofill. That is why we fixed the reference to the table that the information is coming from.

You can name the table of information and use that in the VLOOKUP as well as naming the column that has the lookup value in.

Matt names the lookup value column *Items* and the price list as *Price List*.

Now the formula looks like this:

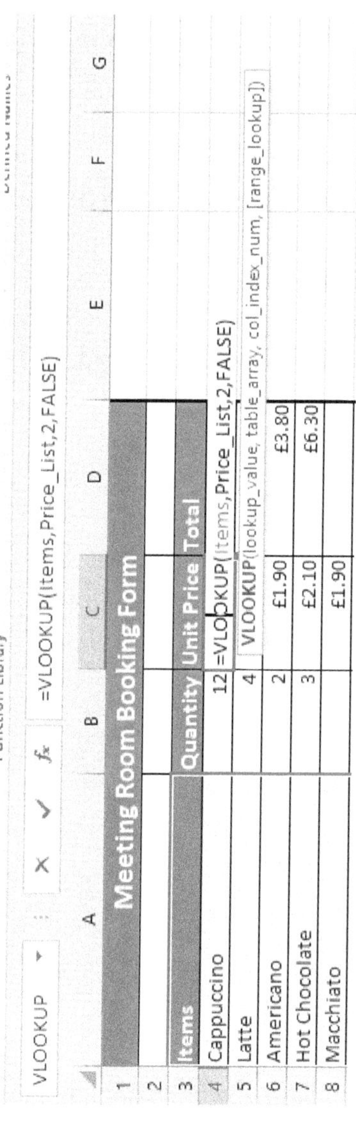
VLOOKUP
=VLOOKUP(Items,Price_List,2,FALSE)
Meeting Room Booking Form
Items
Quantity
Unit Price
Total
Cappuccino
12
=VLOOKUP(Items,Price_List,2,FALSE)
VLOOKUP(lookup_value, table_array, col_index_num, [range_lookup])
Latte
4
Americano
2
£1.90
£3.80
Hot Chocolate
3
£2.10
£6.30
Macchiato
£1.90

Figure 229

It says, look for the value on this row in the *Items* column.

Look for it in the *Price List* range.

When you find it, return the value in column 2.

Make sure it is an exact match.

Now Matt has his order form created, all he needs to do now is show people how to use it.

Protect Part of the Worksheet

Now Matt has an order form for booking out the meeting rooms and ordering refreshments. But he finds his staff are often overtyping the formula so it doesn't work any more. Matt's not thrilled. All his hard work learning how to set it up is gone in a flash.

Lisa shows Matt how to protect part of the worksheet so that only the quantities can be filled in. All the staff need to do is fill in the quantity of each item, and the spreadsheet will do the rest.

Protection is made up of two parts:

1. Locking or unlocking cells.
2. Turning on the protection feature.

Locking or Unlocking Cells

When you start a new worksheet, Excel treats all the cells as locked. This means if you apply protection to the worksheet, all the cells will be locked down, and you won't be able to enter anything into them.

Imagine a hotel with lots of rooms which are all locked when you arrive. You can only enter once you have a key. Then you can get into your room, but not into anyone else's.

That is what locking cells does. However, in this case, Matt needs to be able to enter information into some of the cells whilst keeping others locked. This is done by first unlocking the cells he wants to change (handing over the key), and then applying the protection to everything else so those stay locked down.

Step one – unlock the cells you want people to change.

Step two – apply protection to everything else.

When the sheet is protected, you will see this message when you want to enter data into a cell that you don't have permission to use.

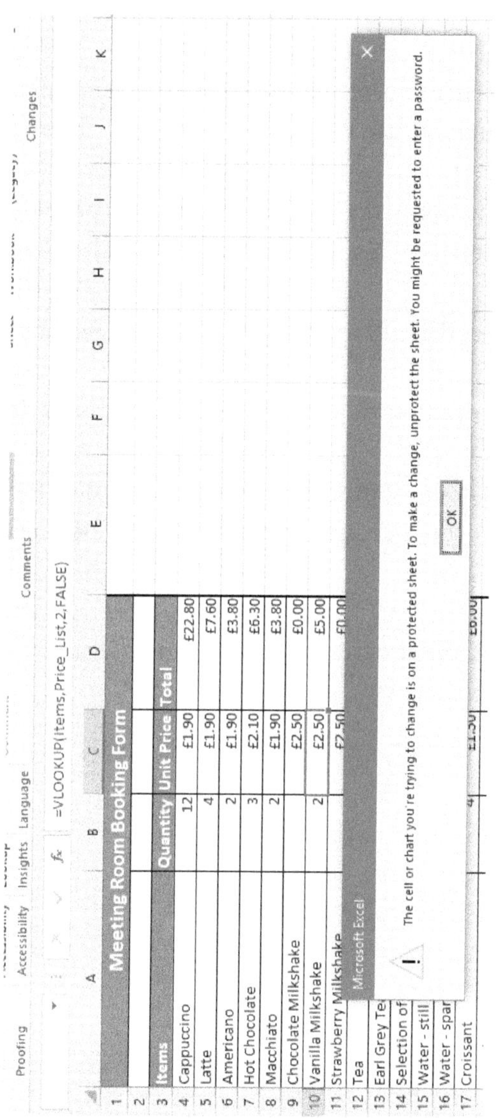

Proofing
Accessibility
Insights
Language
Comments
Changes
=VLOOKUP(Items,Price_List,2,FALSE)
Meeting Room Booking Form
Items
Quantity
Unit Price
Total
Cappuccino 12 £1.90 £22.80
Latte 4 £1.90 £7.60
Americano 2 £1.90 £3.80
Hot Chocolate 3 £2.10 £6.30
Macchiato 2 £1.90 £3.80
Chocolate Milkshake £2.50 £0.00
Vanilla Milkshake 2 £2.50 £5.00
Strawberry Milkshake
Tea
Croissant
Microsoft Excel
The cell or chart you're trying to change is on a protected sheet. To make a change, unprotect the sheet. You might be requested to enter a password.
OK

Figure 230

Unlock Cells to Change

The first job is to determine which cells can be unlocked so the data in them can be changed.

In the order form, the only cells Matt wants people to enter information into are the quantity cells. He will unlock those.

First, select the cells to unlock, in this case, B4:B25.

Click the drop-down under *Format* on the *Home* ribbon.

Note that at the bottom, in the *Protection* group, the locked button is turned on. Click on this button to unlock the selected cells.

Now click the drop-down under *Format* again and select *Protect Sheet.*

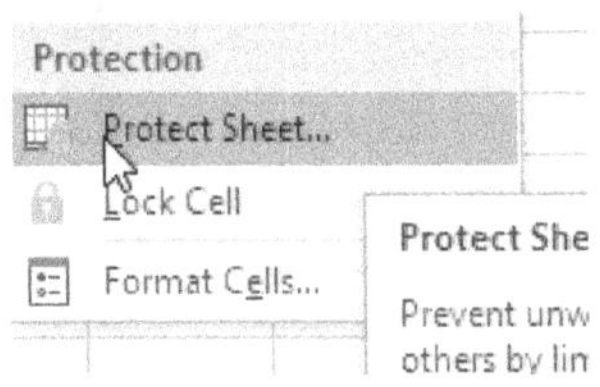

Figure 231

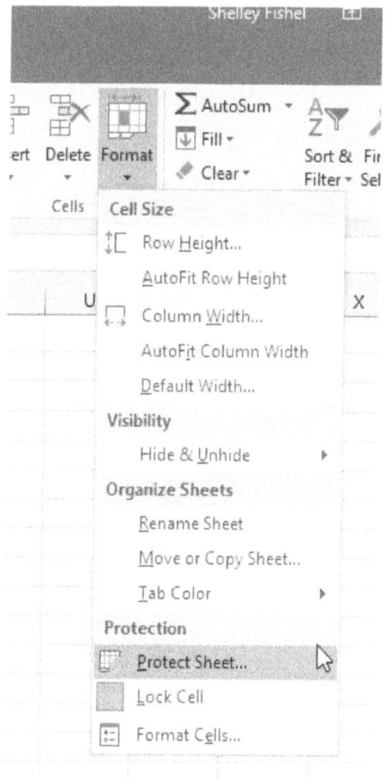

Figure 232

This will apply the protection. There is one more step.

Matt is now prompted to add a layer of security by adding a password and choosing what people can and can't do.

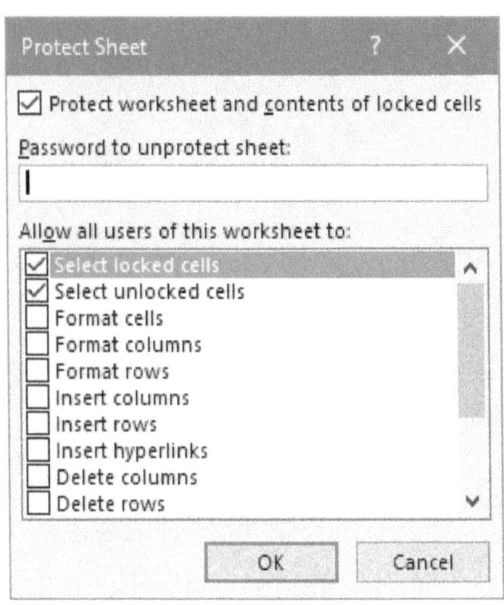

Figure 233

Koffee Says:

If anyone else knows about this feature, it's child's play for them to override your protection. By adding a password, they will only be able to remove the protection with the password.

If you don't add a password, the protection is still activated. It just means that anyone who knows how to protect and unprotect a worksheet will be able to turn it off.

Like this:

Click on the drop-down underneath *Format* on the *Home* ribbon.

Select *Unprotect Sheet* from the list of options. Note, it is the only option as everything else is switched off due to the protection in place.

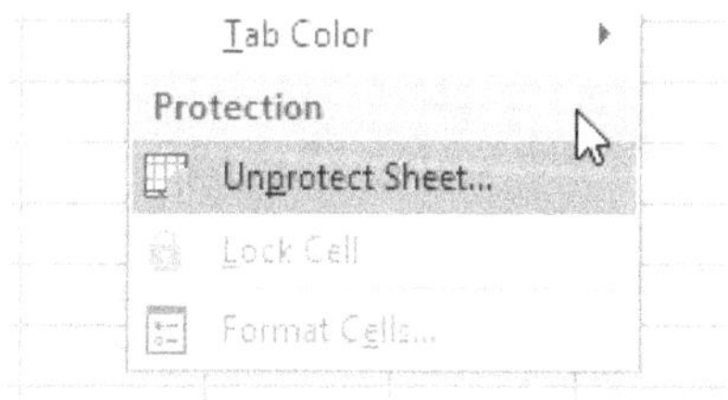

Figure 234

You will be prompted for the password if one is set. Otherwise, the protection is simply removed.

Koffee Says:

BE CAREFUL!

If you set a password and then forget it, you're in trouble. There is no way to retrieve the password, so to save yourself from a nervous breakdown, make sure you set one you can remember, or keep a note of it somewhere extremely safe!

Charts

Let's think about creating charts. Matt knows that in his weekly meeting with team members, some of them will switch off as soon as they're shown a list of numbers. He knows that for those people it's often easier to understand a visual, and this is where charts come in.

What Type of Chart?

The type of chart Matt needs to use depends on the data he needs to represent.

For example, a pie chart is used to show data for one category divided into segments adding up to 100%. A bar or column chart will show comparative data.

Quick Analysis

Excel 2016 has a neat tool called Quick Analysis.

Select some data, and a little button pops up to give you some options. For example, when selecting the data for January sales, this appears:

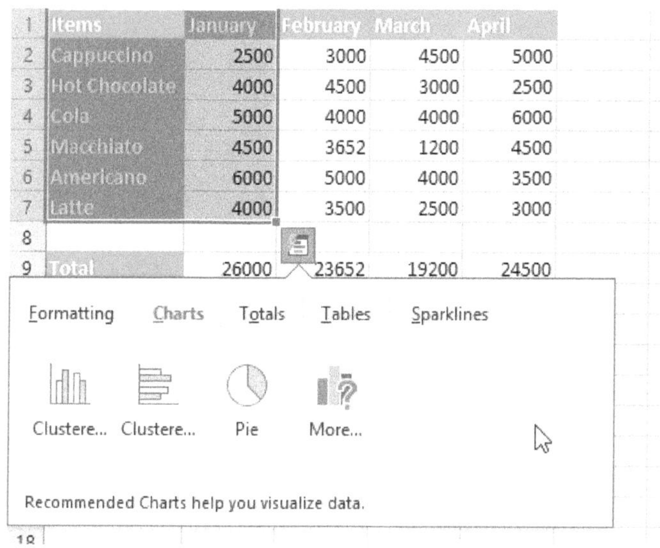

Items
January
February
March
April
Cappuccino
2500
3000
4500
5000
Hot Chocolate
4000
4500
3000
2500
Cola
5000
4000
4000
6000
Macchiato
4500
3652
1200
4500
Americano
6000
5000
4000
3500
Latte
4000
3500
2500
3000
Total
26000
23652
19200
24500
Formatting
Charts
Totals
Tables
Sparklines
Clustere...
Clustere...
Pie
More...
Recommended Charts help you visualize data.

Figure 235

The Quick Analysis button shows options for *Formatting, Charts*, *Totals*, *Tables,* and *Sparklines.* It will show options based on the data selected.

Below, Matt has selected the items and the totals for January, so when he chooses a pie chart, this is what appears:

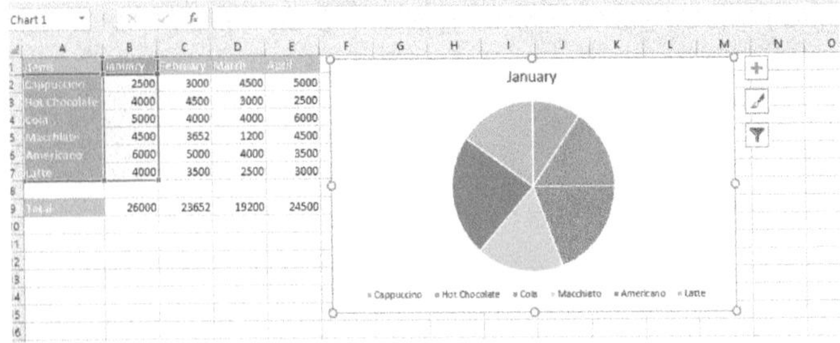

Figure 236

If he were to select all the data and choose a clustered column chart, this would be the result:

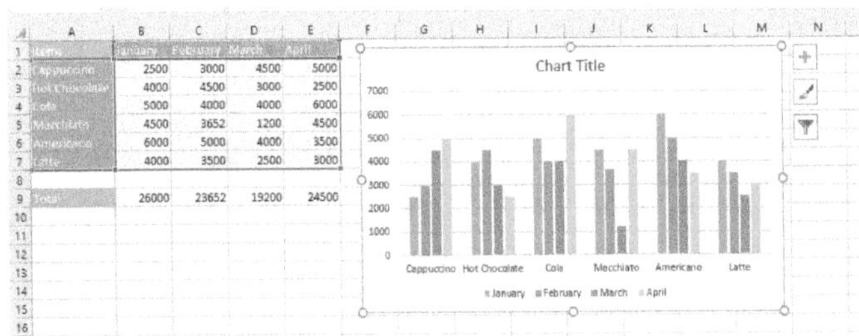

Figure 237

He can, of course, create charts without the Quick Analysis button.

All the different chart types are on the *Insert* ribbon.

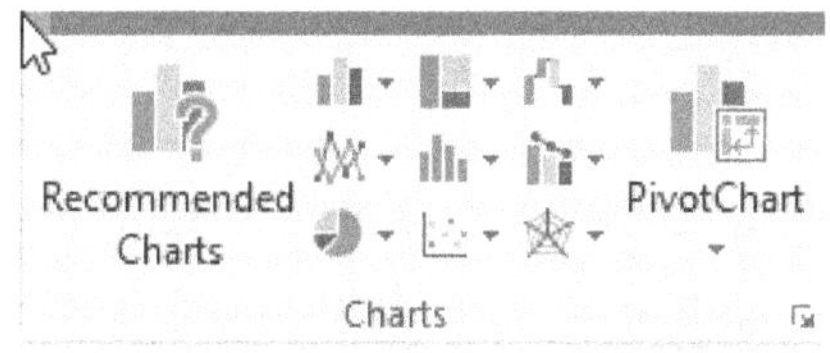

Figure 238

Recommended Charts

Matt can select the data and choose *Recommended Charts* if he isn't sure which one to go for. Click *More* from the *Quick Analysis* box, and Excel will offer a dialogue box allowing Matt to see what different chart types would look like.

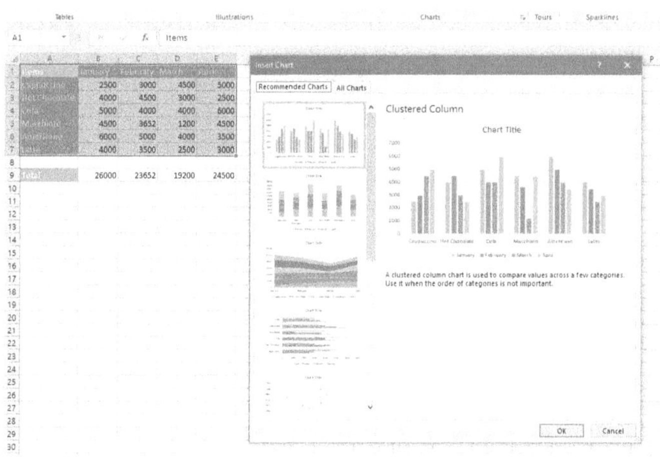

Figure 239

Create a Chart from Scratch

Matt can see the benefit of creating a recommended chart or using the Quick Analysis button, however, what if he wants to create a chart from scratch from any type of data?

When thinking about creating a chart, it's necessary to think about what you wish to show. If the data is arranged as a long list of repeating values, then the data may need to be summarised before a chart can be used to makes sense of it.

Here is an example. A list of the sales of beverages showing where they were sold and which type of drink they were can be useful for totals etc. However, if it's going to be put into a chart, the data needs to be summarised first. If Matt created a chart from all the data un-summarised, it would be unreadable. Like this for example:

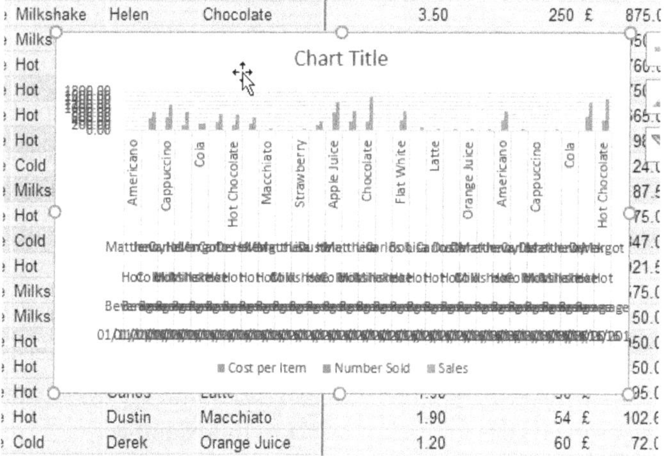

Figure 240

Hmm, needs a bit of work.

Lisa explains that a chart simply takes all the data you select and assumes each line is a category of information. Then it creates a graphic representation of the data. To get a meaningful representation, we need to summarise first. What Matt needs to see is the total sales for each type of coffee in a chart. It could be a pie or a bar/column chart.

First though, here is how to summarise the data.

SUMIF, AVERAGEIF, COUNTIF

When creating a chart, there will often be data clean-up or reworking to perform first. In order to create a chart of sales for each type of beverage, for example, Matt will first need to summarise the data to get the relevant totals.

The SUMIF and AVERAGEIF functions can help Matt do this. The SUMIF function gives a total sum of each criteria as its name suggests. The AVERAGEIF function works out the average sales for each product in this example.

Lisa shows Matt how to summarise the data using the SUMIF command. First, she creates a list of all the items on sale at Koffee Island.

The Structure of the SUMIF

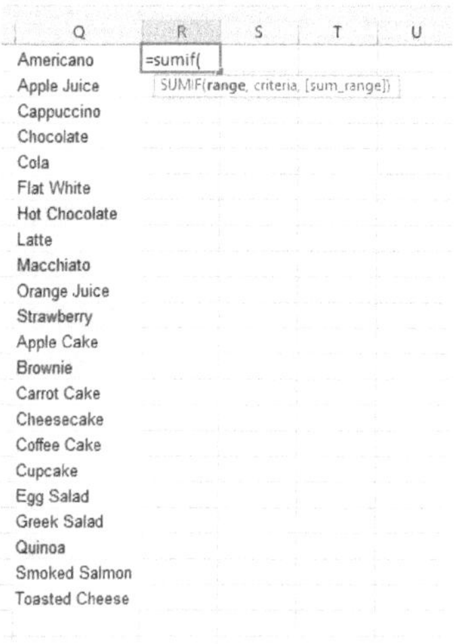

Figure 241

SUMIF – the name of the function to use.
Range – where to look for the criteria to sum.
Criteria – what are you looking for?
Sum_Range – which range of data to sum?

Lisa explains to Matt that he can type the function directly into the worksheet, or he can use the insert function button. Initially, she suggests he uses the insert function button to show how the function is built. Once he's more familiar with the system, he may be just as happy typing it in directly.

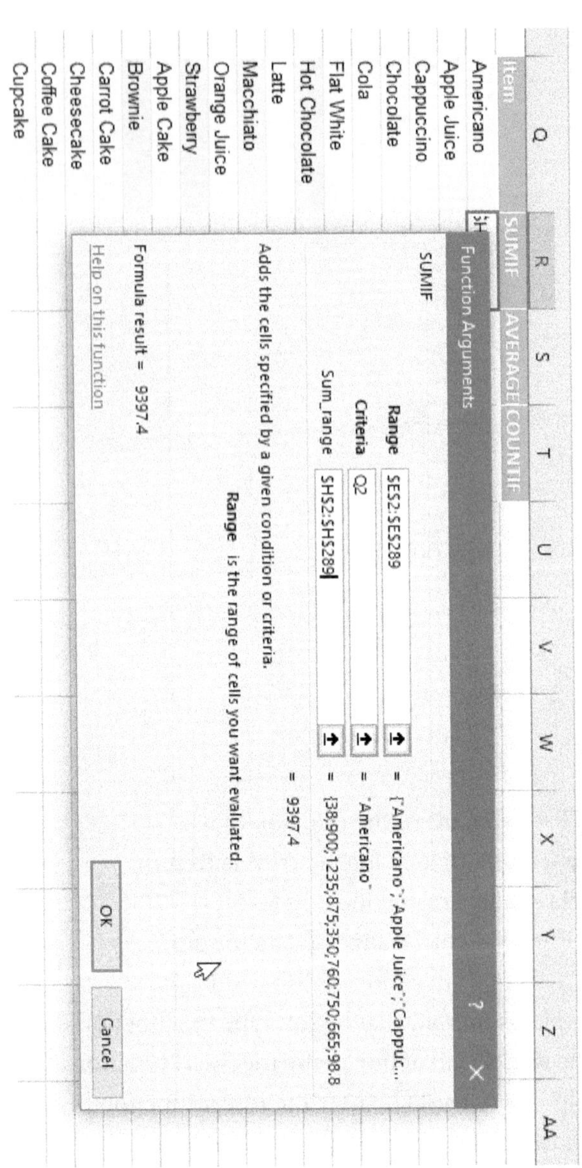
Item
Americano
Apple Juice
Cappuccino
Chocolate
Cola
Flat White
Hot Chocolate
Latte
Macchiato
Orange Juice
Strawberry
Apple Cake
Brownie
Carrot Cake
Cheesecake
Coffee Cake
Cupcake
SUMIF
AVERAGE
COUNTIF
Function Arguments
SUMIF
Range
$E$2:$E$289
= {"Americano";"Apple Juice";"Cappuc...
Criteria
Q2
= "Americano"
Sum_range
$H$2:$H$289
= {38;900;1235;875;350;760;750;665;98.8
= 9397.4
Adds the cells specified by a given condition or criteria.
Range is the range of cells you want evaluated.
Formula result = 9397.4
Help on this function
OK
Cancel

Figure 242

Click into the cell where the first answer is required.

Click on the insert function button on the Formula Bar.

Figure 243

Choose the SUMIF function. (Remember, if you can't see it, search for it instead.)

In the *Range* field, select the range that holds the criteria and remember to fix it with the F4 key as the idea is to copy it to all the cells in the list. We don't want the range to change or move.

In the *Criteria* field, click on the cell holding the criteria to look for – this does not need fixing as it will adjust as the formula is copied down the column.

In the *Sum_Range* field, select the range of numbers to be totalled every time it finds the criteria selected in the range area.

Click *OK*.

Matt has copied the formula to all the cells in the column using the Autofill handle to drag the formula down to all the cells. Now he has a neat summary that can be turned into a chart.

=SUMIF($E$2:$E$289,Q2,$H$2:$H$289)

	Date	Type	Category	Barista	Item	Cost per Item	Number Sold	Sales
2	01/11/2016	Beverage	Hot	Matthew	Americano	1.90	20	£ 38.00
3	01/11/2016	Beverage	Cold	Jenny	Apple Juice	1.50	600	£ 900.00
4	01/11/2016	Beverage	Hot	Carlos	Cappuccino	1.90	650	£ 1,235.00
5	01/11/2016	Beverage	Milkshake	Helen	Chocolate	3.50	250	£ 875.00
6	01/11/2016	Beverage	Milkshake	Margot	Cola	1.00	350	£ 350.00
7	01/11/2016	Beverage	Hot	Carlos	Flat White	1.90	400	£ 760.00
8	01/11/2016	Beverage	Hot	Derek	Hot Chocolate	3.00	250	£ 750.00
9	01/11/2016	Beverage	Hot	Helen	Latte	1.90	350	£ 665.00
10	01/11/2016	Beverage	Hot	Margot	Macchiato	1.90	52	£ 98.80
11	01/11/2016	Beverage	Cold	Matthew	Orange Juice	1.20	20	£ 24.00
12	01/11/2016	Beverage	Milkshake	Lisa	Strawberry	3.50	25	£ 87.50
13	02/11/2016	Beverage	Hot	Dustin	Americano	1.90	250	£ 475.00
14	02/11/2016	Beverage	Cold	Helen	Apple Juice	1.50	898	£ 1,347.00
15	02/11/2016	Beverage	Hot	Matthew	Cappuccino	1.90	485	£ 921.50
16	02/11/2016	Beverage	Milkshake	Lisa	Chocolate	3.50	450	£ 1,575.00
17	02/11/2016	Beverage	Milkshake	Carlos	Cola	1.00	50	£ 50.00
18	02/11/2016	Beverage	Hot	Bob	Flat White	1.90	500	£ 950.00
19	02/11/2016	Beverage	Hot	Lisa	Hot Chocolate	3.00	50	£ 150.00
20	02/11/2016	Beverage	Hot	Carlos	Latte	1.90	50	£ 95.00
21	02/11/2016	Beverage	Hot	Dustin	Macchiato	1.90	54	£ 102.60
22	02/11/2016	Beverage	Cold	Derek	Orange Juice	1.20	60	£ 72.00
23	02/11/2016	Beverage	Milkshake	Matthew	Strawberry	3.50	25	£ 87.50
24	03/11/2016	Beverage	Hot	Jenny	Americano	1.90	500	£ 950.00
25	03/11/2016	Beverage	Cold	Carlos	Apple Juice	1.50	65	£ 97.50

Item	SUMIF	AVERAGE	COUNTIF
Americano	9397.4		
Apple Juice	4981.5		
Cappuccino	8019.9		
Chocolate	9506		
Cola	1941		
Flat White	4770.9		
Hot Chocolate	18165.13		
Latte	9211.2		
Macchiato	5783.099		
Orange Juice	2011.2		
Strawberry	9849		
Apple Cake	20309.42		
Brownie	12441		
Carrot Cake	10692.35		
Cheesecake	28584.64		
Coffee Cake	1320		
Cupcake	1225		
Egg Salad	4822.5		
Greek Salad	15443.65		
Quinoa	6944.5		
Smoked Salmon	29217.15		
Toasted Cheese	14478.75		

Figure 244

The AVERAGEIF Function

This follows the same structure as the SUMIF function. Instead of choosing the SUMIF function from the insert function options, select AVERAGEIF instead. Here is how it looks when complete:

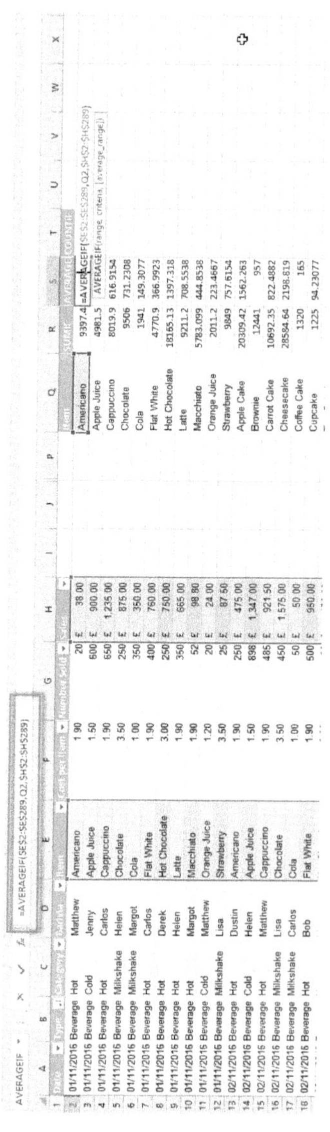
=AVERAGEIF($E$2:$E$289,Q2,$H$2:$H$289)

Figure 245

Note that instead of SUMIF at the start, the function has AVERAGEIF. From that point on, the structure is the same. When you get more confident, you can also type this function into the Formula Bar.

COUNTIF

The COUNTIF function is a little different. This function simply counts how many times the criteria appears in a list.

The syntax or structure:

Range – where to count the number of times the criteria appears.
Criteria – what to count.

In this example:

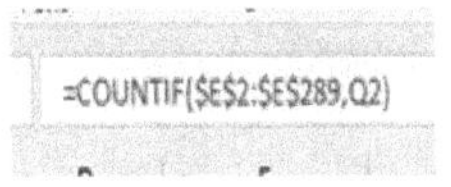

Figure 246

It says, look in the range E2 to E289 (fixed so that when copied it stays the same) and count how many times the value in Q2 appears.

Finished, it looks like this:

Item	SUMIF	AVERAGE	COUNTIF
Americano	9397.4	722.8769	13
Apple Juice	4981.5	383.1923	13
Cappuccino	8019.9	616.9154	13
Chocolate	9506	731.2308	13
Cola	1941	149.3077	13
Flat White	4770.9	366.9923	13
Hot Chocolate	18165.13	1397.318	13
Latte	9211.2	708.5538	13
Macchiato	5783.099	444.8538	13
Orange Juice	2011.2	223.4667	9
Strawberry	9849	757.6154	13
Apple Cake	20309.42	1562.263	13
Brownie	12441	957	13
Carrot Cake	10692.35	822.4882	13
Cheesecake	28584.64	2198.819	13
Coffee Cake	1320	165	8
Cupcake	1225	94.23077	13
Egg Salad	4822.5	370.9615	13
Greek Salad	15443.65	1187.973	13
Quinoa	6944.5	534.1923	13
Smoked Salmon	29217.15	2247.473	13
Toasted Cheese	14478.75	1113.75	13

Figure 247

Now Matt has the total sales, average sales, and he also knows how many times each of the items appears in the data list.

Now the data is summarised, Lisa shows Matt how to create custom charts.

Create a Chart from Summarised Data

Start by selecting the data, and then go to the *Insert* ribbon and select the type of chart to create. There are many to choose from. Matt wants to see a pie chart and a column chart. He also wants to know how to edit the charts to make them look great.

Create a Pie Chart

Matt will create a pie chart, so he selects the pie chart icon from the *Charts* group on the *Insert* ribbon. Then he can choose which type of pie chart to create. He chooses the first one so he can see what it does.

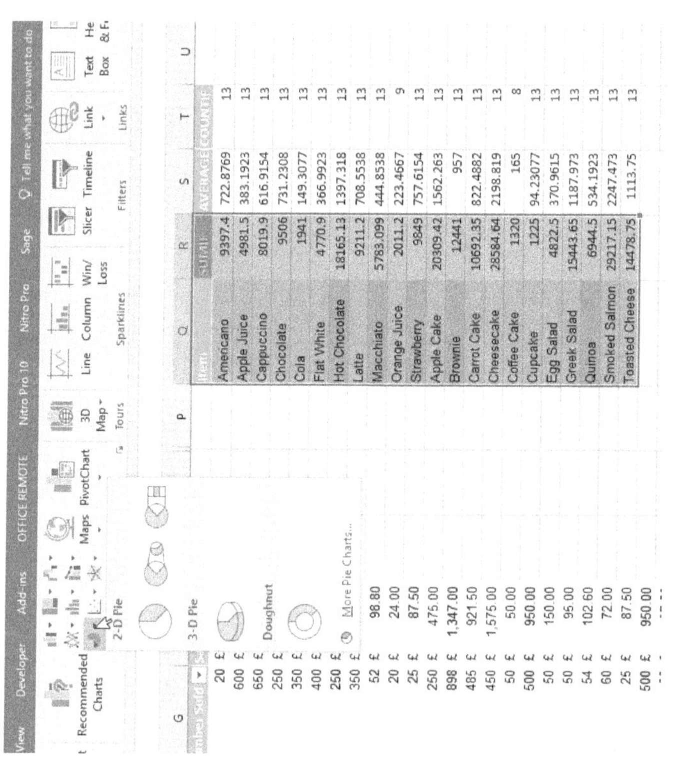

Item	SUMIF	AVERAGE	COUNTIF
Americano	9397.4	722.8769	13
Apple Juice	4981.5	383.1923	13
Cappuccino	8019.9	616.9154	13
Chocolate	9506	731.2308	13
Cola	1941	149.3077	13
Flat White	4770.9	366.9923	13
Hot Chocolate	18165.13	1397.318	13
Latte	9211.2	708.5538	13
Macchiato	5783.099	444.8538	13
Orange Juice	2011.2	223.4667	9
Strawberry	9849	757.6154	13
Apple Cake	20309.42	1562.263	13
Brownie	12441	957	13
Carrot Cake	10692.35	822.4882	13
Cheesecake	28584.64	2198.819	13
Coffee Cake	1320	165	8
Cupcake	1225	94.23077	13
Egg Salad	4822.5	370.9615	13
Greek Salad	15443.65	1187.973	13
Quinoa	6944.5	534.1923	13
Smoked Salmon	29217.15	2247.473	13
Toasted Cheese	14478.75	1113.75	13

Figure 248

He gets exactly what he asked Excel for: a pie chart.

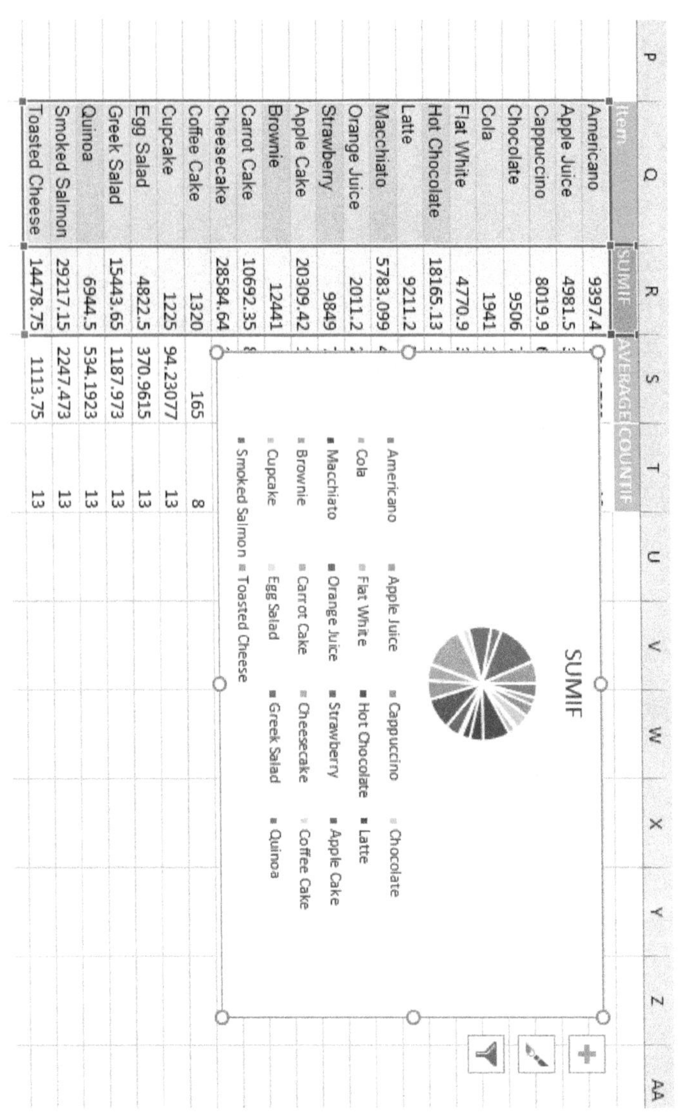

Item	SUMIF	AVERAGE	COUNTIF
Americano	9397.4		
Apple Juice	4981.5		
Cappuccino	8019.9		
Chocolate	9506		
Cola	1941		
Flat White	4770.9		
Hot Chocolate	18165.13		
Latte	9211.2		
Macchiato	5783.099		
Orange Juice	2011.2		
Strawberry	9849		
Apple Cake	20309.42		
Brownie	12441		
Carrot Cake	10692.35		
Cheesecake	28584.64		
Coffee Cake	1320	165	8
Cupcake	1225	94.23077	13
Egg Salad	4822.5	370.9615	13
Greek Salad	15443.65	1187.973	13
Quinoa	6944.5	534.1923	13
Smoked Salmon	29217.15	2247.473	13
Toasted Cheese	14478.75	1113.75	13

Figure 249

Matt wants to make some changes to how it looks, and Lisa shows him how.

Clicking the + in the top right allows Matt to add or remove some elements from the chart:

- *Chart Title*
- *Data Labels*
- *Legend*

The paintbrush is for formatting. Click on it to display a formatting pane to the right or left depending on how much space you have on the screen. Pick the format that does the job you want it to do.

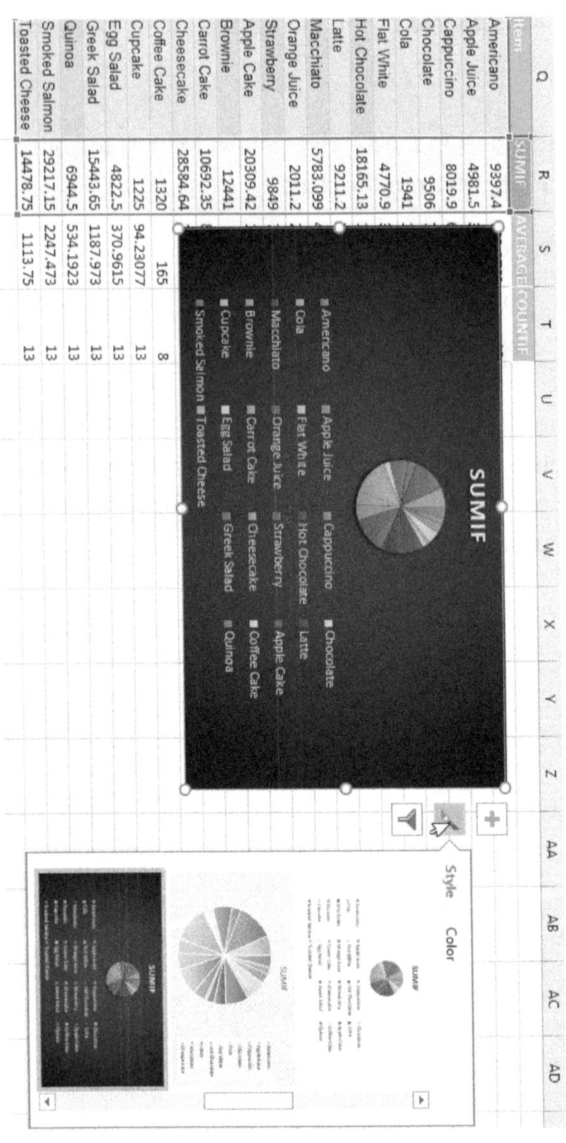
Q R S T U V W X Y Z AA AB AC AD
Item SUMIF AVERAGE COUNTIF
Americano 9397.4
Apple Juice 4981.5
Cappuccino 8019.9
Chocolate 9506
Cola 1941
Flat White 4770.9
Hot Chocolate 18165.13
Latte 9211.2
Macchiato 5783.099
Orange Juice 2011.2
Strawberry 9849
Apple Cake 20309.42
Brownie 12441
Carrot Cake 10692.35
Cheesecake 28584.64
Coffee Cake 1320 165 8
Cupcake 1225 94.23077 13
Egg Salad 4822.5 370.9615 13
Greek Salad 15443.65 1187.973 13
Quinoa 6944.5 534.1923 13
Smoked Salmon 29217.15 2247.473 13
Toasted Cheese 14478.75 1113.75 13
SUMIF
Americano
Apple Juice
Cappuccino
Chocolate
Cola
Flat White
Hot Chocolate
Latte
Macchiato
Orange Juice
Strawberry
Apple Cake
Brownie
Carrot Cake
Cheesecake
Coffee Cake
Cupcake
Egg Salad
Greek Salad
Quinoa
Smoked Salmon
Toasted Cheese
Style
Color

Figure 250

Clicking on the filter button will bring up a filtering pane allowing you to choose which of the items you wish to see. Check or uncheck the boxes to display or hide the options you want. Make sure you click *Apply* to apply your selection.

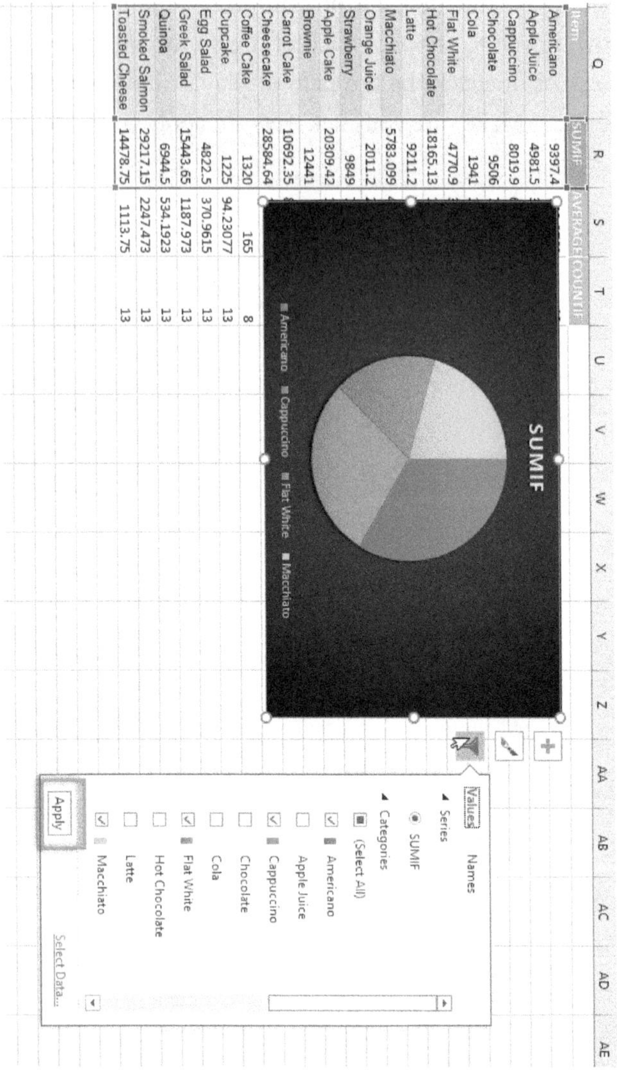
Item
SUMIF
AVERAGEIF
COUNTIF
Americano 9397.4
Apple Juice 4981.5
Cappuccino 8019.9
Chocolate 9506
Cola 1941
Flat White 4770.9
Hot Chocolate 18165.13
Latte 9211.2
Macchiato 5783.099
Orange Juice 2011.2
Strawberry 9849
Apple Cake 20309.42
Brownie 12441
Carrot Cake 10692.35
Cheesecake 28584.64
Coffee Cake 1320 165 8
Cupcake 1225 94.23077 13
Egg Salad 4822.5 370.9615 13
Greek Salad 15443.65 1187.973 13
Quinoa 6944.5 534.1923 13
Smoked Salmon 29217.15 2247.473 13
Toasted Cheese 14478.75 1113.75 13
SUMIF
Americano
Cappuccino
Flat White
Macchiato
Values
Names
Series
SUMIF
Categories
(Select All)
Americano
Apple Juice
Cappuccino
Chocolate
Cola
Flat White
Hot Chocolate
Latte
Macchiato
Apply
Select Data...

Figure 251

The Chart Ribbons

The Design Ribbon

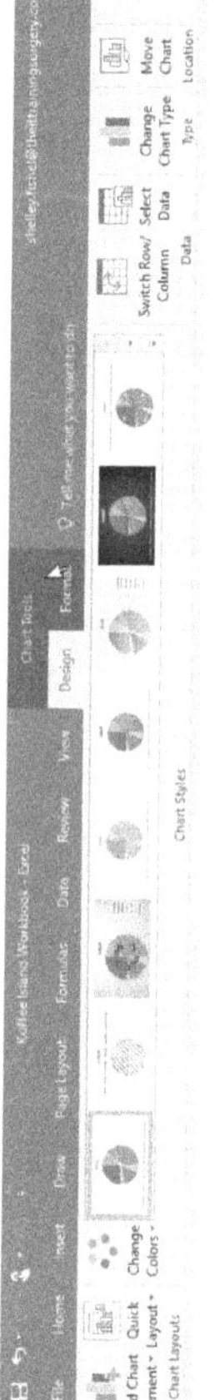

Figure 252

The Format Chart Ribbon

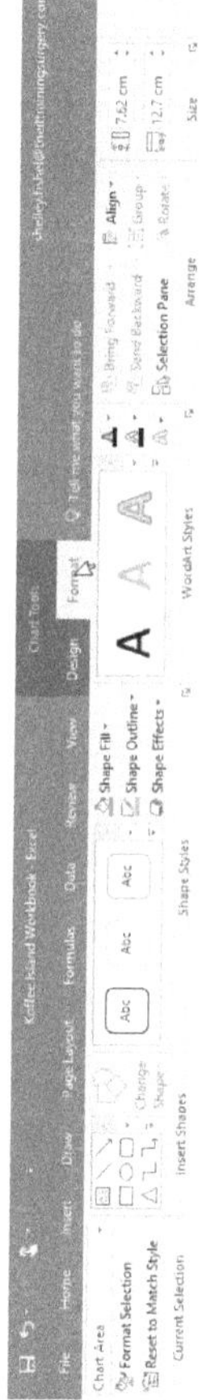

Figure 253

These two contextual ribbons show up whenever you add a chart to a worksheet. They have many more options to offer than the quick icons on the chart itself.

The *Design* ribbon is where you should head to make fundamental changes to the chart, such as changing the data range it is coming from or changing the style. If you have a bar/column chart, you might want to switch the rows and columns around to get a different picture of your data.

The *Format* ribbon does what it says on the tin. Use it to change the format of the chart or the sections of the chart.

Create a Column Chart

Follow the steps to create a pie chart and choose a column chart instead of the pie option. You will be able to decide which type of column chart style you wish to use.

In this chart, Matt is showing both the totals and averages of the sales at Koffee Island, and he has filtered it to show sales for *Americano*, *Cappuccino*, *Flat White*, *Latte*, and *Macchiato*.

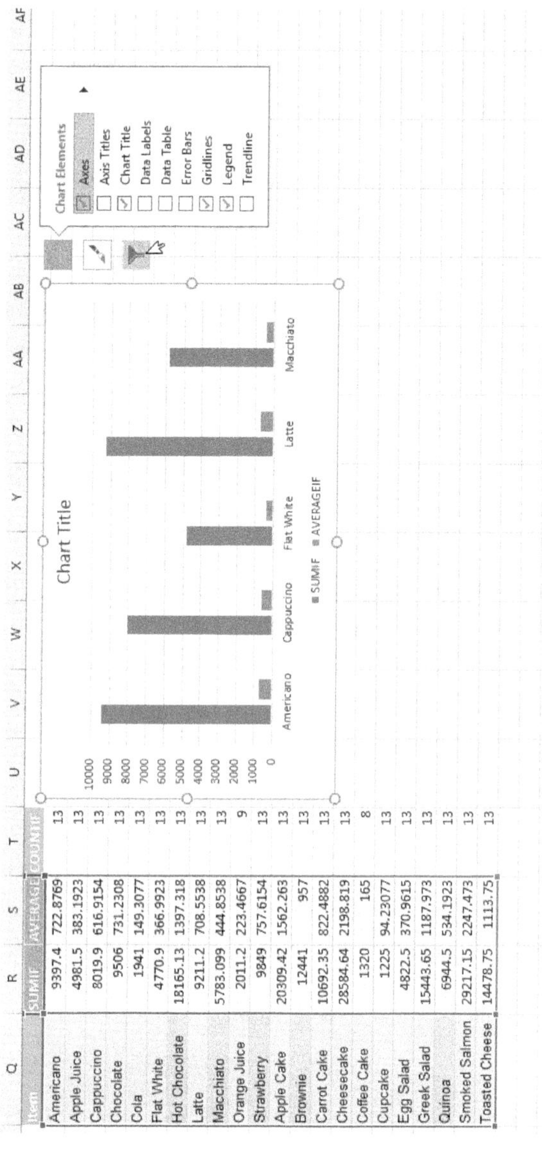

Item	SUMIF	AVERAGE	COUNTIF
Americano	9397.4	722.8769	13
Apple Juice	4981.5	383.1923	13
Cappuccino	8019.9	616.9154	13
Chocolate	9506	731.2308	13
Cola	1941	149.3077	13
Flat White	4770.9	366.9923	13
Hot Chocolate	18165.13	1397.318	13
Latte	9211.2	708.5538	13
Macchiato	5783.099	444.8538	13
Orange Juice	2011.2	223.4667	9
Strawberry	9849	757.6154	13
Apple Cake	20309.42	1562.263	13
Brownie	12441	957	13
Carrot Cake	10692.35	822.4882	13
Cheesecake	28584.64	2198.819	13
Coffee Cake	1320	165	8
Cupcake	1225	94.23077	13
Egg Salad	4822.5	370.9615	13
Greek Salad	15443.65	1187.973	13
Quinoa	6944.5	534.1923	13
Smoked Salmon	29217.15	2247.473	13
Toasted Cheese	14478.75	1113.75	13

Figure 254

Note that just as with the pie chart, there are three icons that allow you to add extra elements to the chart, select a quick format, or filter the chart.

For more substantial changes to the chart, use the ribbon as there are many more commands there.

Lisa shows Matt just one command which may come in handy. It is how to switch the columns and rows. Sometimes when creating a chart, it is not obvious which data should be on the Y or vertical axis and which data should be on the X or horizontal axis. Excel has a go at deciding for you, but sometimes it may not be what you need.

To change the axis around, click on *Switch Row/Column* on the *Chart Tools Design* ribbon.

Have a go at working out what all the chart icons do and how you can modify a chart quickly and easily.

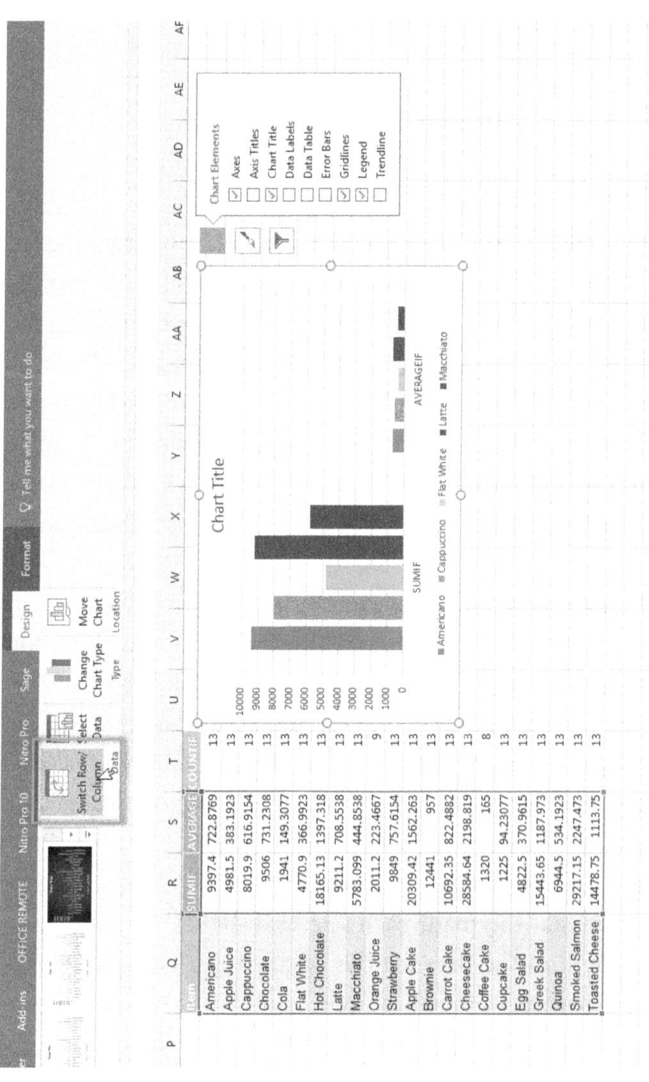

Item	SUMIF	AVERAGEIF	COUNTIF
Americano	9397.4	722.8769	13
Apple Juice	4981.5	383.1923	13
Cappuccino	8019.9	616.9154	13
Chocolate	9506	731.2308	13
Cola	1941	149.3077	13
Flat White	4770.9	366.9923	13
Hot Chocolate	18165.13	1397.318	13
Latte	9211.2	708.5538	13
Macchiato	5783.099	444.8538	13
Orange Juice	2011.2	223.4667	9
Strawberry	9849	757.6154	13
Apple Cake	20309.42	1562.263	13
Brownie	12441	957	13
Carrot Cake	10692.35	822.4882	13
Cheesecake	28584.64	2198.819	13
Coffee Cake	1320	165	8
Cupcake	1225	94.23077	13
Egg Salad	4822.5	370.9615	13
Greek Salad	15443.65	1187.973	13
Quinoa	6944.5	534.1923	13
Smoked Salmon	29217.15	2247.473	13
Toasted Cheese	14478.75	1113.75	13

Figure 255

SUMIFS – Working Out Who Sold What

Matt's head is spinning with excitement as he learns more and more. He's rapidly discovering that Excel is an absolute necessity for his business. He can see that summarising the sales to find out totals for each item and making a chart is not as difficult as he would have imagined. What if he wants to see who the best coffee seller is and which type of coffee they sell the most? He is thinking of having a Barista of the Week award and needs a way to find out this information.

Lisa, of course, has a solution for that. Having shown Matt how to use SUMIF, she tells him there's another variation called SUMIFS – note the 'S' tagged on at the end. This allows you to add up data that meets more than one criteria. If you want to find out the total sales for an individual plus the type of coffee they sold, this is the function to use.

Lisa quickly adapts the spreadsheet to show the name of the barista who made each sale, and she sets up the area to the right of the data for the calculations. Lisa also makes sure that each range has been named. It is much easier to understand a SUMIF function when using named ranges.

G	H	I	J	K	L	M	N
ber Sold	Sales			Criteria		Total Sales	
20	£ 38.00			Barista	Bob	24841.75	
600	£ 900.00						
650	£ 1,235.00						
250	£ 875.00			Barista	Bob	2006.4	
350	£ 350.00			Item	Cappuccino		
400	£ 760.00						
250	£ 750.00						
350	£ 665.00						
52	£ 98.80						
20	£ 24.00						
25	£ 87.50						
250	£ 475.00						

Figure 256

Lisa has added a couple of headings: *Criteria* and *Total Sales*. The criteria that we want the function to look for will be typed in the criteria column, and the total cell is where the calculation will take place.

So far so good. The first calculation is a SUMIF, which Matt learnt earlier when summarising the data for his chart.

=SUMIF(Barista,L2,Sales)

It says, look in the range named *Barista*, and when you find the value in cell L2, add up the total in the *Sales* column that matches that criteria.

Bob has made sales of £24,841.75. If Lisa then changes the value to Jenny, we can see that Jenny sold more than Bob with £30,364.98!

Now for a SUMIFS. Matt wants to know the value of sales for a particular barista when they are focussed only on one particular item. In this example, cappuccino. What was Bob's total sales for cappuccino?

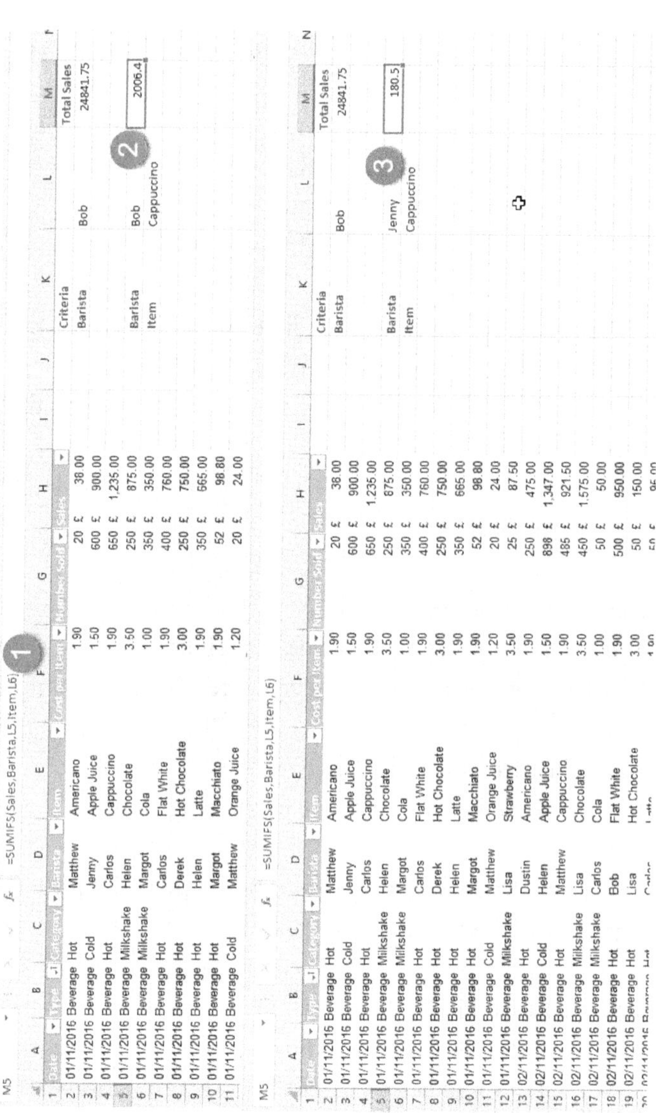
=SUMIFS(Sales,Barista,L5,Item,L6)
Total Sales
24841.75
2006.4
180.5

Figure 257

In the top image is the function to find out the total sales of cappuccino for Bob (1).

=SUMIFS(Sales,Barista,L5,Item,L6)

The SUMIFS structure is different to the SUMIF.

It starts with the range to sum first and follows with the criteria to look for. You can keep on adding criteria. First, tell it where to look for the criteria and then what the criteria is.

In our example:

Sales – the range to sum.
Barista – the first range to look in for criteria.
L5 – find whatever value is listed in cell L5 in the range *Barista.*
Item – the second criteria range.
L6 – find whatever value is in L6 in the range *Item.*

In Figure 255, we can see that Bob sold £2,006.40 of cappuccino (2) and Jenny £180.50 (3).

Matt then asks Lisa if he could find which of the baristas sold the most in the first week they were open. Lisa suggests a pivot table would be easier. Just because a function exists doesn't mean you have to use it. Sometimes there is a more elegant way. As Matt has already learnt about pivot tables, he sets about applying what he's learnt to this question.

Finding Out Who Sold What When?

First, Matt summarises the data with a pivot table.

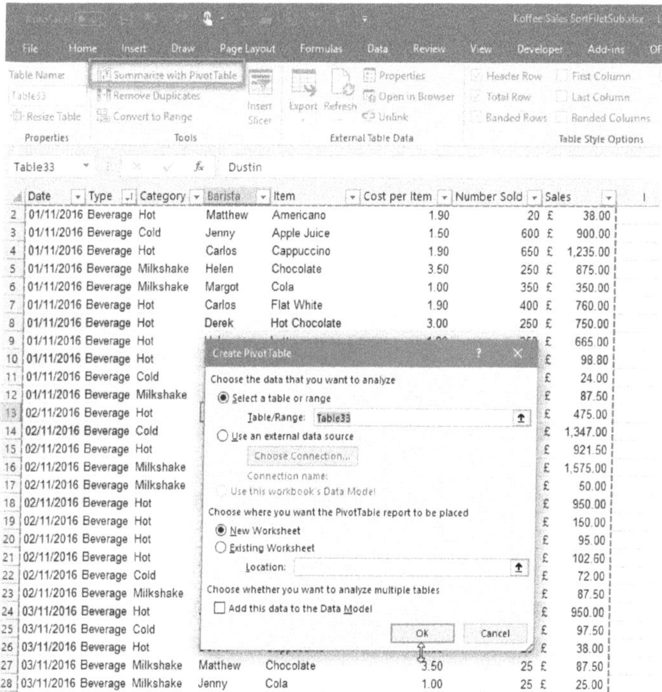

Figure 258

He puts the new pivot table on a new worksheet to help him see what he is doing.

He adds *Date, Barista,* and *Sales* to the pivot table (1) – these are the fields he wants to summarise.

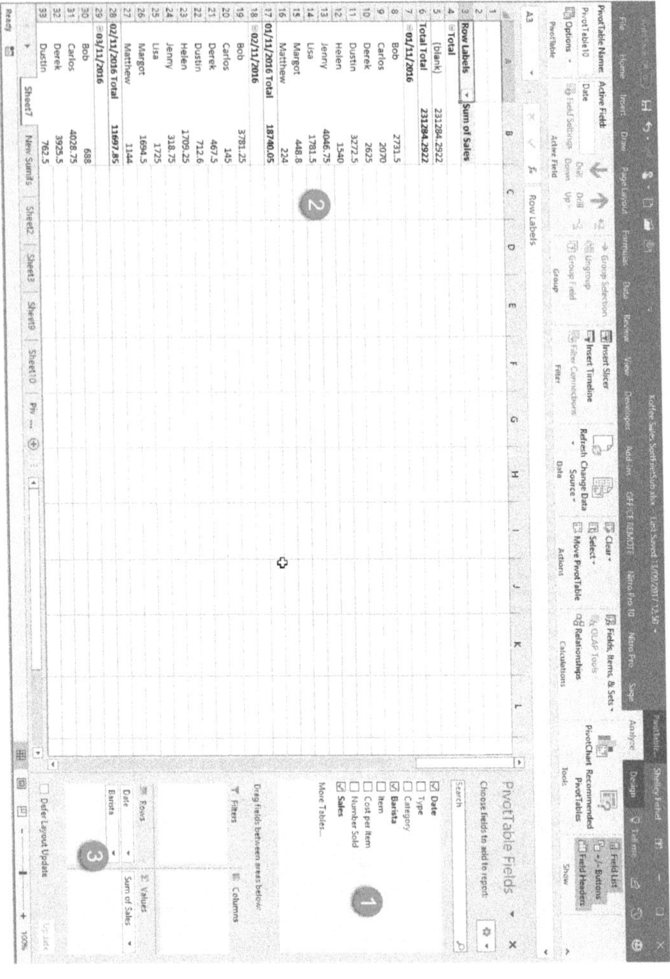

Figure 259

He sees how the pivot table has started with the fields arranged on the spreadsheet (2) and in the pivot table quadrants (3).

However, this isn't what he wants to see. He can't see the totals of each person next to each other, and he seems to be looking at the sales for every day, not for a range of dates.

He drags the *Date* field to the *Column* quadrant and the layout changes.

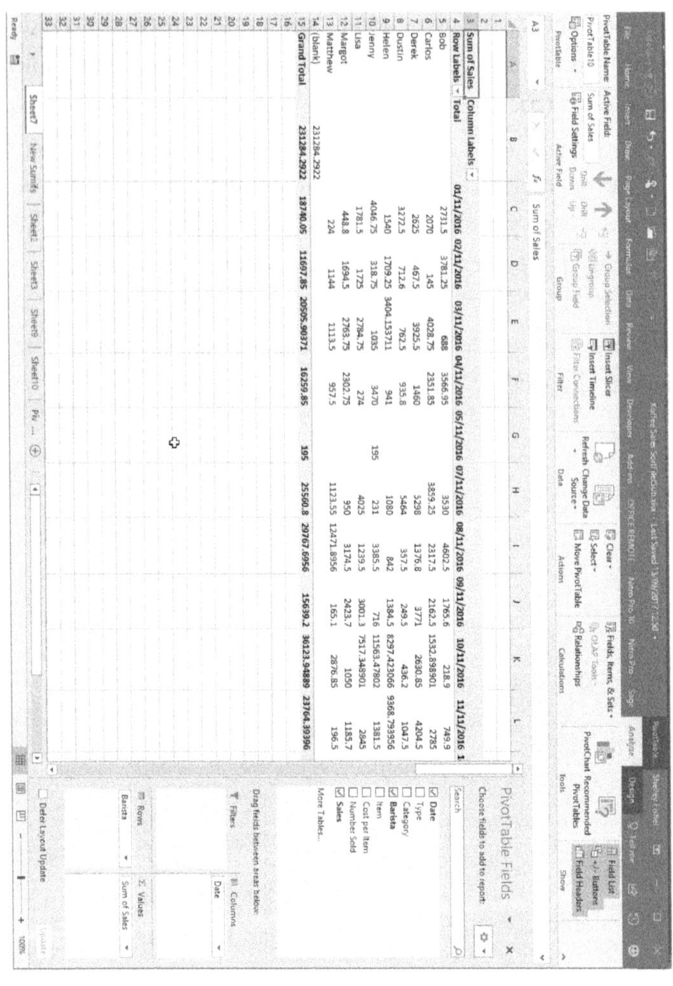

Sum of Sales	Column Labels										
Row Labels	Total	01/11/2016	02/11/2016	03/11/2016	04/11/2016	05/11/2016	07/11/2016	08/11/2016	09/11/2016	10/11/2016	11/11/2016
Bob		2731.5	3781.25	688	3566.95		3530	4602.5	1765.6	218.9	749.9
Carlos		2070	145	4028.75	2351.85		3859.25	2317.5	2162.5	1532.898901	2785
Derek		2625	467.5	3925.5	1460		5298	1376.8	3771	2630.85	4204.5
Dustin		3272.5	712.6	762.5	935.8		5464	357.5	249.5	436.2	1047.5
Helen		1540	1709.25	3404.153711	941		1080	842	1384.5	8297.423066	9368.793556
Jenny		4046.75	318.75	1035	3470	195	231	3385.5	716	11563.47802	1381.5
Lisa		1781.5	1725	2784.75	274		4025	1239.5	3001.3	7517.348901	2845
Margot		448.8	1694.5	2763.75	2302.75		950	3174.5	2423.7	1050	1185.7
Matthew		224	1144	1113.5	957.5		1123.55	12471.8956	165.1	2876.85	196.5
(blank)	231284.2922										
Grand Total	231284.2922	18740.05	11697.85	20505.90371	16259.85	195	25500.8	29767.6956	15639.2	36123.94889	23764.39396

Figure 260

Now to filter on the dates so that he can focus on just the first few days.

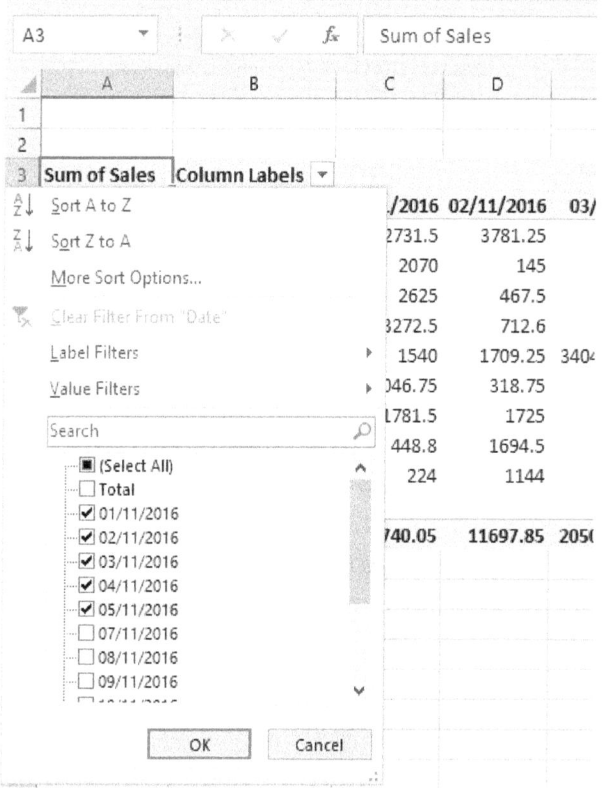

Figure 261

Now the pivot table is showing the total sales for each barista in the first week.

Sum of Sales	Column Labels					
Row Labels	01/11/2016	02/11/2016	03/11/2016	04/11/2016	05/11/2016	Grand Total
Bob	2731.5	3781.25	688	3566.95		10767.7
Carlos	2070	145	4028.75	2351.85		8595.6
Derek	2625	467.5	3925.5	1460		8478
Dustin	3272.5	712.6	762.5	935.8		5683.4
Helen	1540	1709.25	3404.153711	941		7594.403711
Jenny	4046.75	318.75	1035	3470	195	9065.5
Lisa	1781.5	1725	2784.75	274		6565.25
Margot	448.8	1694.5	2763.75	2302.75		7209.8
Matthew	224	1144	1113.5	957.5		3439
Grand Total	**18740.05**	**11697.85**	**20505.90371**	**16259.85**	**195**	**67398.65371**

Figure 262

All Matt needs do now is a little bit of formatting.

First, he chooses a design from the *Pivot Table Design* ribbon – a green one, in line with the Koffee Island branding.

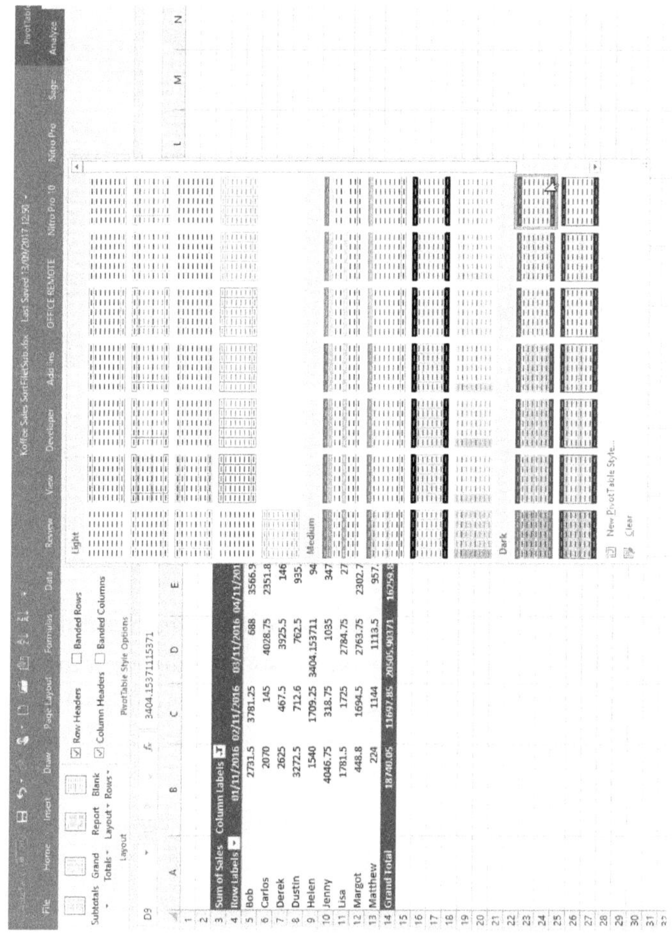

Figure 263

Then he wants to show the values in pounds with a currency symbol and only two decimal places.

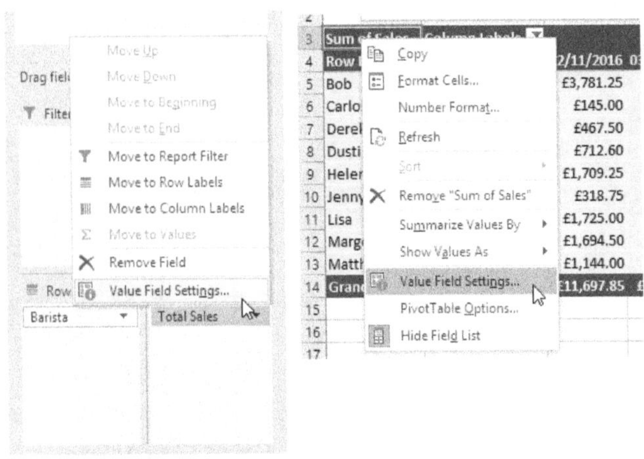

Figure 264

Matt can either right-click on the *Sum of Sales* heading or click the drop-down arrow on the sum of sales heading in the *Values* quadrant. Either way, he needs to select *Value Field Settings*.

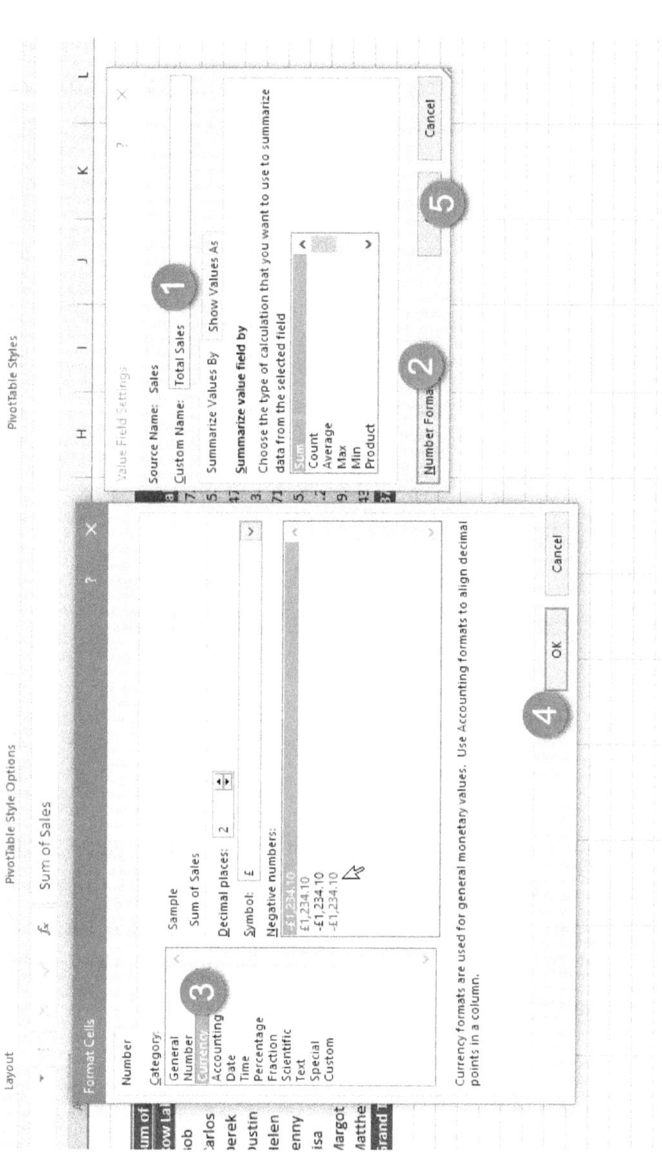
PivotTable Style Options
PivotTable Styles
Sum of Sales
Format Cells
Number
Category:
General
Number
Currency
Accounting
Date
Time
Percentage
Fraction
Scientific
Text
Special
Custom
Sample
Sum of Sales
Decimal places: 2
Symbol: £
Negative numbers:
-£1,234.10
£1,234.10
-£1,234.10
-£1,234.10
Currency formats are used for general monetary values. Use Accounting formats to align decimal points in a column.
OK
Cancel
Value Field Settings
Source Name: Sales
Custom Name: Total Sales
Summarize Values By
Show Values As
Summarize value field by
Choose the type of calculation that you want to use to summarize data from the selected field
Sum
Count
Average
Max
Min
Product
Number Format
Cancel
1
2
3
4
5

Figure 265

Once in the value field settings dialogue box, Matt changes the heading to read *Total Sales* (1), then clicks on *Number Format* (2) and chooses *Currency* (3), clicks *OK* (4), and then *OK* again (5).

Now his pivot table is looking more like it!

Total Sales	Column Labels					
Row Labels	01/11/2016	02/11/2016	03/11/2016	04/11/2016	05/11/2016	Grand Total
Bob	£2,731.50	£3,781.25	£688.00	£3,566.95		£10,767.70
Carlos	£2,070.00	£145.00	£4,028.75	£2,351.85		£8,595.60
Derek	£2,625.00	£467.50	£3,925.50	£1,460.00		£8,478.00
Dustin	£3,272.50	£712.60	£762.50	£935.80		£5,683.40
Helen	£1,540.00	£1,709.25	£3,404.15	£941.00		£7,594.40
Jenny	£4,046.75	£318.75	£1,035.00	£3,470.00	£195.00	£9,065.50
Lisa	£1,781.50	£1,725.00	£2,784.75	£274.00		£6,565.25
Margot	£448.80	£1,694.50	£2,763.75	£2,302.75		£7,209.80
Matthew	£224.00	£1,144.00	£1,113.50	£957.50		£3,439.00
Grand Total	£18,740.05	£11,697.85	£20,505.90	£16,259.85	£195.00	£67,398.65

Figure 266

Matt can clearly see Bob has sold the greatest value with sales of £10,767.70. No surprises there as Bob is the most enthusiastic barista around, and if it hadn't been for Bob being there right at the beginning, Matt didn't think he'd have made it this far.

Excel Really Does Do the Business!

Matt was able to harness the power of Excel from day one, making sure his business was set up and run the right way from the very beginning. He knows he can use his knowledge to keep on track and make sure Koffee Island stays profitable.

Matt knows there is much more Excel can do, and he is looking forward to practising the skills he's learnt before delving into more detail.

Apply what you have learnt about using Excel to your business and see the benefits.

Useful Keyboard Shortcuts

CTRL + N	Create a new workbook.
CTRL + O	Open an existing workbook.
CTRL + S	Save a workbook.
CTRL + P	Print worksheet.
CTRL + W	Close workbook.
CTRL + A	Select whole worksheet.
CTRL + Home	Move to cell A1.
CTRL + End	Move to bottom right of data.
CTRL + SHIFT + ↓ (Down Arrow)	Select all cells from current cell to bottom of data.
CTRL + Shift + Plus	Insert row/column.
CTRL + Shift + Minus	Delete row/column.
CTRL + Pipe (key to left of number 1)	Show/hide formulas.
CTRL + F	Find a word in worksheet.
CTRL + B	Make selected text **bold**.
CTRL + I	Make selected text *italic*.
CTRL + U	Make selected text underlined.
CTRL + 1	*Format Cell* dialogue box.
CTRL + ;	Insert today's date into cell.
CTRL + SHIFT + ;	Insert current time into cell.
CTRL + Z	Undo last action.
CTRL + Y	Redo last undo.
CTRL + X	Cut.

CTRL + C	Copy.
CTRL + V	Paste.
SHIFT + F11	Insert new worksheet.
F1	Help.
F3	Bring up list of range names.
F4	Create an absolute cell reference (adds dollar signs!).
F7	Check spelling.
F11	Create chart from data (must select data first).

Index

V

Lightning Source UK Ltd.
Milton Keynes UK
UKHW02f1653020118
315430UK00010B/93/P

9 780993 592942